"A Cheshire Way of Life"

With Best Wishes

Ivor Goodliy

© 2008 Ivor Goolding

This book is sold subject to the condition that it shall not, by way of trade or otherwise, be lent, resold, hired out, or otherwise circulated without the publisher's prior consent in any form of binding or cover other than that in which it is published and without a similar condition including this condition being imposed on the subsequent publisher.

The moral right of Ivor Goolding is asserted as the authors of this work.

ISBN 1904623654

First published in Great Britain 2008 by WriterPrintShop

Typeset by e-BookServices, New Delhi

Design by Rubell Print Ltd Tarporley, Cheshire

"A Cheshire Way of Life"

by
Ivor Goolding

Ivor Goolding

Born in Sale, Manchester in 1937, the story is about growing up in Cheshire villages and towns from the early 1940's to the early 1960's.

His father being a policeman, plodding beat for over 25 years, retiring at Ellesmere Port as a Sergeant. A strict disciplinarian and prone to very quick mood changes.

Having to move around Cheshire every two years the author would make many friends in places such as Runcorn, Little Budworth, Stockton Heath, Hoole, Crewe, Shavington & Ellesmere Port.

Educated at Crewe Grammar from 1950-54, leaving with 4 'O' levels. Joining Rolls Royce as an apprentice in engineering eventually finishing at Castrol Oil, Ellesmere Port.

After completing his apprenticeship, it was straight into the Army for National service with The Royal Welch Fusiliers in 1959-61.

If you were at Crewe Grammar or Rolls Royce also Ellesmere Port & in the Army in the late 50's at the time of the book it will be of particular interest to you.

For

IRENE

*I would like to thank Irene my wife for all the help she gave
me during the writing of this book.*

*Irene has since died and I would like to make a donation
from the sale of every book sold to*

The HOSPICE of the GOOD SHEPHERD

At Backford, Chester

Acknowledgements

I would like to thank John & Bernadette Pennington for their encouragement, advice and proof-reading skills in getting this book completed.

To Rubell Print Ltd of Bunbury, Cheshire for their technical assistance & organising the production.

To all the people mentioned & apologies to those who I may have missed out.

Table of Contents

CHAPTER ONE

Bombs, Balloons and Swastikas

"*We're on the move again.*" These were the words used by my Mother almost every two years as my Father was transferred around the County of Cheshire when serving with the Cheshire Constabulary. Most of his service would be spent plodding the beat, although on occasions he would be called to do some training with the CID; although unfortunately he never made the grade because, even in civilian clothing, he looked like an out and out copper.

My Father had spent the earlier days of his recruitment on the Wirral around New Ferry - in those days a supposedly rough area, where the police went around in pairs on a Saturday night. The trams were still running from Birkenhead Woodside to New Ferry Toll Bar, and Cammell Laird was in its heyday, employing most of the people in and around the area.

The men were working seven days a week at Cammell Laird, building and repairing many of the ships that travelled the high seas and, quite naturally, would let off steam after work in the pubs around the New Ferry Toll Bar where there was a pub on every corner. Knowing my Father, he would have been involved in any skirmishes that may have occurred after closing time outside the pubs.

This is also where my Mother met my Father, at one of the dances at Hulme Hall; the dance hall in the middle of the Port Sunlight Village. My Mother said they had become engaged within a couple of months of meeting one another, and after my Father had plucked up enough courage to ask my Grandfather for her hand in marriage, they were married in December 1936.

In those days the police authority would vet the woman a constable wanted to marry to ensure she was a respectable, law abiding person. Also, as they were offering them, as a married couple, rent-free housing, then everything had to be above board.

My parents were married at St. Andrew's Church in Lower Bebington where my Granddaughter, Rebecca Louise, was christened; a fact I am extremely proud of. My Mother was 26 and my Father was 24 when they tied the knot.

Not long after they were married, my Father was transferred to his first beat as a fully fledged copper. The town was called Sale and it was situated on the outskirts of Manchester, and they were to live at 9 Bamber Avenue.

This was where I was born, at Sale Memorial Hospital on 14th November 1937. My Mother explained that it was a typical November night for those days with thick freezing fog swirling around the hospital. Fog was common then due to the heavy industry surrounding the Manchester area. She also told me that my Father, who was on duty that night, would appear at the window every hour to see if I had arrived. I was born just after midnight on Sunday 14th November; a fact my Mother was very relieved about, as she was an extremely superstitious person. "Thank God it wasn't 5 minutes earlier," she has often said.

We were not at Bamber Avenue long before we moved to a small place on the perimeter of Knutsford called Mere, where we lived near a busy road junction on the main A556 from the South to Manchester. It was a semi-detached house - big and rambling with large gardens both to the front and the rear. There were mature beech trees at the front, and the main road was about 30 yards from the house. Telephones were installed *"for police work only."* A fact emphasised often by my Father, but my Mother said that the next door neighbour, also a policeman's wife named Myer Hughes and her would have some fun with the phone while the men were on duty. I can't think what they could have been up to, but there we are; my Mother had simple tastes and simple things made her laugh. Perhaps that's why she laughed a lot at me over the years.

I can remember quite clearly while I was still in my pram watching the red squirrels running around and our police dog, Lady, chasing them but never managing to come within ten yards of them. I can also remember a big black cloud appearing every so often; no doubt my Father either going on or coming off duty. Did I remember these things or did my Mother tell me about them so often that I thought I remembered? After all, I would only have been just over two years old.

It must have been a very happy time for my Mother, for she often talked about Myer, her Husband Alan, and Lady, the police dog who had been commended on several occasions for catching burglars while she was out with my Father plodding the beat.

The pattern was now set for the next 25 years or so, and our next move was to Runcorn, a chemical town on the Manchester Ship Canal. The town was also flanked by the River Mersey. The ICI was the largest chemical works in Europe at the time and it employed a high percentage of the people in the town.

ICI originated in Northwich, not a stone's throw away up the River Weaver. This was where salt was first discovered and mined, causing widespread subsidence to a lot of houses in the streets of Northwich and of course houses had to be shored up to prevent them from collapsing. This was where my Father spent his boyhood - 61 Huxley Street, Castle.

It was at Runcorn that I commenced my education at a school called Victoria Road Church of England School.

It was now late 1941 and the war was in full swing with German bombers over most nights, either on their way to Liverpool or Manchester and on odd occasions dropping one on the ICI or thereabouts. The news was pretty grim from the war front in Europe; the Germans had occupied most of it and were now contemplating whether to invade England.

Victoria Road School had been built in the last century and, of course, was in the traditional style of the Victorians with its smooth dark clay bricks and the odd row of bright yellow to break the outline up and give it that architectural finish. It was not a very big school but I can remember the playground having a twenty foot wall all around; exactly the same as a prisoners exercise yard and it was very dark, even on the sunniest of days. It was, however, there for a reason, since there was a sheer drop on the outside.

Each morning my Mother would plant my little brown beret on my head and away we would go; my Sister, Susan, often tagging along to get her out of the house because my Father had just come off nights at 6 o'clock and needed some sleep. Some days my Mother would realise with alarm that my Sister was missing and after a quick search around the house, she would hare down to the school and appear at the classroom window looking very distraught. Then, seeing my Sister sat next to me, her face would change to one of relief and she would enter the classroom smiling, full of apologies to the teacher. The two of them would then leave and wind their way back to Langdale Road; my Sister no doubt getting a mild scolding.

It was whilst at Runcorn that I first got a taste of my Father's discipline, initially in the form of a telling off in a very loud voice, much to my Mother's disdain. On one occasion, when my Sister was standing on one of the new chairs (only purchased the week before), she toppled the chair over and broke the back of it. Well, my Father went berserk with her! He didn't seem to be worried whether SHE was all right or not; his main concern was for the chair. The incident was mentally noted by me and I managed to evade any telling off for a while. My Father had some strong principles and how we suffered for them.

One of his main principles was that he would not buy anything on credit or, as he put it, *"on tick"* or *"on the slate,"* so it was understandable later on in life why he was so annoyed over the broken chair; the suite had cost them a lot of money.

The arguments between my Mother and Father were now becoming more frequent and although they may not have been serious arguments to them, to my Sister and I they always seemed very heated.

My Father would often be late reporting off duty due to the war and the security screening, according to him. On one particular Friday, planned weeks in advance, we were off to my Gran's house in Parkside Road, Lower Bebington on the Wirral. My Mother had dressed up to the nines and instructed us not to move in case we messed ourselves up. We stood there like that for an hour until eventually, lowering the lace curtains, my Mother shouted, "Here he is, the so and so!"

My Father, arriving one hour late, rushed up the path and in through the back door, and as he came through the living room door he pulled off his bike clips and said, jokingly, " What a morning I've had," and innocently sat down for his dinner which had been drying up in the oven. He had genuinely forgotten that we were going to my Gran's, or had he? My Mother came racing through the door with the roast dinner balanced on a tea towel and tripped over the threadbare mat and the dinner was launched through the air, landing smack on the front of my Father's police uniform splattering everywhere. There was gravy running down onto his lap, sprouts over his face, and bits of steaming hot potato on top of his baldhead. My Sister and I had made a very swift exit and were sat on the stairs not daring to move. Next we heard my Father scream. It was a very high pitched scream. "I've been scalded," and he stood up lunging towards my Mother.

"Don't you lay a finger on me, it was an accident," she shouted.

Of course we'll never know if it was an accident, because over the years she has never said yes or no, so I give her the benefit of the doubt; although my Father had his own ideas about it and he was always convinced that she did it on purpose. Anyway, he ran out of the room past me and my Sister, glaring at us as if we were in on the plot with my Mother and screamed again. "Oh, ouch, I'll be marked for life," before disappearing into the bathroom switching on the cold water tap. Then he must have buried his head under the cold water because all we could hear were gurgled screams every so often as his head started to cool off.

In the meantime my Mother had tucked my Sister under her arm, grabbed my hand and away we went to Parkside Road, before the screaming red-headed bull came out of the bathroom. I could imagine my Father standing in the living room like one of the bulls in the bullfight looking around quite dumbfounded with nothing to vent his fury on when the bullfighter disappeared behind the board.

A visit to Parkside Road was an exciting occasion for my Sister and I; seeing my Gran and all my Mother's relatives. This was a journey we were to make many times during our early years.

Over the years my Mother gradually refrained from arguing with my Father and just nodded in agreement with him, which appeared to annoy him even more, so she didn't know what to do for the best really. After arguments my Father waged psychological welfare; this consisted of not speaking to anyone

5

for weeks and this really hurt me and my Sister. It caused real mental anxiety for us and no doubt for my Mother as well.

After the weekend at my Gran's it was back to 62 Langdale Road and my Father, where all seemed to have been forgotten about the previous Friday's argument and my Father's head only showed a few red marks. We now entered a silent meal period where my Mother would say, "Tell your Dad his dinner is ready." Therefore, I suppose in a way, they were speaking again.

During the war, changeover of shift would not always be at the police station as it was thought to be a good tactic to confuse the enemy if the changeover was done at different locations around the town. (As if the might of the German army was watching the changeover of two policemen in the middle of nowhere!).

One particular night is quite crucial to my story as my Father was to change shifts with another policeman at the bottom of Langdale Road at the Air Raid shelter. With the location only 5 minutes down the road, my Father decided to have a last cigarette and toast his legs by the fire before going out. He did this every time he went on duty in the Winter and the warmth would last him until he got to the police station. My Mother didn't want him to go on duty this night because she said she *"had a premonition."* My Father looked at her quite bemused and stared into space for about 5 minutes stumped for words. My Mother was always having premonitions so we took little notice of her. However, no sooner had my Mother spoken than there was an almighty bang. The Germans were early that night, but Father insisted on going, saying that the other policeman would be waiting. My Father met the other policeman coming up to meet him and no doubt tell him how he was nearly blown to Kingdom Come.

My Father was more than pleased to see him, because if he had been on time at the shelter, they both would have been killed. He was very morose for months afterwards; why, I don't know, because they were both still alive. So it was fate really that my Father didn't go on duty the usual 15 minutes early, which he always liked to do and of course my Mother's premonition had kept him back a few minutes, although my Mother didn't get any credit for that!

When we lived in Runcorn my Mother would often take me and my Sister over to Widnes market on a Friday; a day out she really enjoyed. We'd start off early in the morning and walk down to the Transporter bridge as it was called. The Transporter was a magnificent piece of engineering because it was a complete bridge similar to a swing bridge but held by giant lashings and pulleys and would travel, suspended over the Mersey from the Runcorn bank across to Widnes. The complete journey took about 20 minutes. Running parallel with the Transporter was the main railway line from London to Liverpool carried by a viaduct which also spanned the river; although the viaduct was about a mile in length. Both these constructions were about 300 feet above the Mersey. As the Transporter arrived at the other side, the barrier would lift and the vehicles and passengers would disembark to their various destinations; some to Liverpool but the majority to the market. The Transporter had shortened the journey for passengers and vehicles so that they did not have to travel to Warrington. Most routes went to Liverpool then as it was one of the biggest ports in the World for both cargo and passengers.

After spending most of the morning rushing around the market looking but not really buying anything, my Mother would say, "We'd better get back to the Transporter now; I have to get your Father's tea ready." Winding our way through the crowds my Mother yanked me off the footpath shouting, "A ladder! ...don't walk under that, it's unlucky!" The window cleaner, hearing my Mother's shout, stopped whistling and in one movement knocked his bucket and some of his water streamed down drowning my Mother. My Mother always wore a hat, trilby style, usually with a feather sticking up. As we looked up apprehensively at my Mother, she burst out laughing. Seeing my Mother laugh instantly brought roars of laughter from my Sister and I. It was great to see my Mother laugh for a change.

I still can't recall my Mother ever having any luck in her life, even though she was very superstitious; never cross on the stairs, always put your right shoe on first, if you spill salt always throw a pinch over your shoulder - they went on and on! Some of these things did rub off onto me and I still abstain from walking under a ladder.

We arrived home in time for my Mother to make my Father's tea and, unusually, every one was happy on this particular day. There would always have to be three large meals a day - a fry up for breakfast, a cooked dinner and a tea - usually consisting of a salad followed by cake.

It was about this time that my Father decided to start disciplining me for minor things and fear of my Father was instilled into me for ever; he was very strict and I could understand him being so later on in my upbringing, although the punches were somewhat heavy at times. The reasons for the beatings seemed rather trivial to me - like riding my bike with no lights and worst of all, letting him see me. I have spoken to other policemen's sons over the years and most of them also suffered some heavy handed discipline. Looking back, I now believe that if I had been brought before the Courts, even for a minor offence, my Father undoubtedly would have lost his job. I don't know if that applies nowadays, but it certainly did then.

The war had now been on for almost three years and there was no sign of it ever ending. We were still diving under the table after the siren sounded and my Mother would listen very intently for the sound of the German bombers; she claimed she could tell the German plane by the long drone it made as it struggled to get its load of bombs to its target for the night. Once the siren went there was never enough time to get to the shelter at the bottom of Langdale Road; well, what was left of it after the stray bomb had blasted half of it away a few weeks before! Once my Mother had herded us under the table she was quite happy - although what protection that would have given us I hasten to think! At that tender age it was all a big joke to me and my Sister, Susan.

To break the monotony of the relentless bombing raids, a circus suddenly appeared from nowhere and set up on a piece of waste land on Weston point. This was my first experience of a circus and my Mother assured me I was going to enjoy it. We took our seats and the trumpets blared to announce the start of the show. The clowns then raced out, faces all white and with big red lips and enormous eyes. They rolled about doing silly things and the older children were laughing loudly - why, I didn't know. I had never seen clowns before and as they moved towards me, I jumped up in fright and away I went, straight out of the marquee and up the road to nowhere, with my Mother racing after me shouting, "They're only clowns with lipstick on, come back!" As the years rolled by I was to meet many more clowns, but most of them were not in the circus!

On my way to school one bright frosty morning, I had this feeling of being watched and as I made my way along Langdale Road, I saw what can only be described as a "thing" suspended in the sky like an aeroplane without wings, grey, oval and casting a shadow over me - as if I hadn't got enough to worry about! There were a lot more dotted around the area 500 feet above. Apparently they were the latest deterrent for the German bombers, anchored by wire which allowed them to sway around and if an unfortunate German pilot happened to catch one of these, he and the plane would be blown up when the gases inside ignited. They were painted grey to match the surroundings and to blend in with the sky and at night they would reflect light all around the area, giving the impression of the Northern lights. If one of the barrage balloons were hit by enemy aircraft, then pieces from it would be scattered all over the district and people would collect the odd bits and use them to make clothes.

Runcorn was now, supposedly, a prime target for the German bombers with the chemical industry all around working all out making the constituents for explosives. There were not many bombs dropped on Runcorn but I can recall many bangs during our stay there, mainly in the distance and probably Liverpool, which was under constant attack during the early part of the War.

At Runcorn my Father went for his first training as a would-be detective and teamed up with a man with whom he was to spend most of his service on the CID - Dixie Davenport. He was a real Phillip Marlowe character with his trilby set at an angle, cigarette drooping from the side of his mouth stuck to his bottom lip as he talked, the Gabardine raincoat with the belt twisted at the back and missing some of the loopholes. My Father could not live up to his standards as he had to be smart with everything in place, even his trilby peak over the eyes and square to his shoulders; but he obviously enjoyed himself while he was on cases with Dixie.

Much to the annoyance of my Mother, my Father would be out all night *making enquiries* and would often arrive home with a faint smell of alcohol and a strong smell of mints on his breath. Dixie would often be round at 62 Langdale Road explaining to my Mother that they had been on a case and it was a very important part of my Father's training. The Waterloo Pub was mentioned. My Mother appeared to believe him, because Dixie had this certain smile as well as being one of the most convincing liars one could ever wish to meet, and no doubt my Father was thankful for him in that respect.

My Father, in uniform, was a true copper and unfortunately for me this also applied at home, but while he was on CID service he seemed to be a lot happier. It's a pity he didn't make a better go of it because the whole family would have had a happier time.

Occasionally my Father would be called up for Army training. Although he was exempt from military service, he was called up for 18 months to a place called Shoeburyness on the South Coast. He had been in the Army for 4 years prior to the war breaking out and it was now necessary for him to retrain as he had been out of the Army since 1934 and things had moved on. More modern methods were being applied, and of course he had to train in case we were occupied by the Germans; as things progressed in Europe and Hitler was eyeing the "White Cliffs of Dover" this was becoming a possibility.

My Father, in his infinite wisdom, advised my Mother to go to her parents, taking my Sister and I to where it would be safer and she would also be with her family and friends. We went, but what a surprise she was in for, especially on the safety front! However, back at Parkside Road my Mother was happy with her relatives, talking about the good times she had working at Levers in Port Sunlight, although she had to terminate her employment with them as soon as she got married; obviously a condition laid down by the police authority in those days.

I can recall many incidents which occurred while we were staying at Parkside Road during the Air Raids and the May Blitz of Liverpool in 1941. Parkside was a crescent about half a mile in distance, with the Birkenhead to Chester main line railway bordering it to the north and Bebington road to the west. I would be just over 3 years old and my Sister still a baby, about one year old, so we were a handful to carry around, especially when the grown ups had to sprint to the shelters in Meyer Park.

One night, after being there a couple of days and enjoying a bit of freedom away from my Father's watchful eye, there was an unfamiliar noise. It was the sound of the air raid warning. It meant nothing to me at that time but to my Mother and my Grandparents, it struck horror into their very being. The noise went on for about 5 minutes; a constant wailing similar to a ship's foghorn only many notes higher. The routine became regular. Immediately my Granddad heard the noise he would shoot upstairs followed closely by my Gran, and then with even more speed they would come down the stairs covered in blankets and heavy coats. In the meantime my Mother would put my coat on and wrap my Sister up in extra blankets, trying to smile but looking very harassed; looking at the window, noting the flashes of the searchlights as they strove to pick up the German bombers as they headed for Liverpool. My Mother would have the pushchair ready for me, and my Sister, Susan, who would be fast asleep, would be handed to my Granddad. As soon as Granddad had confirmed that we were all ready, he would open the door and instruct us all to move fast. Then we'd race down the road heading for the shelters in Meyers Park, panic stricken faces shouting to each other to keep the pace up before the Germans arrived with their payloads of destruction.

As we raced along the footpath past the pig farm there were a few grunts as the pigs were woken up from their slumber by the noise. People would be shouting, some crying and many falling in the dark in their nightly anxiety to get to the shelters. During the blackouts and with the nightly raids, my Mother's nerves became very taut; that wasn't surprising really with two babies to look after as well as herself and her parents. Of course, many people were in the same predicament and many nerves were shattered. I can remember many screams and shouts as bombs intended for Liverpool dropped close to 106. The whole house would shake and I could never understand why it never came down with the constant shaking every night, and this was only from the blast of bombs, say, a mile away.

If the Ack-Ack got too hot for the German bombers over Liverpool they would veer over the Mersey to Birkenhead and get rid of their bombs and then head for home as quick as their engines would carry them. Unfortunately some of the bombs would drop anywhere and it was either your luck running out or the next street's. Many planes were shot down as the search-lights locked onto them and many landed in the Mersey.

"They're getting closer - we'll be pushed for time tonight." These were often the cries of my Gran as we raced on and on. "They were late with that siren tonight," she would mutter as she strove to get her breath.

My Granddad often dropped back and had to lean on the fence trying to get his breath; he was well into his 60s now and a veteran of the 1st World War, having fought and been wound-ed on the Somme. Whether they were late or not was neither here nor there, because they knew if they didn't get into that shelter before the "Gerries" came over, we would be done for. I soon learnt that the siren was followed by the Bombers and we had to move very fast if we wanted to make the shelters. In the mad panic things would be dropped. My Mother would pause but it was a waste of time going back because it was pitch black. My Mother and Gran would hang back for Granddad to catch up as he had the baby as well and she was the main concern for everyone. My Mother never left us for a second on those nightly dashes. As I peered through the night I could see the searchlights wavering across the starlit sky and sometimes, for a few seconds, they would lock onto one of the German bomb-ers and I could clearly see the Swastika on the tail. Then it was gone into the cool night air, only to be picked up again later. They moved very slowly with a full payload of bombs, and once the searchlights locked on, the Ack-Ack would start up and the noise was terrifying for everyone, even more so for me as I did not understand what it was all about.

The Blitz was now well under way and would continue re-lentlessly for a whole month night after night with the same routine - the siren, followed by the bombers, the race for the shelter and remaining there for most of the night in the pitch black, wrapped in blankets waiting for the "All Clear Siren." My Granddad's spirits were kept up by my Sister's smiling face as she looked up at him thinking it was all a game. I thought the same as well.

Finally the shelter would come into sight. It was up a slight hill and my old pushchair would often topple over on the last bend as my Mother spotted the shelter door open and an ARP man welcoming us and pointing with his torch to our benches for the duration of the bombing raid. My Gran seemed to take it all in her stride, as if war had been part of her life for ever. She would come out with such statements as: "They've cheated tonight coming early!" She thought they shouldn't come over during meal times and that there should be a referee to see fair play - pity the Germans didn't know that! "Typical Gerry trick," she would mutter.

Anyway, night after night we would settle into the shelter and listen to the bombers overhead. The noise was deafening with the bombers droning and circling, the Ack-Ack firing constantly and the muffled sound of the bombs dropping on Liverpool, only a couple of miles away over the Mersey. Many a poor soul in that shelter was driven to the edge of a nervous breakdown before the War had finished; unfortunately it was to continue for another four years yet. Pieces of everything would fall from the sky - bits of the bombers, spent shrapnel, still red hot the next morning as we trampled our weary way home, shoulders hunched over, heads bowed, not looking up until we reached 106. As my Mother pushed me back to 106 in the early morning darkness, I could see the sky lit up as if there were a million bonfires lit over on the other side of the Mersey. Liverpool had been almost totally flattened - those poor people.

The German bombers would arrive early most nights now, drop their payload and scoot back to the fatherland. There were some laughs in the shelters though. There was one old dear who made a point of getting down there even before the siren went off so she could have the same seat every night; she would then fall fast asleep only to be woken by the ARP. One morning we were all roused by a delayed action bomb going off about a mile away. It woke the old lady up and she sat straight up and shouted, "Is that the milkman?" Being a milkman then must have been a risky business. People in the shelter either burst out laughing or crying as they all realised they were still alive and the fear gradually drained out of their system.

Back at 106 my Granddad usually made a pot of tea - the cure for all ailments and the best moral booster of all. He would then bring out his accordion and play all the old First World War tunes and sing along for a while, and the activities of the previous night would be forgotten.

My Granddad must have had a hard life having had his shoulder blown in on the Somme and now having to endure another War. Being responsible for the family's safety and well-being, knowing that his only Son was fighting somewhere in France, must have made it a very anxious time for him, but he kept going cheerfully.

One day a neighbour arrived and told my Mother and family about an unexploded bomb with its tailfin showing out of the ground at the bottom of Parkside Road. My Mother took hold of my hand and away we went to have a look at this piece of the German war machine. When we got there, there were hundreds of people milling around peering and some brave ones actually dared to touch it. Actually, everyone believed it to be dead until the Bomb Disposal Squad arrived and told everyone to clear the area immediately. My Mother didn't need a second telling and off we went, back to 106 to tell the tale. Just as we reached the front door there was a terrific explosion and my Mother knew instantly what it was. She grabbed me and hugged me very tightly, crying with fear and relief. "Lucky we came away when we did," she sobbed.

"Lucky!," that was the understatement of 1941. I never found out whether the Bomb Disposal men had blown it up deliberately or whether it went off of its own accord. In any case, it was the second time in 24 hours I had had my eardrums shattered.

Waking up after my mid morning nap I could hear lots of grunting and talking in the back garden. I ventured curiously out into the back but all I could see was lots of dirt being thrown out of a big hole about 10 feet from the back door. Edging closer to the hole I could see my Granddad and a neighbour digging a great hole for all they were worth; it must have been about 6ft deep by this time and 8 x 6 in length and breadth. Apparently they were digging it out in order to assemble the ultimate in shelters - "The Anderson." It was made up of sheets of corrugated iron, galvanised and radiused at one end. It more or less came in kit form with a couple of planks thrown in to sit on. I could see my Granddad scratching his head a few times as he tried to figure out the way the sheets went, while my Gran was having a good old laugh behind the lace curtains in the kitchen. Sometimes she would overdo it and the laughter would drift to my Granddad's ears and he would glare in the general direction of the window, being only too aware that my Gran would be watching most of the time.

The shelter, when complete, would hold about 6 grownups - 3 sitting on either side on the planks. This was much better than having to scurry down to the shelters every night carrying blankets and babies, and dragging pushchairs. No shelter was absolutely 100% protective - they were only meant to stop the blast and the shrapnel and a direct hit would obviously kill everyone within 50 yards of the explosion.

Anyway we eventually progressed from diving under the stairs to the ultra modern in shelters. My Gran took it upon herself to be the organiser once she heard the siren going.

"Quick - down under the shelter; the Gerry will be here soon!"

Most mornings, once we had been given the `the all-clear', my Aunts and some of my Uncles would arrive to see that everyone was alright, and to amuse us in the best way they knew how. My Aunty Ethel would lead with her very infectious laugh and in no time at all she would have us all laughing; my Mother would be the loudest of all, with tears running down her face.

We remained at Parkside for about a year through most of the heavy bombing of Liverpool, and were shook by every bomb that dropped in the vicinity of Bebington. Of course, they were mostly strays because most of them were meant for Liverpool and many for the Birkenhead docks and, of course, Cammell Lairds. 24 people were killed in one night in Bebington alone after a large number of "incendiaries" and high explosive bombs were dropped in early March 1941. The scars are still visible on many of the house roofs today around the Corona Road area in New Ferry, where tiles had been replaced after shrapnel and blast from the bombs had lifted them. Some houses were totally destroyed further down towards the "Shore" with the loss of many lives.

Back at Runcorn, my Father had now returned home from his military refresher course and Ack-Ack duty; we remained there for a while longer before my Mother informed us that my Father was being moved to the Country to a place called "Little Budworth."

CHAPTER TWO

Selkirk Cottage

The small furniture van weaved its way through the narrow lanes of the mid Cheshire plain en route from my Father's previous posting in the town of Runcorn in the chemical making belt of the North Cheshire area. We had spent 3 or 4 years in the Runcorn area but were now heading for the Country.

As we moved deeper and deeper into the rural plains of Cheshire, the scenery became more stunning as the hedgerow flowers were in full bloom and the grass was a lush green. I can recall asking my Mother if we would be staying here for long. There was a long pause as my Mother stared at the wonderful surroundings; "A few years ....I hope," she eventually replied, all the while not moving her eyes from the view ahead.

After several more miles she told me that my Father would have to move around the county a few times before he completed his service; this was an understatement, as we were to move around 10 times in total.

The furniture van swayed as it wove its way along the lanes, touching some of the oak tree branches hanging over the narrow lanes and knocking some off as it veered around the acute angle bends - originally cart tracks trodden by the cattle of a bygone age. We were heading for the small village of Little Budworth on the Oulton Park estate owned by the Egerton Family; a well known Cheshire Gentry family who lived in and around the Mid Cheshire area for hundreds of years. As the lanes became narrower, the furniture van was forced to slow down to a snail's pace and let's just say that `some colourful language' was uttered by the driver - a little bald headed man who could hardly see over the steering wheel! As he attempted to move the gears up and down the gearbox, his face would contort with every crunch of the gears. I knew nothing about gears then, but I do recall thinking to myself that there would not be much left of that one once the van reached its destination.

Eventually we rounded another right angled bend by the Old Mill and Little Budworth pool and there, in full view, was the outstanding feature of the village - St Peter's Church. There had been a church on this site for centuries; initially as a look-out against enemy soldiers during the Civil War and then as a church in its present form (although in much need of renovation). It stood proud like a castle on top of the hill guarding the surrounding district. Directly opposite the church was the Red Lion public house, an old 17th century building converted into a pub, although the original watering hole for weary travellers was the centre house of the church mews cottages where the owner would set up a table outside the house and sell his potent brew in exchange for whatever wares the travellers of the day were selling - mainly salt and trinkets from the market towns of Winsford and Northwich, a couple of hours walk away in those days.

After travelling down a slight hill we passed the local Post Office and the Church Hall on the left hand side. Churches, of course, were usually built on line from east to west and this naturally applied to the church in this village, with the road running parallel being Vicarage Road. At last and with a long sigh of relief from the driver, the furniture van literally ground to a halt outside our new abode - Selkirk Cottage which stood right opposite the Church Hall.

Selkirk Cottage had been built just after the First World War (1919) by a member of the Egerton Family for one of their Scottish relatives. The whole building consisted of two houses - semi detached cottages to give them their proper country name. Our new neighbours were the Tushingham family whose Son, incidentally, was also on the police force at that time. Mr Tushingham, a small, dapper man sporting a grey handlebar moustache, had been in service to the Egerton family mainly as a groom over many years. Although well into his 70s, he would still venture to the lodge on odd days in the week and chop logs for the Oulton Park Lodge fire which in those days was occupied probably by the Squire.

Jumping down from the furniture van, my Sister and I raced up to the new house; the approach was quite stunning with the quaint little garden at the front leading up to an arched open porch. We had arrived in "Little Budworth."

Exploration of the house revealed plenty of nooks and crannies for hiding in. It had three bedrooms with fantastic views over the Little Budworth pool. My bedroom was at the rear of the house which was very spacious but very cold in the winter, facing north. Looking out from my bedroom window was an exhilarating sight first thing on a sunny spring morning, with the early morning mist clearing and the ground laden with a heavy dew reflecting the sun's rays towards my window like sparkling diamonds. The garden at the rear of the house stretched back for about 30 yards with a slight gradient towards the pool. My eyes were drawn gradually as if admiring a recently finished landscape painting with the colours not yet dry moving on across a field of young green corn, larks rising in their ever spiralling ascent up into the shimmering blue early morning sky. Eventually Little Budworth pool would drift into vision with all its fascinating wildlife.

Surrounding the pool were tall bulrushes where the moorhens and the coots paddled in and out, foraging for more food. All this scenery appeared to have been orchestrated on this same day in spring of 1943. A gap in the reeds brought my eyes to the pool itself. There, as if mustered on this single day, were all the animal and birdlife in all its glory scurrying about the pool, busying themselves with all the chores of spring, collecting bits of flotsam for nesting, searching for a mate, preening etc, the local mallard population with young chicks already hatched and making arrow-like waves as they took their first paddle across the pool in search of more food. Pike were jumping for dragon flies as they skimmed back and forth over the water, wings blurred, blues and light greens of their colouring reflecting in the sunlight. Cattle drank their fill at the pool. The pool ended abruptly with the reeds on the far side of the water and the eyes would be drawn upwards onto a gentle slope from the water's edge and gradually up into the clear blue Cheshire sky - so warm and peaceful and seemingly endless.

The stream which fed the pool had its origins to the north west of the village, near the White Hall Farm. The water, on leaving the pool at the east end, went under the road to feed a water wheel in the mill which has long since shut down. During our escapades around the pool, strands of reeds would be picked and individually marked before being thrown into the duct which went under the road. The rush of water would carry them through to the other side, the winner obviously being the first through on the mill side. After leaving the mill the stream flowed east and wound its way across country, eventually joining the River Weaver, south of Winsford. In those days the pool was full of fresh water mussels, often used as ammunition to throw at the pool daredevil as he basked like a whale in the middle of the pool inside a large rubber inner tube. Scattered around the pool were moorings for fishermen to pass many hours with a rod and line. Our little bent pins on the end of willow sticks kept us occupied for hours, although never tempting a fish to bite.

After a few months I got to know the area within a radius of about 1 mile of Selkirk Cottage. Even at that age I had a sense of adventure in my blood; probably inherited from my Great Grandfather on my Father's side who had moved around frequently, eventually to arrive in Gloucester City where he worked as a blacksmith.

CHAPTER THREE

Swallows, Hens and Flowers

On many occasions I would be out of the house virtually all day, but I always managed to get home for my tea in the late afternoon, usually covered in soil, greenery and blackberry juice - most of which would be on my face and very difficult to wash off - as my Mother was to discover when she attempted to remove the stains from my grey diamond patterned pullover - the traditional garment of the day.

At times, as I passed through the back garden to the house, I would have to run the gauntlet of the diving young swallows that had nested in our coal shed, testing their flight feathers and brushing my head as they swooped in very low; it was a game to them, shrieking as they passed. The same family of swallows came back every year and renovated the same nest in the coal shed. There would usually be 5 chicks chirping away for weeks on end as their parents darted in and out through the narrow gap at the top of the coal shed door, their beaks full of flies caught in flight. The fledglings seemed to sense that the parent was close by, because they started chirping a long time before the parent arrived, seemingly chirping "me first, me first."

One quiet, sunny summer afternoon whilst the village was at rest, I thought I would take a peep inside the nest. Placing an old orange box on top of the coal, I was able to peer into the nest and see 5 little yellow beaks permanently in the open position. As I attempted to stroke one of the young birds' heads, its head moved forward as if expecting food off my finger, pecking frantically then realising there was no food and moving back very dejectedly. As I strove to get into a better position to see all the birds, the box moved and I came tumbling down onto the coal, which luckily broke my fall. I scrambled down the pile of coal eventually reaching the bottom, covered from head to toe in coal dust - and bird droppings! Iwent into the house after evading some swooping attacks from the parents of the young swallows, looked in the mirror, sang a few choruses of one of Al Jolson's hits and tried to get the stuff off - but to no avail. My Mother then arrived home from shopping and could not believe her eyes. I thought I'd done a very good job of removing the black mess, but she had other ideas and into the sink I went to be scrubbed with carbolic soap and cold water. I was often threatened with the carbolic soap and cold water if I should ever get into similar states - which I did!

At the rear of the house there was a very long and narrow garden, stretching down to a pigsty at the bottom. My Father would grow rows and rows of vegetables to supply the kitchen table during the course of our stay at Little Budworth. Very often he would exhibit the produce at the Police Show which would be held once a year, along with the Sports Day. It was a good day out for both parents and children. My Father won many prizes at this event. The pigsty, although never used, did come in very useful for a long time as a hiding place.

On the Tushinghams' side there was an old farm - the oldest in the village I am led to believe, farmed by a member of the Rutter family, a well known farming family of the district. A hen from the farm had decided to make its nest in our pigsty and laid eggs for weeks and consequently my Mother had an endless supply of fresh eggs for quite a while. The best taste in the morning is a fresh fried egg with rashers of local farm bacon, and my Mother made sure we had a good breakfast every morning. I can smell, and even taste, those eggs sometimes when my mind wanders back to those far off, young and innocent days of childhood.

In the Tushinghams' garden stood the highest sycamore tree for miles around and it would be a collecting point for all the starlings in the vicinity. As more and more arrived, the branches would be weighed down to almost breaking point and then, as if from a given signal, they would all take flight as one, circle overhead for a while and then disappear over the pool to some unknown destination.

At the side of our house my Mother would grow chrysan-themums. She was very proud of her efforts and sometimes she would enter them in the annual Police Show.

My Mother was always taken in by tales of woe and lis-tened attentively, although I'm sure on many occasions she knew she was being told a sob story. One Friday morning as I was on my way to school, I remember my Mother standing talking to an old lady (whether she was from the village or not, I cannot recall). She asked my Mother if she could have a few bundles of the flowers to take to her Sister in hospital at Northwich. My Mother readily agreed and even helped her to pick quite a number of large bunches. My Mother said that the old lady could hardly see over the top of the flowers, there were that many of them as she shuffled down to the bus stop by the Post Office.

My Mother's highlight of the week was a trip on the bus to Northwich Market, picking up in Little Budworth at 11 o'clock every Friday morning. As she strolled around the stalls, most-ly admiring and not buying, she came to a very well set out flower stall with bunches of chrysanthemums. Mother was standing there comparing them with her own flowers at home when a dear old lady turned round and went to smile at my Mother, but to her amazement she realised who it was and quickly turned away. My Mother was speechless and carried onto the next stall.

"That was the woman who I gave the flowers to this morn-ing," my Mother muttered under her breath. She would always moan after the event. Needless to say, the nice old lady didn't stop outside our gate again - in fact, we never saw her in the village again!

Chapter Four

Happy Times Around the Village

Our Labrador Retriever, Jock, was a true friend and joined me on many of my escapades around the county of Cheshire. My Father had brought him home from a farm in Eaton on a cold and wet night - a little ball of fluff! My Mother fell for him instantly. He soon grew into a very large playful pup and then an even larger fully grown Labrador of very high intelligence.

Every Sunday when he was off duty, my Father would take the family on a walk around the Oulton Estate keeping to the public footpaths where Jock would run forever. He was brown in colour and it was very difficult to see him as he mingled in the bushes and trees of the estate in the late evening light. He would always end up in the pool whether he wanted to or not - my Father would see to that! The pool was covered in white lilies and an iron bridge straddled the pool where it tapered into the banks at either side. The gardens had obviously been laid out by a professional gardener during the latter end of the 19th century and still held their glory, although the Estate Hall had now gone. The bridge was made of wrought iron and the sides were trellised with a gate at either end. The whole scene was reminiscent of Monet's garden at Giverny outside Paris which he designed himself, surrounded by oak trees, conifers and all types of rhododendrons. In the Spring on a cool misty morning there is no better sight in Cheshire.

On arrival at the bridge, Jock had disappeared into the undergrowth knowing very well that my Father was going to shut the gate once we were through, much to the annoyance of my Mother. After my Father had whistled and shouted his name he reappeared, covered in mud and bits of flora. It was understandable why my Father wanted him to go into the water.

We would all be in the middle of the bridge, the gate shut and barring poor old Jock's way, he would be running around in circles and the expressions on his face would make my Mother and Sister plead with my Father to let him through, but to no avail. Jock knew his fate. As we walked on across the bridge, the loose wooden planks rattling with every step, Jock was still testing the water with his paws. As we reached the other side there was an almighty splash and Jock had now launched himself into the water and was swimming for the opposite bank. I could never understand why he made such a fuss over going in the water, because he loved to swim. My Father would say, "That'll get rid of all the fleas he has collected this last week." Once at the other side, he would slither and scramble to get out, eventually managing to get out and run as fast as he could towards us, wagging that very strong tail and shaking all the water off as near to my Father as he dare, soaking my Father and then scurrying off into the bushes, remaining there for at least 10 minutes, knowing by that time my Father would have cooled down. After the time had elapsed, my Father accepted the laughter from us all and I noticed a hint of a smile on Jock's face as he came out from under the bushes again.

Our weekly walk around the estate was a happy time for me because for one day my Father took some interest in my Sister and I. My Father was a very moody man and could change in an instant from laughter to anger, so we had to be on our guard most of the time. Meal times were the worst times, as my Father insisted on strict discipline whilst at the table. If I should laugh or do anything he thought was out of order, there would be a clip around the ear for me.

After our Sunday evening stroll around the village, my Father would walk up to the Egerton pub. If it rained he would stay in and, as he thought, amuse poor old Jock. He would fiddle around with the wireless for hours trying to get bagpipe music and once found he would turn it up full blast. Jock would then twitch his ears, stand on his front legs, head pointed straight up at the ceiling and howl for all he was worth. This would go on for a while and my Father would be laughing that much he could hardly get his breath (this was good to see), ending up on the floor clutching his sides and pleading with my Mother to switch the wireless off. None of us would be in any fit state to do that, because on the rare occasions that we saw Father laugh, it was infectious and we all enjoyed it while it lasted.

After a while the novelty of the wireless and Jock's singing wore off and Father would disappear down the garden to the outside toilet laughing a raucous laugh every time he thought of the poor old dog singing his head off. Jock's ears, when not being entertained by my Father, would always be in the permanent alert position ready for any mood change that may suddenly occur. In fact, Jock knew better than anyone else if a mood change was imminent.

Jock's proudest moment came when my Father went shooting down by Little Budworth pool, mainly at ducks and rabbits - after all, he was a gun dog and rabbit pie was one of my Mother's specialities! I would have to skin and gut them; a task I wasn't too fond of doing - my Father saying he had the hardest job shooting them. Jock would nod in agreement. Many a time I had chewed on a piece of cooked rabbit only to crunch my teeth on a piece of lead pellet - very painful!

Jock remained with us until my Father's last posting. Unfortunately, he could not adjust to the traffic and the concrete. When I think back at the narrow escapes that poor dog had over the years - being hit by a wagon and lying unconscious for hours, and on other occasions being gored by a bull and the vet recommending that he should be put down, my Mother nursing him back to health, spending hours bathing and nursing him day and night until he was fit again.

CHAPTER FIVE

Lock-Ins, Artists and The Village School

Whilst at Oulton Park my Father made many friends - and some enemies, mainly because he was a very thorough copper. I can understand why he was like he was. He was only safeguarding his job, because whilst he was employed at ICI as a teenager, he was sacked on the spot for playing cards in his lunch hour. My Uncle said "The next they heard of him he was in the Army in India with the Royal Artillery." He stayed in the Army for four years, coming out in 1934 and joining the police force.

My Mother regaled us with plenty of tales about my Father during his service with the police around Cheshire - some funny and others he would not mention to her, mainly off duty. In the rural area of Tarporley, he had to report every time he went on duty. It was a 4 mile bike ride along narrow country lanes with no lighting at all through winter, summer, wind, hail or rain with a very dim battery light front and back to help him make his way for his 8 hour shift.

On one cold winter's night my Father had not arrived home from his 2-10 shift and my Mother was very worried. Apparently he said he had to investigate rumours that the landlord at the Red Lion pub at Eaton was having lock-ins. The then landlord had plied him with a few pints of beer until he eventually forgot what he was there for! When he finally left the pub, somewhat the worst for wear, it took him several attempts to get onto his bike, up the slight incline from the Red Lion, but once he got to the Mill corner he picked up a bit of speed and it was mostly down hill to Oulton Mill pool where unfortunately for him he turned sharp right instead of left, and went straight into the pool - bike as well! In his drunken stupor he had managed to surface and scramble up the bank and immediately fell asleep. There was only the one motorised police patrol car in the whole of that division in those days and they searched most of the night, eventually finding my Father asleep and soaking wet! I never did find out who the policeman was that found my Father. Whoever he was, he saved my Father from losing his job, (although off duty, he was still in uniform) and he didn't book the landlord for having illegal lock-ins either - I wonder why???

In the warm months of summer an artist would appear from nowhere and set up his easel and start painting the picturesque cottage next to the Church Hall. I can recollect the black and white half timbered walls of the cottage being covered in red roses. I would sit and watch the artist for hours. He had an old army great coat on, tied with a piece of string and to look at him you would have thought he was a tramp. He sported a very bushy grey beard which had been neither cut nor washed for weeks, and he wore an old trilby on his head to keep the sun out of his eyes as he painted. He would more or less set his easel up at the same time every day in order to catch the same sunlight and the same shadows to give him the correct angles of shade. My Mother would sometimes take him out a cup of tea in the mornings - that was if my Father was on the early shift. It was generally believed that the artist was living under a makeshift shelter of bracken and branches somewhere on Little Budworth Common. His finished paintings were masterpieces to me; the reds and greens were so fresh it was as if he had taken the colours directly off the roses. The following year he did not come back; maybe he had moved onto more colourful pastures.

After a few days settling down into my new surroundings, school was mentioned and the following day I was taken to the village school opposite the Smithy where I was introduced to the Headmaster, a Mr Evans, and Mrs Booth, the teacher of all the lessons at junior level. As it was wartime, they had to make do on a shoestring as all the stationery had to go to the war effort. However, they did a very good job with the limited supply of material they had. The dinners were delivered in insulated canisters every day at noon. Our school must have been the last dropping off stage, because the dinners were often starting to cool off, even worse because as soon as they entered my mouth, I would start to baulk. The very dark green cabbage was not much better with bits of grit and the odd caterpillar; it also had a very bitter taste.

Every day with good intentions my Mother would get me ready for school, plonk my little brown beret on my head and then lift me onto the back of her Sit Up and Beg Bike, and away we would go. I can remember getting as far as the Alms Houses about 200 yards from Selkirk Cottage and I would jump off and run across the fields; how I hated those school dinners! My Mother would catch me and threaten me and say "I'll get your Dad to bring you tomorrow!" I would jump off a few times but eventually we would arrive at the school and Mrs Booth would greet her with a nice smile. We were more or less forced to eat all our dinners because during Wartime they were deemed to be good for us and gave us extra calories. They probably were, but how those broad beans made me ill!! I eventually did get used to the dinners, because a blind eye was being turned to the leftovers on my plate, mainly the broad beans. I am sure one of my parents would have had a word with Mr Evans. I started to look forward to going to school after that escapade.

Mrs Booth, a lovely old lady who looked like a real school ma'am, lived about three miles from the school and would bike across the common, winter and summer, and I can never recall her missing a day whilst I was there - even in the heaviest snowfalls. Years after I had left Little Budworth I would go back occasionally on my bike and always made a point of calling in and seeing Mrs Booth at her small farmstead on the top of Chester Road.

I suppose Mrs Booth's scripture lessons every week had more effect on me than she realised, for in my child's mind I had the village neatly divided up into biblical locations. To the side of the Red Lion pub there was a narrow lane which went out into the fields, and on the right hand side, half way up the land, was a pile of stones covered on either side by two hawthorn bushes which formed an arch over the stones. This, to me, was similar to the place of the Resurrection where Christ was buried before ascending to heaven on the third day. Now a bowling green hut has been built on the very same spot; I only noticed this very recently.

Little Budworth Common was an area of land about a mile square, mostly covered in silver birch trees dotted here and there with pink heather and carpeted with bracken. The Coach Road out of the Oulton Estate bisected the Common right up to the top Tarporley Road. During the summer months the trees would have grown over the road forming a tunnel and travelling along it gave the feeling of going down a rabbit's burrow. Here, I imagined that the Good Samaritan would walk. The Old Smithy opposite the school was where I imagined the birth of Jesus. Jesus with the fish and the loaves was near Little Budworth pool on the far bank from the church.

The Garden of Gethsemane was in a very picturesque corner of the churchyard on the north west wall. It was such an isolated place in the churchyard and by scrambling up the sandstone wall I could look out onto the pool from a different angle and this I thought was the best view of all.

Another bible location to me would be along Booths Avenue and into the wilderness. I would not venture along this route for fear of not ever coming back! As a child these were the pictures of the bible I had dreamed up and this is the first time I have ever thought to mention them.

Most of the children in the infants were in the same class and I became very good friends with three of them. Namely Ken Dobson, Ted Dean and Derek Bratt - the gang of four if you like. Ted lived on a small farm on Well Lane to the east of the Church; he was the eldest by a couple of months. Ken lived on a small farm west of the village and Derek lived in the end house in a row of cottages next to the church. Thrown together by chance, we have kept in touch on and off over the years. Playful fights were often the order of the day as we went on our escapades around the village and they would often take place on a piece of grass surrounding the War Memorial; the most inappropriate place when you come to think about it really! They would only last until one pegged his opponent's arms to the ground for the count of three; sometimes a very slow three and it was usually Ken who came out the winner!

All along the route to school there were numerous distractions - investigating birds' nests, badger sets on the common, climbing the very high wall around the Egerton Estate and peering over whilst hanging by my finger nails - eventually slipping and falling into the well compacted bracken at the bottom which broke my fall. Once I hit the ground I would go into a routine of forward rolls which would take me down to the dell where all the rabbit burrows were - sometimes scattering the young rabbits as they had their early morning stretch and play.

Chapter Six

The Witches Cottage

The Oulton Park Estate was about two miles square and landscaped in the 18th century, originally with a huge hall which unfortunately burnt down in the 1920's and consequently was never judged viable to rebuild. It was strictly forbidden to venture inside the grounds in those days by order of my Father. Originally a road had been etched through the common up to the main road to Chester. The approach to the estate was very picturesque. Directly opposite the Common was the Lodge, built at the same time as the hall itself and occupied by the groom and the gamekeeper. The Lodge was painted in cream with a touch of sunburst yellow and no doubt built of local sandstone. The Lodge straddles the road that approaches the Estate Hall and has an arch in the middle which in days gone by was high enough to let a coach and six horses through up to the Main Hall, hence the name - *The Old Coach Road*.

The Coach Road would also cut across the Northwich to Tarporley road and come out half a mile further on opposite Mrs Booth's farmstead, our school teacher. The Lodge is still there today. The gates of the Oulton Park Lodge are made of wrought iron and have probably been renovated over the centuries. The Park Lodge has been well designed with recesses similar to the Georgian house in London. I would imagine that it would be very cold in the winter, although the Gamekeeper kept a well stocked pile of logs to last through any emergency and no doubt there would be, knowing the winters and the isolation in those days! Once through the Lodge gates the track would wind round eventually arriving at the Hall itself, with its well laid out gardens, tennis courts and lawns for croquet. Around the immediate vicinity of the Hall, the pool would bend in and taper to give a beautiful view across the Cheshire countryside, covered with white water lilies and fringed by rhododendron bushes of multi-colours, straddled by the metal bridge with its latticed sides and wooden boarded walkway.

On many occasion on my way to school I would move off the road onto the Common to see if I could spot the rabbits or the foxes washing out the sand from their fur, after a night's sleep in the burrows and dens. I had often seen them, but on this day it appeared that they were having a lie-in - maybe they had been out all night hunting prey for their young. I was about to tread my way back to the road when suddenly about 20 yards away, a rabbit appeared, closely followed by her kittens out for their morning warm up. I watched for a while but by this time it must have been well past 9 o'clock so I dashed through the wet bracken and even wetter grass, eventually arriving onto the road with my feet soaked. I squelched along for about 20 yards and then decided it would be better if I took my socks off and try to dry them in the early morning sun which was now flickering through the silver birch trees and which must have given off a little bit of heat, because my socks started to steam. After half an hour I gave up and hopped into school half an hour late!

I turned sharp right through the school gates and on into the class, getting a very disapproving look from Mrs Booth, who by this time had given up asking where I had been until now. After the lesson she took me to one side.

"Don't you like assembly Ivor?" she asked.

I did, but I preferred to roam around the Common and find things out for myself.

The school was also built of the local sandstone as was the Church and Lodge, and no doubt the Oulton Hall, well built and of a similar design to many of the schools throughout the Mid Cheshire region. I can recollect it having two large sycamore trees in the playground often used as a base for many games and they had been well etched over the years, with hearts and the initials of girlfriends and boyfriends. The playground was divided into two by a fence which was 6 feet in height with iron railings. One half would be for the juniors and the other half for the older children, and it was strictly forbidden to enter into each other's areas.

It was after school that our education would really start. Turning left outside the school gate instead of right for home, we would head for the small Hamlet of Rushton having received information that there was a swan's nest on the lake in the estate grounds, just visible from the top of the wall. Knickerbrook, which was in spring flood and running over the road into the estate pool, was fed from the Oulton Mill pool. After spotting the swan's nest in the distance and the swans busy gathering reeds etc for the nest, we carried on to Shaws Farm and on into the hayloft playing around for hours, swinging in the beams and throwing hay and straw at one another - no doubt the laughter could be heard all over the village, and not realising that time had moved on quickly and it had now become twilight, verging on darkness.

When the three of us realised it was so dark and knowing that we had to pass the Witches' Cottage, glances were exchanged as we each waited for someone to make a suggestion. It was agreed silently as we all moved in unison towards the loft ladder, out of the barn and down the lane towards Knickerbrook, the only way home. The bats were now fluttering around squeaking and diving low to investigate the movement down below them; how they managed to miss the telephone wires was a mystery to me! The road swept around parallel to the estate wall and then curved away from the wall and there, in front, was the Witches' Cottage, and as we moved closer my stomach started to tighten. We were almost level with the cottage and about to make a run down Knickerbrook Hill when a big black cat jumped off the wall, landing right in front of us, turning to look at us with evil green eyes, spitting and screeching, before darting across the land and into the bushes on the other side. We had now frozen on the spot, only to be aroused by someone chopping wood at the back of the cottage. Smoke and sparks were flying out of the crooked chimney stack built up the side. Fear had now started the adrenaline flowing and we were about to make another run when an owl made our minds up for us. The owl hooted above our heads from a branch of the large beech tree, and this immediately put another 10 miles an hour onto our speed, as we raced down the hill, not stopping until we were out of earshot of the owl and, what we thought, was the witch chopping sticks. It was now pitch black as we caught our breath and all that could be heard was the flow of the water as it ran from one side of the road to the other, gently lapping over our shoes.

We had now calmed down and were on the move again when, across the still night air, came a tapping sound. It was a noise similar to a man moving on a wooden leg.

"Pirate" said Ken, and no sooner had he said it, than we dived under the hedge on the bend out at Knickerbrook, trembling with fear as the terrible apparition drew closer and then passed by. We eventually opened our eyes when it was about 20 yards passed and, to our utter relief, it was one of the farm labourer's with a walking stick! Enough is enough, I thought to myself and both Ken and Derek obviously thought the same, so we decided to get a move on and not let anything else distract us.

The country has its own night sounds when all the nocturnal animals come out to hunt their prey. I know for sure that we heard most of the sounds that night! After that escapade my Mother set a very strict boundary as to where I could venture after school, and the limit was Knickerbrook - as if I would have ventured any further after our night of turmoil!

CHAPTER SEVEN

Messages from the Trenches

On my way to school I would press my ears against the telegraph pole - this was my own innocent way of listening to the world. The wind blowing across the telegraph wires was like the sound of a thousand guitar strings vibrating together and giving off messages, going to all parts of the globe. With the War at its peak, I would imagine messages being relayed from Hitler to his Generals and deciphering them, and when I eventually arrived at school I would tell my friends many stories. On many a morning I would be greeted with "So, what's the latest from the trenches then Ivor?", whereupon I would make something up quickly, such as "Hitler's had his moustache shot off." That would get a laugh because we would all make up our own little ditties and sing them around the playground, all aimed at the Nazis, not knowing who they were of course, just that they were the enemy.

The police had now installed a telephone at our home so that they could get in touch with my Father more quickly. Little Budworth 367 - that was the number; it sounds like a Glen Miller tune, but it was actually our telephone number - strictly for police business mind you.

I spent a great deal of my time on my way to school learning the ways of the country, calling in at Park Farm, Tom Rutter's farm and watching Mrs Rutter making cheese in the churn, turning it over many times to solidify the milk and, eventually, produce a curd from which that lovely creamy Cheshire Cheese would emerge. By adding the by-product, whey, she would make that even tastier Cheshire butter and would give me a crust of bread with a spread of the butter about half an inch thick, before sending me on my merry way to school .....oh, happy days!

The early morning fragrances that floated around the village could have helped me to find my way to school blindfolded. Leaving home I would walk on the right hand side, passing the vicarage on the left, almost opposite our house. About 50 yards further on, on the same side as the vicarage, was Tom's farm with the very well rotted manure on the midden in the middle of the farmyard, on a frosty morning steaming and wafting over the wall and along the country lanes like a regiment of will-o-the-wisps. The mass of the midden waiting to be spread over the fields to enhance the growth of the corn, potatoes, mangold-wurzels and many other crops.

Opposite Park Farm were the Alms Houses on the same side as "Selkirk Cottage" and again built of the local sandstone. The Alms Houses were small and compact with four or five rooms and bedrooms which housed the elderly people of the village, and were maintained by the Church. Leaving the Alms Houses and the smell of the hedgerow honeysuckle, another 20 yards on we arrived at the War Memorial - a monument to the men of the village who had laid down their lives in the First World War, with flowers left on the sandstone shelves from previous Remembrance Days. The memorial stands outside the Egerton Pub on a triangle of well maintained grass. On leaving the memorial I would jump up onto the other sandstone wall, walking along and balancing precariously until reaching the end. The smell of the hawthorn flowers was overwhelming. Then, crossing Park Road heading for the Common area opposite the Oulton Park Lodge, would come all the wild flowers - foxgloves, honeysuckle laden with pollen, bees darting in and out in their never ending search for more pollen to keep the Queen Bee going and to ensure that the hives survive for another summer. The fragrance of these flowers drifting from the common will stay in my memory forever.

Winter in the village was often very cold and the frost and fog would hang around for days. It would be very eerie at dusk when the winter sun started to set behind Eddisbury Hill casting long shadows through gaps in the fog and giving the appearance of dancing icemen with their yellow and red shawls swirling in the light breeze. On occasions the village would be cut off from the outside world for days if there had been a very heavy snowfall which had drifted up the hedges for several feet.

And what transport there was could not get through and this was when the Shire Horses would come into their own. They could plough through anything, pulling a cart behind full of mangolds for the cattle in the fields.

However, no matter how bad the weather was, school would always remain open and Mrs Booth would not worry about what time people arrived; she always managed to get there on her Sit Up and Beg Bike. Heating was from an old cast iron fire in the centre of the room. On arrival at school the place would be freezing until Mr Evans got the fire roaring with logs and everyone would try to get as close as possible to try and thaw out and dry their saturated gloves and scarves ready for the next snowball battle. I can remember the plasticine being like blocks of ice and having to roll it in my hands for hours in order to soften it up to make farmyard animals.

After the short lesson it was time for our dinner - cabbage and broad beans...yuck! In the playground attempts were being made to build giant snowmen by different groups. This kept most people busy and so retain the heat that had been absorbed in the classroom. It was one of those days that we were all huddled against the sandstone wall sheltering from the cold easterly wind - actually, waiting for the bell to ring and, as it was so close to Christmas, to go back into the classroom to sing Carols.

Making my way home from school at the end of the day, the sun throwing out light across the snow giving off beautiful hues of yellow and orange, it would take me hours to arrive home - mainly due to snowballing and rolling down the banks of fresh lily white snow, clothing saturated. This was the first deep snow I had made my way through alone. For me the winter could go on forever - the cold and numb fingers never seemed to bother me at all!

CHAPTER EIGHT

The Chaffinch and Blackbirds Nests

During the early spring I would examine the chaffinches nest in the throes of construction. I first discovered the nest one morning after quietly watching two of them flying in and out of the hawthorn hedge. They were carrying horse hair, teasel and chicken feathers in their mouths to build the nest. I carefully noted the position and left a stone on the top of the bank directly under the nest, before carrying on to school to be late - as usual. The chaffinches nest took about 7 days to complete and I had watched most of its construction and was filled with wonder.

I always kept to the right side of the road when going to school, past the War Memorial and then arriving at the nest neatly tucked away in the hedge - well protected by the thorns on the branches. It was just the right height for me to peer in without stretching and balancing on tiptoe.

One Monday morning, to my amazement, there was an egg in the nest, beautiful in colour - white with reddish scrawl marks all over it. It was so fragile to hold that I had to put it back quickly before it cooled off and cracked. The Mother bird appeared on top of the hedge not too far away looking concerned, so I moved away quickly.

I called at the nest at about the same time every day and there would be a fresh egg in the nest . Five – the usual number for a chaffinch. One of the birds would be sat on the nest every day for about a fortnight and then, eventually, one mid-May morning, there in the nest, clawing around on top of the remaining eggs, was what could only be described as the scrawniest looking thing I had ever set eyes on, with little bits of fluff stuck here and there with a great big yellow beak stuck right in the middle, permanently open. A total of five chicks eventually hatched out and the parent birds would be kept very busy, darting in and out of the nest with mouths full of caterpillars, flies and grubs of all colours and sizes, to fill the ever open mouths. I didn't tell a soul about the nest because there would no doubt be egg collectors around, and I always checked at the weekend to see that they were alright. What I could have done, I don't know, but in my innocent mind I thought it would keep the predators away and give them some protection.

During the summer holidays the fledglings were overflowing out of the nest - legs and beaks hanging everywhere, testing their wings for lift-off. Then, one morning, I arrived at the nest and to my disappointment they had all flown. It was a sad day for me because I looked forward to visiting them every morning and talking to them, noting how things progressed, and the parents did not seem to mind once they had got used to seeing me, chirping away in that very distinct song they have - "little bit of bread and no cheese."

A few days later Ken and I were wandering around the village throwing stones at telegraph poles etc.

"I see the young chaffinches have flown then" he said.

"Which chaffinches?" I replied innocently.

"The ones by the War Memorial," he said abruptly.

He had also been watching them from the beginning and, unknown to both of us, the birds had been receiving double protection, in a manner of speaking.

There would be many occasions when I would come into contact with nature, mostly admiring from a distance, but there would be several incidences when I would come off second best.

One day after meeting at Ken's farm, having a natter about places we should visit in the area during the course of the day, it was decided we would go to the American dump down by the White Hall. Our main interest would be the "Yanky Comics." We always shared things we found. Sometimes we would strike it lucky finding tins of cigarettes (sometimes with quite a few in them) - which we would save for a rainy day. We would also occasionally find sweets and chewing gum still in the boxes and their wrappers, so they would be quite safe to eat.

On our way down to the "Yanky Dump" down the lane, more or less directly opposite Ken's farm which continues straight up to the White Hall built on a slight hill and overlooking the village from the west, we passed the filter beds covered in sand and sprouting giant watercress (incidentally picked during the last century for the tables of the big Cities). We ate a couple of stalks but spat most of it out as we found the taste of it very hot, sharp and gritty - probably due to the sand in the filter beds - once the sewerage system for the Oulton Hall estate. Thinking back, we were very lucky we didn't catch typhoid or some other disease come to think of it! I did have some stomach upsets, but would always blame the school dinners.

Down from the White Hall flowed a freshwater stream to the Little Budworth Pool from the West, and alongside there was a brick building with parts of a broken pump inside; possibly used by the Water Board or maybe even to collect fresh water from the stream to supply the villagers of the last century. Inside it was dusty and rafters were rotting away, but we still decided to climb up and look for a rare birds nest. As I clambered around the rafters, one snapped and I fell to the ground which, luckily for me, was covered in well compacted straw. The crack of the rafter disturbed a female blackbird off its nest and she swooped low and through the unhinged door. I immediately climbed back up but could not see into the nest, so Ken gave me an extra push and I managed to get my grubby little fingers into the nest where I felt four very warm eggs. In the meantime, Ken's usually very steady shoulders started to wobble with my weight, and the next thing I know I'm back on the ground again, and we're both roaring with laughter. Unfortunately I had brought one of the eggs down with me and it had landed on top of my head, splattering, and was now running down my face in yellow and white stripes. I tried to rub most of it off with some grass, but it matted into my hair - which was now starting to stand up vertically like the crest of a cockerel and the more I tried to flatten it, the worse it would go.

All the way back to Ken's farm, we would periodically burst out laughing, rolling into the grass bank and holding our sides with pain. Why I was laughing, I don't know, because I couldn't see what a mess I looked, but just to see Ken laugh was enough for me, and away I would go again with tears running down my face mixing in with the egg, and creating an even bigger mess. We eventually parted company at the Pinfold, as Ken was almost home. I quickened my pace as I came towards the Alms Houses, but unfortunately one of the old codgers was leaning on the gate puffing on his pipe so I darted across the road. He gave me a long hard stare, his eyes following me, head not moving and then blinked and muttered "Modern day kids....I know what I'd do with them!" I almost answered him, but thought better of it and instead I gave him a wry smile and crossed back onto the other side of the road, and so on passed Tom's farm. Tom was busy organising the cows into the shippon for milking so I knew it was teatime. He gave one of the cow's a smack with his bare hand and glanced over to me.

"How long have you been wearing Brylcreem then, young Ivor?" he asked with a smile, still gripping his pipe in between his teeth. I told him the story over a distance of about 20 yards and the shouting brought Mrs Rutter out. She volunteered to clean me up with one of her milk concoctions, but I declined her offer and ran the rest of the way to Selkirk Cottage.

When I arrived home my Father was busy digging in the garden and as he grunted and turned another clump of earth over, he glanced at me with those puzzled eyes. As usual he never uttered a word and continued digging. By this time I was round the corner of the outside WC and proceeded into the house where my Mother was making the tea.

"What happened to you?" she asked. I didn't answer and went straight upstairs to my bedroom where I looked through the window to see how my Father was taking it. He was leaning on his spade with a bemused look on his face and I thought I saw a hint of a smile there - just maybe! My Mother spent hours washing my hair and combing the yoke and egg white out, and the next day my hair had a beautiful sheen to it - as if it had been washed in one of those modern-day shampoo products. However, I resented Ken and Derek calling me "Spike" for a few days afterwards!

CHAPTER NINE

The `Over' Fair

A rumour was circulating around the school that a fair had arrived in the small village of Over, which was about 4 miles from Little Budworth and bordering the town of Winsford. As soon as school was over, Ken and I made our way across the Common, passed the Pool and walked all the way to Over. I had never been to a fair before but I knew it would cost money, so I took about two and six pence (half a Crown), which my Granddad had given to me on his recent visit to Budworth; he loved coming to the village.

As we drew closer to the fair I could hear the music from the pianola playing as the waltzers whizzed round and round. We had a go on many things and I was particularly fascinated by the Roller Penny, as there was a slim chance I could win some money. I was just happy to be there and stare in amazement at all the activities that were going on around me. We wandered around for hours looking at the flashing lights and the speed of the roundabouts. Of course, I would love to have gone on everything, but my funds would not stretch that far.

After spending all our money we had not realised that night had fallen. Finding our way to the fair was relatively easy, but going home in the dark would be another matter. We had walked for a long time and at last came to the turnoff into Park Lane, and eventually back along the lane that went passed Ken's farm. We had managed to pick out some of the milestones on the route which assisted immensely, but they only gave the distance between two towns, or villages in our case. We would turn signposts round to point to the opposite direction - this was said to confuse the enemy; if there ever was an invasion by Adolph!! It was now very dark as we arrived at Ken's farm, and we had no idea of the time. Ken went in to face his parents who would no doubt be concerned, while I carried on again passed the Pinfold, The Egerton Pub and as I rounded the Alms Houses I saw down the lane my Father just going out on duty for his 10 o'clock shift. He was just cocking his leg over his bike. That was enough for me! I went through the Egerton Pub grounds, over the stile at the rear and into Ken's fields, before running as fast as my little legs would carry me into the barn of Mr Dobson's farm, disturbing half the poultry as I settled down for the night on the straw bales.

As I settled down in the barn there was a commotion and people were scurrying around everywhere.

"You go that way, and I'll cut him off this way" I heard them shout.

I then heard the most frightening sound of the click of a twelve bore shot gun and that was enough for me. "Don't shoot....it's me - Ivor Goolding!" I pleaded.

Apparently what had happened was that Ken's cousin, Phil, had been having a wash in the kitchen and glanced through the window. He noticed a dark shape ghosting across the top field and heading for the farmyard. With no hesitation he shouted, "Fox heading for the chicken coops!"

The whole family ran out of the house and surrounded the barn and the chicken coops. After calming me down, Mr Dobson took me home to Selkirk Cottage and explained to my Mother what had happened.

"It's a good job your Father's not here!" she scolded - telling me off in her own way. Little did she know that I had seen my Father going on duty, thinking that he was looking for me.

Ken's Father's farm was a playground for us and if we didn't meet at Tom Rutter's then we would meet there. Ken would sometimes borrow his Sister Anne's Sit Up and Beg Bike; he could ride it, but I hadn't learnt at that time. I tried for hours to get my balance, but to no avail.

"Tomorrow we will go to the hill between the Church and the Old Mill where you can learn to ride the bike," announced Ken - more through frustration than anything else!

After school the next day we called at the farm, picked up a couple of "Slobber Chops Pears," Ken jumped on the bike and we made our way to St Peter's Church. At the top of the hill I attempted many times to get my balance but without success. After 20 minutes Ken must have thought I would never get the hang of it, so he held the back of the seat, positioned me on the bike right at the top of the hill, and gave me a push as he ran alongside. I was concentrating on the front as I careered down the hill, picking up speed, wobbling everywhere and going up and down the kerb. I managed to stay on, thinking that Ken was holding the bike. Thank goodness there was no traffic around. Gathering more speed I glanced around to ask Ken how he thought I was doing but, to my horror, he was standing at the top of the hill waving and laughing uncontrollably! I was on my own and speed increased as I gathered momentum, with a few extra wobbles for excitement and going at 50 miles an hour - as I thought! I was so overjoyed at staying on the darn thing that I couldn't have cared less what was around the bend. Faster and faster I went, and pulling on the brakes made no difference at all at that speed until, eventually, I lost control of the bike and at the corner of the mill I jumped off, with the bike continuing ahead passed the mill, with me landing in the ditch on top of a bed of very wet nettles. I jumped up covered in stings and shouted, "I've done it!" not caring one bit about the pain of the nettle stings. I could ride a bike!!

At the top of the hill as I arrived back pushing the bike (as the hill was so steep), Ken was rolling around on the grass clutching his sides as he laughed. After that momentous day in my life I would often be seen wobbling around the village on the old Sit Up and Beg Bike.

Chapter Ten

Locked in the Bell-Tower

Well Lane, which was situated just passed the Church, was another area where we could get lost for hours in the kale fields. The kale towered above our heads like a thick forest and gave rise to all sorts of games. It was very easy to hide once in there, but often difficult to find our way out! It was laid out in rows like giant corn stalks. The stalks of the kale were very thick and where stalks had broken off, the very sharp edges would cut our arms and yank pieces out of our pullovers. After a game or two and a few bites at the smaller stalks, which tasted very similar to mangold-wurzels, we decided to venture down Well Lane which was out of bounds to me (why, I do not know, because it was only a marshland, but my Mother said it was a swamp). The whole field would have lapwings' nests scattered around tucked away in the grass, eggs camouflaged to match the surroundings and the Mother flying around, shrieking a warning when we came near to the nest. We did inspect a few of the nests and admired the eggs which were mottled and warm. Lapwings' eggs were supposedly eaten in the 19th century - I believe they have a very rich taste, but I certainly wasn't going to find out!

I saw my first grass snake slithering along through the nests, taking the odd egg here and there - it was about 3 feet long.

After running away from the snake we decided to head for the Churchyard. We climbed the lyche gate, making sure we didn't tread on any of the gravestones, mostly flat, and made of huge pieces of sandstone with the names of people who had lived and died over the centuries in the village of Little Budworth. It was a small graveyard with some graves headed with marble angels dotted about, mainly family graves.

We decided to climb the yew trees with their distinct smell and survey the district from the top, or as far as we dared to climb. The yew trees were planted in the churchyard to ward off any evil spirits, and I thought they did a good job because I had never seen any or wanted to! The Church of St Peter can be seen for miles around and it was originally built in the 16th century - not as high as it is now though. It was then restored and extended in the 18th century. It had a tall castle-like tower to hold the bells which peeled out every Sunday, summoning the community to the morning and evening services. The Cheshire sandstone has gradually eroded over the centuries and the Church is now in need of extensive restoration. Inside the Church, to the west end, there was an organ pumped by hand which gave out a beautiful tone - mainly due to the very good acoustics which enabled the music to flow around the ceiling and reverberate, seemingly, for ever. Immediately opposite the organ, looking to the east, was the pulpit where many a sermon was orated to the villagers over the years. The organist had a mirror so that he could get an indication from the preacher of when the next hymn was about to start - sometimes a little late, dare I say it, and much to the annoyance of the preacher!

That evening, immediately after tea and after running amok all afternoon in the kale fields (where we found the energy I don't know - it must have been the fresh farmhouse butter and milk), we decided to climb to the top of the Bell Tower. The Church tower had a square parapet with three turrets on each of the four sides and had made a good lookout post over the years. We really believed that from the top of the Church tower we would be able to see in the distance the edge of the world.

After managing to swing the big oaken door open between the three of us, we ventured nervously inside it. It became very dark and we could smell 300 years of flaking sandstone and dust, which was no doubt created by birds and bats over the centuries. Ken suggested we forget the whole idea and I tended to agree with him. However, something was urging us on - almost against our will. We nudged each other forward and, after the first few steps, we seemed to pluck up the courage, but after about 10 paces inside, the big oaken door (which we had purposely left slightly ajar), slammed shut with an echoing bang that must have been heard for miles, as it went on echoing around the Church and the Churchyard in the dusk. That was a signal for me to move rapidly up the spiral staircase, followed closely by Ken and Derek. We then paused halfway up and listened for a while. All was silent as we stood in the shafts of light that shone through the narrow slits in the wall of the Church. We then heard a scratching sound on the door, like an animal of some sort trying to get into the Church. As we scurried right up to the top of the spiral staircase, passing the bells which were also covered in dust, we arrived at the small trap door that led onto the top of the parapet at the top of the Church tower. We pushed it open, scrambled onto the parapet and froze for about 10 minutes; our little hearts racing, our eyes flickering everywhere. How we managed to get up that spiral staircase so quickly, I will never know, because it was very narrow and the steps were worn with the constant running up and down by the lookouts and bell ringers over the previous centuries.

At last we recovered our composure and walked over to the castle turrets where we clambered up and peered over. By this time it was now dusk, and as we squinted down at the ground below us it seemed to be miles away, and houses in the immediate vicinity looked like dolls houses. After a while I became dizzy and fell back onto the floor of the parapet. We then unanimously decided to call it a day and there was a mad dash for the trap door.

Peering over the parapet I had noticed the pinafore shape of my Mother standing outside Selkirk Cottage looking up and down the land, wondering where I was - little did she know how close I was!

Two barn owls decided to swoop low over the Church top, again frightening the lives out of us and giving off loud shrieks as if warning us to get off their hunting territory. This dampened our enthusiasm for adventure even more as we again struggled to get through the trap door.

In the panic I can recall two of us getting through the small trap door together - no mean feat, as we were all stocky lads! Our dash onto the spiral staircase was halted by the absolute blackness that enveloped us as we groped our way down the steps. Every half dozen steps there would be a flickering of light through the small slits and our arms and legs were cut by the rough sandstone walls as we moved stealthily down to the bottom, looking at one another every so often to make sure we hadn't picked up another being - either human or spiritual! It appeared to be alright, because all I could see in the gloom were two very ashen faces looking straight at me - eyes frozen and wide open.

Eventually we reached the bottom of the steps and made a dash for the oaken doors. I felt for the latch and tried to pull the door open but it wouldn't budge. The three of us tried, but it still would not move. We were trapped and our sighs of relief quickly turned to sobs.

We banged on the door and the sound echoed all around the spiral staircase. If the word "panic" had not been thought of up to that time, I think this was going to be the time and the place. Seven and eight year old children in a flat panic, trying to think logically! Finally we decided to return to the top of the tower and shout to anyone who may be passing down below. Unfortunately, at this time of night most of the villagers would be settling down to their warm cup of Ovaltine - a wartime concession issued by the Government. Others would either be inside the Red Lion or on Dads Army duty, or combining the both.

We waited until 10 o'clock and eventually the regulars started to make their way home, filing out one at a time through the narrow door. We shouted at most of them but no one heard our shouts for help from that distance - and in any case they probably thought it was the local owl population airing their tonsils.

Eventually Tom Rutter appeared and stood outside the door, looking around him and taking deep breaths of the warm summer air. At last he glanced up at the Church clock, pulled out his Fob watch and shook it to confirm that the Church clock was correct by his, and then put it back into his waistcoat pocket. He then decided to roll some thick twist to load up his pipe, filled the pipe and lit it. He gazed everywhere except up to the top of the Church. He was never going to hear our shouts, what with the bats and the owls, and the cows coughing in the adjoining fields - it was a hopeless task.

At last there was a lull in the cries of the night and we managed to get into harmony and, between the three of us, compiled a really loud scream.

Our wailing voices drifted across the Churchyard which had obviously reached Tom's ears because he immediately took his pipe out of his mouth, squinted his eyes and tried to focus in the direction of the screams. First he looked into the Churchyard through the wisps of the early evening mist which swirled around the gravestones and the yew trees. Initially he ignored our frantic shouts - he probably thought he'd had one too many and was hearing things. However, we persisted in our cat wailing and Tom looked straight at us peering through the parapets and whispered, "Who be that up there?"

Tom moved towards the Church steps and there was another mad scramble to get to the bottom of the spiral staircase. At last we stumbled to the bottom and the door was opened by Tom who had a concerned look on his face at first, because at this point he was unable to see who it was in the gloom and dust. He said that someone must have been having a joke with us because the door had been tied with a piece of string on the outside. We never did find out who the joker was, but we all had our own ideas and I noticed that Ted kept well away from the group as we told our story in the school playground the next day.

Tom, not for the first time, took me home where I had to explain to my Mother what had happened. Fortunately my Father was on duty.

Some days after our little escapade on the Church roof, I passed Mr Salmon, the Vicar, and he stopped me and began telling me about certain children in the Parish venturing into the Church at night. I wonder who that could have been. He continued on to highlight the dangers of climbing steep steps at night and assuring me that "the bats in the belfry could inflict a nasty bite if disturbed."

The message got home to me instantly, and I never dared go up that spiral staircase again.

Chapter Eleven

Our War Effort, VI's and VE Celebrations

On my way to school one winter's morning in late 1943, not really bothered whether I got to school or not, I glanced into the Alms House windows quickening my pace as my gaze latched onto one of the resident's staring straight at me - their eyes not blinking. As I passed the War Memorial I could see Ken waving frantically from the small field behind the Egerton Pub, and as I got closer I thought the field was flooded, but on further inspection I realised that it was strips of silver paper. Neither Ken nor I had any idea what it was doing there and on arrival at school we told Mrs Booth and she asked us to pick as much up as we possibly could; she even allowed us to go home early to do this. Apparently it had been dropped by German pathfinder aircraft to throw our radar system out and allow their heavy bombers a clear run into the big cities of Liverpool and Manchester.

We did pick most of the silver paper up and thought we had made a contribution to the war effort but, alas, the bombers did find their targets on many nights and the cities were heavily bombed night after night.

Mrs Booth was proud of our little effort, "But don't be late for school again," she would say in her best scolding voice.

Also at the time the RAF were starting to get the better of the Luftwaffe and there would be plenty of vapour trails to be seen, spaggettied in the skies above Cheshire as they twisted and turned in the many dog fights that went on for hours, and the odd German fighter spiralling down to earth to explode in a ball of smoke and fire, and then silence.

Even then we had been so hyped up to hate anything Nazis that we felt no remorse for the poor pilot who had obviously died a horrific death in the inferno.

As the War progressed I began to notice how things had started to speed up considerably in the air. I can still visualise the scene one bright summer's morning when a Lightening Twin Fuselage aircraft flew very low over the village, swooping in from the Common over Selkirk Cottage and banking around the Church, and then over the pool and away to some unknown destination at a very high speed. The camouflage was useless against the clear blue Cheshire sky.

The village of Little Budworth was isolated from the outside world in those days; the nearest main road being about 2 miles from Lodge corner. The same families have lived there for centuries going about their daily country life.

The local landowner then was Sir John Egerton and he lived inside the Oulton Park Estate. The original hall was burnt down in the 1920's but there is a very good painting of it in The Egerton Arms pub, which is now owned by Ken. The Egerton family treated the villagers of Little Budworth very well and in return they worked hard for their employers.

Oulton Park was unfortunately turned into a race track in the early 1950s and all the top drivers of the day would compete at the very picturesque track, with its natural undulations, large oaks and mature chestnut trees dotted all around.

Just before the end of World War II things begun to change very rapidly, with improvements in travel and general living conditions, but for the people of the village the change came gradually. Some did not want to change their lifestyle and preferred the old traditional way of life, and if I'd have had the good fortune to have stayed in the village, I certainly would have preferred the same way of life also, and let the world go by at its own speed if it wanted to.

I absolutely loved the village at Christmas time and if it snowed then that would be an added bonus, because it would resemble many of the traditional Christmas card scenes sent through the post.

I spent three Christmas's at the cottage and to me, as with most children, Christmas was a very exciting time, especially searching around the bedrooms to try to find our presents. We would stay awake on Christmas Eve hidden under the clothes, just in case Father Christmas did come down the chimney - which I had in my room. Yes, I think that was a very exciting part of my childhood and I can't think of any other time, apart from watching my own two children opening their presents on a Christmas morning.

The local Vicar, Mr Salmon, would organise a Carol Singing march around the village. Most of the people and some of the children would congregate outside the Church before moving on like sheep following Mr Salmon to our first destination, which was usually on the corner of Well Lane and Mill Lane. It was impossible for the Vicar to get the ensemble to sing harmoniously and in the end most would be singing out of tune. The children usually ended up singing their favourites, such as "Away in a Manger" and "Hark the Herald Angels Sing," apart from the main group.

Snowballs were lobbed around indiscriminately - much to the annoyance of the Vicar, who would be the main target, along with the verger and they would be stood right in the middle of the choristers. The verger would be holding the lantern above the Vicar's head and trying to concentrate on his singing as well.

The whole night would be extremely enjoyable, with most people contributing warm mince pies and money, and over the course of the evening a considerable amount of money would be collected which was used to go towards the Church requirements; mainly to the Alms Houses and any repairs that the Church needed.

In those days village life tended to revolve around the Church to a greater extent than it does today; although this is probably due to the many other distractions that are available today.

Reverend Salmon only died a couple of years ago at the age of 94. On a Sunday morning watches could be set by his movements around the village, as if he were letting everyone know that the Sunday morning service was imminent and they should be preparing to leave for Church. He appeared to glide along the footpath, as if on castor, his surplice gown flowing in the fresh morning breeze as he made his way along, humming one of the hymns that he had selected for that particular Sunday in the Church calendar. He would have a copy of the Bible neatly tucked under his arm and he would be waving his other arm around as if giving a sermon to an imaginary congregation, his shoes gleaming like a guardsman's on muster parade.

Eventually, on arrival at the steps of St Peter's, Reverend Salmon would give one last flutter of his arms and he would be up the steps - two at a time, and into the Church to lay out the prayer and hymn books. He was a perfect example to all the parishioners - young and old.

Reverend Salmon often organised functions in the village for the War effort. There would be sports days and fancy dress competitions, displays by the Fire Brigade and the ARP. The make-up on the victims legs, all put together with many different coloured plasticines, made the wound appear even more horrific and realistic, and many people could not bear to look, for fear of passing out, and to me it was real! But the whole practice was done mainly for the benefit of all the villagers in case the real thing did occur - God forbid, and Hitler did invade "The Green and Pleasant Land."

A detachment of the local reserve (Dads Army) would give a display of nerve racking rescues, sliding down a wire with a man on their backs as if over a wide river in full battle dress, finishing in a heap at the bottom with the injured man yards away. If not injured before, he certainly was now, as he limped back to his rescuer!

As team after team went down the fixed wire, it became more and more sagged in the middle and every so often it would recoil near the bottom, catapult the poor victims over the hedge at the bottom of the field, and into a holly bush. Maybe the wire had been deliberately lined up with the holly bush to give an added obstacle to think about.

The fancy dress event was a very glamorous occasion for all the girls and also the Mothers who had made the dresses, mainly with tissue paper. Mothers had sat up many nights piecing the costumes together - I know my Mother did. My Sister came third in her competition and my Mother was very proud. My American uniform did quite well too!

Once the fancy dress competitions were over it was time for the judging of all the garden produce and the flower arranging in the big tent. Jams were made of every fruit that could be picked in and around the village, along with pickles, beetroot etc.

The next event, later in the afternoon when most children had eaten their fill of cakes and scones, was the sports, egg and spoon races, sack races and three legged races - mainly all the types of races that would no doubt make the children very sick!

This occasion in the village stands out in my memory, not only for the enjoyment it gave to all us youngsters, but for all the work that must have been put into the event by "All" the villagers. This event had been going on for hundreds of years and a little upstart like Adolph was not going to stop it now. It was one of the main functions in the Church calendar of traditional village life and would, hopefully, continue for centuries to come.

When all the events had finished, most of the villagers would descend on the village pubs where they would down several pints of their favourite ale. Reverend Salmon would join them and relax, smiling proudly that every event had run smoothly and that all the effort he had put into the event had born fruit, so to speak.

All the money that had been raised would go to the War effort.

CHAPTER TWELVE

Garden Fetes, "The Yanks" and Joe Louis

Almost every summer there would be several garden fetes organised inside the Egerton estate grounds. The local children were all invited and at the same event they would be presented with their Sunday School prizes for good attendance - this would usually be in the form of a book. I found one of the books just a couple of years ago after my Mother had passed away. It was in her little bag of favourite possessions and titled "Peter of Yellow Gate," and was still in mint condition. Written on the inside cover was "To Ivor Goolding for good attendance, from Lady Grey Egerton." I never did get around to reading that book. I couldn't read very well at all in those far off days, but anyway, my favourite hobby then was being out in the countryside.

The whole fete was laid out in front of the Estate House - a very beautiful setting with all the tents with their pelmet fringes giving the appearance of looking into a Renoir painting. Rows and rows of stalls like penny bazaars where one could roll pennies, knock tin cans down with mop heads, and if lucky winning many prizes of homemade sweets etc.

Cakes and buns were provided and very quickly consumed by the children of the village - some must have starved themselves for days judging by the amount of food that disappeared. I was quite ill myself after eating a large cooking apple - one of the prizes for knocking three cans down, coupled with half a dozen buns; I was quite bloated and spent a while around the back of the stables only to reappear when the magician started his act in the stables, or did he make me appear? Who knows? He was that good! I had never seen a magician before and judging by the audience - mouths agape, eyes popping - neither had a lot of them!

My day was complete when the magician called me out to the front - probably because my mouth was open much wider than anyone else's. The quickness of his hand never ceased to amaze me as he brought florins from out of his mouth, down his nose from behind his ears and eventually bringing two shilling pieces from out of my ears and presenting them to me as a gift for helping him with his act. At the end of the act I sat down, still staring at the two florins in my hand feeling behind my ears to see if there were any more. I sat and watched more of his act - completely hypnotised, as he pulled yards and yards of different coloured scarves out of a tin which seemed to go on for hours.

I went home full of ideas and asked my Father for a two bob piece to show him a trick. He looked at me more suspiciously than usual but he eventually gave me a florin so that I could try the trick on him. He was amazed.

Transport was scarce during the War, mainly due to the fact that petrol was also in very short supply - most of it going to the War effort. Even so, there would be a bus every Friday morning to take people who wanted to go to the market at Northwich or Winsford. It was an old battered maroon coloured bus and could be heard in the distance as it approached the village, banging and spluttering on the regular low octane wartime petrol. It would pull up outside the Red Lion pub and the more people that got on, the slower it would travel. Luckily for the driver, it was all downhill from the Church down to the Old Mill and so on up to the main Northwich road. The driver would have a good old sing song and all the passengers joined in, as the bus appeared to sway back and too to the rhythm of the songs. "There'll be bluebirds over the White Cliffs of Dover," was the number one hit at the time, and that got a very good airing, along with "Run Rabbit, Run Rabbit."

Sometimes it would seem that there was no War at all, although the villagers all contributed in their own little way to the War effort by working very hard on the land, and making sure the harvest was in on time; because in a way there were two families to feed - the troops in Europe and the people at home, so they were entitled to a little relaxation.

Morale was always kept high as people had to make the best of it, whether they were in the frontline or waiting for their Husbands or loved ones to come home from the War.

During 1943 - 1944, after a very cold winter, "The Yanks" arrived at Oulton Park. It was a transit camp for final training before embarking for the Normandy beaches. My first sighting of them was on my way home from school. They had landed at Burtonwood and were now in convoy to the Oulton Park Estate, where they would be billeted. I arrived at Lodge Corner just as the first truck went past and as it went on for hours, I was unable to cross the road.

The Yanks were waving and smiling at me and throwing sweets, chewing gum and oranges - items I had never before seen in my life. My Mother made me wear a little brown beret for years and that day it came in very useful, for I filled it with all the goodies! On arrival at Selkirk Cottage very late, my Mother could not believe her eyes; she thought I had taken the goodies from the Post Office and she hurriedly pushed me into the house, taking the goodies from me to return them as quickly as possible. I told her the whole story and the reason I was late home.

I had also seen men in uniforms with black faces - something which I could not understand, as they were the first coloured faces I had seen. My Mother attempted to explain, saying that they had come from a very hot Country where the sun had tanned their skin black - but she eventually gave up.

Once the GI's had settled in they started to do their training using the Common and the estate. It was also the first time I had seen a bulldozer, as about half a dozen of them had cleared the right hand side of the Coach Road right up to the Tarporley Road, and then all the training obstacles were erected along with trenches.

Many a peaceful morning was disturbed by the sound of gunfire as the squaddies scrambled over the Common, with their Sergeants screaming their orders at them. This area has now completely regrown with the silver birches along with the bracken and the heather, as if nothing had ever occurred there.

Another early morning noise that became a regular occurrence at 6am every morning was the camp band as they marched around the village, passed the Red Lion and up to the top road and around eventually passing Ken's farm, and back into the camp. Of course, my Mother would already be up at that time when my Father was on the early shift and she would be very amused as they passed our house. She was particularly amused by the big drummer who had the appearance of a very fat Jerry Colona, with a red face putting every amount of energy into banging that drum, as if he wanted to wake the whole village - a case of, "We're awake, so everybody else should be too!"

The GI's were a constant reminder that the War was still not over as they moved around the village. On my way to school some mornings, the tannoy from the camp would be playing music I had never heard before. Glen Miller would be wafting through the silver birch trees; apparently it was known as "Swing." The next morning there would be a new beat which was much quicker than Swing, and this was known as the "Jitterbug." I liked this tempo and on arrival at school some of the children would be doing a quickstep to the music, although this would be the forerunner to the jive and eventually "Rock and Roll" - something very much in the future yet.

Looking back at my time spent at Oulton Park, I think the most outstanding period was when the Yanks were there. They really thought the world of the village children - throwing parties and treating us to chewing gum and sweets, bananas, oranges and a lot of items that many of us had never seen before.

At Christmastime the Yanks would throw the biggest party imaginable for all the children in the village - again, expense was no object. The party would be held in their cookhouse on the camp and each GI would be allotted so many children to look after and make sure each and every one enjoyed themselves. I had never seen so much food - turkeys the size of ostriches, and all the vegetables, and mince pies, Christmas puddings steaming hot and, last but not least, crackers - a rarity in War-torn Britain.

We were also given presents to take home; a box would be filled with everything we had during the course of the afternoon.

The Yanks treated us as if we were their own children.

Not long after they would be gone, and a lump often comes to my throat when I think of those Yanks. Most of them tragically died on the Normandy beaches for the sake of this Country, and I sincerely hope that we, as Britains, never forget the debt we owe to those men.

Law and order somehow seemed irrelevant when the Yanks were probably going to give their lives on those French beaches for the British people. In the event, most of those lads that were at Oulton Park were in the first draft and not many survived the German onslaught on that date of the 6th June 1944.

The American MP's kept their own law and order whilst stationed at the camp, and if any of the squaddies did go astray, they were dealt with immediately. I can recall Ken telling me of one night when two GI's had broken out of the gaol on the camp and had made a run for it down past Ken's farm and towards the pool, when two MP's caught them, and the next day they were shot for desertion. This was a common punishment during the Wartime for all the allied forces.

On one occasion the great Joe Louis came to the camp to give exhibition bouts with GI boxers. Most of my family went and I sat with Ken, I remember it so clearly. The man we had stayed up at nights to listen to on the wireless was actually there at Oulton Park in the flesh - both myself and Ken idolised him.

The exhibition took place in a dell and all the GI's were there cheering. Joe Louis was the idol of the day and, in my opinion, would have beaten any of the modern day fighters, although maybe Cassius Clay would give him a run for his money when they were both at their peak.

It was a very warm night and the arc lights which the GI's had rigged up, were not very bright but I could still see the bronze figure of Joe Louis dancing and weaving around the ring - the punches being thrown were at lightening speed. Joe would throw a punch so fast that it could hardly be seen by the naked eye; until it landed fairly and squarely on his opponent's jaw!

Ken and I mused over him being so fast as to catch flies off the wall - we also tried it, but failed miserably.

Joe was a man who had worked his way up from poverty to be Champion of the World and to be one of the greatest heavyweights ever. They were called `Hungry Fighters.'

Many years later Ken told me that my Father had wanted to go in the ring with Joe Louis, but the Police Authority prevented him from doing so because they pointed out that my Father's life insurance did not cover such events - much to the relief of my Mother! Instead he had to be satisfied with his autograph on the back of his notebook.

My Father had been a very good heavyweight amateur boxer in his younger days, and had won many prizes over the years. One of his most treasured possessions was a large cut glass vase which was won in one of the Police Championships and proudly displayed on top of the bureau and cleaned every day by my Mother. My Mother would warn us not to go near the bureau in case we knocked the vase off. In the next breath she would say, "You can tell it's cut glass because you can see hundreds of rainbows when you hold it up to the light - but please don't dare attempt to do that."

Ironically, my Father and his drinking partners (incidentally, all policemen), on one of their weekly booze-ups, arrived back at our house for supper - sandwiches cut by my Mother and a few more night-caps. I was just dozing off when I heard an almighty crash. My Father had accidentally knocked the bureau and consequently the vase came tumbling down and smashed into a million pieces all around him and his mates. There was a deathly silence and the remainder of the night remained very quiet.

The next thing I heard were my Father's mates leaving and saying goodnight to my Mother. I thought I heard a few sobs in the night, but I think it must have been Jock dreaming.

The following day our house was like a morgue - my Father would just stare at the bureau for minutes on end, hoping that the vase would reappear again; he just couldn't believe that he had smashed it. Thank God I didn't do it!! I felt like saying, "You had a smashing time last night, didn't you," but thought better of it.

It was not unusual for my Father to go quiet for weeks on end; he was very moody, but my Mother put up with it, although why, I will never know.

CHAPTER THIRTEEN

Park Farm and Tom Rutter

The local farm, Park Farm, where I was sent every day to pick up the milk at about 5 o' clock, was farmed by a thin-faced, ruddy complexioned farmer by the name of Tom Rutter.

Tom was a humorous, pipe smoking man with a typical farmer's gait, a battered old trilby angled on his head - the front of it smoothed down due to years of leaning against the cows during milking time. Milking was of course all done by hand.

Tom was a practical joker and on my way past his farm one day, he called me over. He had a bundle of straw and feathers cupped in his hands. "Look, a nest of baby rabbits," he said. He gave them to me to take home to my Mother - they must have only been a day or two old, as they had no fur as yet, and their eyes were still shut. Tom knew that my Mother loved animals and that she would not harm anything. She rescued wasps, bees, spiders and earwigs and threw them back outside.

When I arrived home my Mother was overjoyed at the sight of the baby rabbits and told me to put them in front of the fire to keep them warm. I told her the sad story that Tom had told me about them being deserted by their Mother and that he had saved them from certain death.

When my Father arrived home from plodding the beat, he enquired as to what my Sister and I were cuddling in front of the fire. My Mother repeated Tom's story and he came over to have a closer inspection, turned a couple over with his finger (much to the distress of my Sister and I), and then, without any warning, picked the complete nest up, walked out of the house, strode at a fair speed to the bottom of the garden and lobbed the whole lot into the middle of the field.

After glaring at the nest, he turned and came back into the house and looked directly at me, my Mother and my Sister.

"That lot was a nest of rats and I'm going up to see that Tom Rutter!"

He went up to the farm but Tom was nowhere to be found. Only ten minutes earlier he had said, "Goodnight Constable" to my Father. My Father thought he had detected a slight grin on Tom's face.

Vicarage Lane was the main route through the village from the Church up to Lodge Corner, and along the lane there were several farms. They were mainly cattle farms for milk production and the milk would be collected every day. A flat wagon would pick the churns up and take them to the main dairies in the towns to be filtered again and then put into bottles. Some of the milk would be sold to the many cheese makers dotted around Cheshire.

Whilst at Little Budworth I had many encounters with farm animals. At Tom Rutter's farm they had a lovely sheep dog in a kennel outside the entrance to the farmhouse; I can't recall his name but I stroked this dog every night for years whilst on my nightly errand for the billycan full of milk. He would make a fuss of me, lick my face and roll over as far as his chain would allow.

Then, on one particular night, I went over to him and he just leapt straight out of the kennel and went directly for my throat. Luckily I had the sense to roll away, but he managed to bite my leg and my arm before I got out of reach. As the chain snapped tight around his neck, he swung back to the kennel but continued barking and snarling at me. I managed to roll further away holding my leg which was now bleeding quite freely. I ran into the farmhouse, blood streaming down my leg. Tom saw my leg but no sympathy was forthcoming, as he said, "Fallen in the gooseberry bushes again have you?"

When I told him what had happened he became very concerned and shouted Mrs Rutter. She came and immediately grabbed some of the Muslim cloth that was used to filter the milk, wrapped it around my leg several times and then tied it with some string. The bandage had some of Mrs Rutter's old fashioned ointment on it to stop the bleeding - what it actually was, I will never know, but it also eased the pain.

Once Tom had mopped my brow and cleaned most of the farmyard muck off my legs, he gave me the milk can filled to the brim, and away I went, giving the not so very nice sheepdog a very wide berth! His eyes followed me right across the farmyard and as I was approaching the gate he made another lunge towards me, barking and snarling. However this time Tom came out and made a threatening gesture with his hand and the dog immediately shot into the kennel, without looking back.

Apparently, that very same day, the dog had broken his chain and Tom had given him a good talking to, so to speak.

Since that day I have always been very wary of any dog.

I arrived home with half a can of milk as the other half had been spilled in my haste to get away from the dog. My Mother was very concerned and I heard the word "rabies" being mentioned. I had visions of going to hospital for a long time.

My Father started to sniff; his head moving around the room attempting to locate where the smell was coming from. Eventually his eyes became transfixed on my leg.

"What did Tom Rutter put on that leg - hen muck?"

"No," I said indignantly, "It is a special remedy made up by Mrs Rutter from secret herbs."

A couple of days later I saw Tom and my Father leaning on the five bar gate outside the farmyard laughing and slapping one another on the back - I wonder why, because only two days earlier my Father was going to give Tom a good telling off! Oh well, that's grown-ups for you.

Ken and I spent a lot of time at Tom's farm, mainly getting in the way but trying to help by doing the odd jobs like chopping mangold in the hand-operated slicer. At harvest time we would follow Tom up to the field opposite Ken's farm, tying the wheat sheaf and stacking them into a neat formulation, as we thought, to be picked up by the horse and flat wagon later.

We also chased rabbits darting out of the last few square yards of uncut wheat as they raced for the nearest hedgerow. Swallows would swoop and dive at us and we would make gestures as if trying to catch them. They knew that we hadn't any chance of getting within 10 feet of them, as they swerved away at the last moment, gave a little chirp and climbed high into the sky again and then return at twice the speed. This was a game that would go on for hours - I don't know who enjoyed it more, the swallows or us! Their chirps seemed to turn into laughter as we got to know one another quite well.

One particular day during the harvest, Ken and I stood by the gate chewing a piece of wheat stalk watching Tom going around on the horse-drawn cutting and binding machine - we knew when to kept out of the way. The old binder was prone to breaking down frequently so consequently Tom's patience would be stretched to breaking point, so to speak. He had cut half of the field when suddenly the binder gave off a crunching sound and the two horses stopped immediately, sensing that there was something wrong. Luckily Tom had not been thrown off, but jumped off in temper landing 2 or 3 yards away from the binder. He threw his cap to the ground and then picked it up, muttered and kicked the binder.

I can recall there were a lot of `b's' in the phrases as he told the binder what he was going to do to it if it didn't mend itself right away! All the cursing and the swearing didn't help and in the end Tom had to get underneath and see what the trouble was. Ken and I were chuckling to ourselves and we were about to move to other pastures when we glanced back into the general direction of the binder. Tom was on his back pulling at the binding wire that had jammed the arm that threw the sheaves clear of the machine. Suddenly there was a scream and at first we thought that Tom had been trapped, but then he shot out from under the binder dancing and jumping around, waving his arms about and swiping frantically into thin air - Ken and I were mystified.

As we dared to move closer we noticed some sort of insects flying around Tom. Apparently he had disturbed a hornets nest and they had gone down his breeches and inside his shirt, and in his general panic to get rid of them he had no doubt hit some and they were stinging him thick and fast. To us watching it was one of the funniest things we had ever seen in our short lives.....Tom disappearing up the lane in a cloud of hornets - they just would not leave him alone, the poor man.

The tale goes that Tom made his regular appearance in the Red Lion pub that night with his face covered in blue spots - one of Mrs Rutter's cure for stings; probably iodine. The locals said it was also one of the funniest sights that they had ever seen - they thought he had been hit by a blackberry pie! Tom saw the funny side of the situation and roared with laughter with them all.

Park Farm was always a centre of attraction for me and my pals. We would either meet there or at Ken's farm.

One hot summer's day when the potato harvest was in full swing, Ken and I decided to give the potato pickers a hand (although I think we were more of a hindrance than a help). Tom didn't object as he went up and down on the horse-drawn potato thrower. Tom gave me the responsibility of going for the 10 o'clock brew back to the farm.

I took the route straight along the public footpath which came out by the Alms Houses, over the stile, turning right and into Park Farm, where Mrs Rutter had the billycans ready full of tea. I decided to change my route on the way back and went through the orchard and the gooseberry bushes at the rear of the farm where I selected a nice juicy apple and then headed up the bank, under the barbed wire and so on into the field next to the potato field. Striding across the field I would swing the two billycans around in a full circle not spilling a drop - a trick I was extremely proud of; although Tom was not very pleased as he watched from a distance.

As I approached the middle of the field, whistling one of the tunes of the day, I glanced over to the potato field and noticed all the workers and Tom waving frantically - some were pointing.

"Alright," I shouted, "I'm going as fast as I can with the billycan," - that rhymes, I thought! Almost as soon as I had finished shouting I heard a noise I had never heard before - a snorting gurgling roar and then, out of the corner of my eye, I saw this large shape racing towards me at high speed. My fear was confirmed as I turned around - it was the largest bull in the neighbourhood and it was about 10 yards away and closing.

My first reaction was to freeze on the spot, but an unknown force inside me sent me to the left and the bull carried on until it ground to a halt by the hedge and turned.

By this time it was a matter of survival as he started to close in once more. I had managed to get up a bit of speed, still holding the billycans and no doubt fear had put an extra 10 miles per hour on my little legs, as I headed back to the hedge at the other end of the field from whence I had started. I didn't know the record for 100 yards sprint, but I can assure you it was broken that day!

The bull was getting closer and in my anxiety to get away I threw the billycans in the air - this startled the bull and he stopped and looked puzzled, but by the time he had recovered I had jumped the barbed wire fence easily (that fence must have been 2 feet higher than me!), landed on the other side, rolled down the steep bank and eventually, after hitting the hen coop, I ended up in the gooseberry bushes covered in feathers and scratches and, with a sore ankle, staggered into the Park Farmhouse again.

When Mrs Rutter saw me she was more concerned about the tea than me!

"Have they drunk it already?" she asked.

I told her what had happened and she gave me buttered bread crust, and off I went again with two full billycans. This time I made sure I kept to the public footpath.

In the meantime, Tom had raced back to the farm and skidded around the corner by the Alms Houses where he had spotted me

"Where's the bloomin' tea?" he asked, realising that I was alright because he had seen everything that had happened and I know he was very concerned for my wellbeing really. He rolled his eyes back to the top of his head, nodding his head upwards at the same time, patted me on the head and took one of the billycans, and we walked across to the now very thirsty workers.

The summers seemed to go on forever in those far off days, just like the winters did; maybe it was the school holidays or just being left to our own devices all day - time seemed to stand still then. I have no doubt that if either of my parents knew of the escapades that we got up to during the course of the day, they would have been quite alarmed and no doubt would have kept us in for weeks on end!

Early one Saturday morning we ventured into the shippons on Park Farm; Tom had just finished milking by hand and had turned the cows out into the fields. He was now cleaning all the muck left from the previous night and the morning, and barrowing it out onto the midden in the middle of the farmyard, steaming fresh to be taken and spread onto the fields later in the year - a fully organic farm.

Back and forth through the shippon door he went, muttering to himself about 12 bore shotguns and foxes. At last we managed to attract his attention and he came over to us and told us that a fox had got into the coop in the night and killed most of his laying hens. A fox will not just take one hen and go; it will go on chasing and killing whilst the hens are flying around and most of them will die of fright.

Tom suggested that the Hunt should meet more often. Tom said the Hunt usually only killed one fox during the course of a day's chase and for what good that did he might as well stay up all night and shoot them with his 12 bore shotgun, or at least frighten them away. (In modern times there are more foxes killed on the motorways than are killed by the Hunt every year.) The country people have a way of controlling everything concerned with the wild - they should know, they have been doing the same thing and using the same methods for thousands of years.

Tom appeared to be a lot calmer now he had told us all about his misfortune, and he ambled off to start cutting mangold in the slicer. We offered to help but he declined our offer.

I didn't like to see Tom down in the dumps - he was such a happy character usually. Even with the hard work he had to put in every day on the farm, he still managed a laugh and a joke.

After a while we sauntered over to the orchard giving the old sheepdog a wide berth - although he was wagging his tail as if beckoning us over and asking for forgiveness for sinking his teeth into my leg, but I would not be lured into a second trap! I also remember the well known saying, `Once bitten, twice shy.'

In the orchard most of the fruit was ripe - pears, apples, plums and damsons, but we decided to try the very ripe gooseberries. We ate our fill for about half an hour and then moved on through the front gate - feeling very bloated!

I felt intoxicated - as if I had been drinking alcohol, and Ken was the same, swaying all over the place and singing raucously "Hitler has only got one ball...." etc. After a while the gooseberries started to ferment in our stomachs and we had terrible pains. I felt as though my stomach was going to explode. As I walked along it sounded similar to someone swinging a gallon of water around in a Wellington Boot. I bade Ken farewell the best I could and then swaggered home - laughing uncontrollably and singing "We'll meet again...."

Oh did I suffer for hours after - spending many hours in the toilet!

After several visits to the toilet my Mother's curiosity got the better of her and I had to confess all. She was quite amused, but my Father wasn't - he never seemed to be amused.

CHAPTER FOURTEEN

The Threshing Machine and Ken Dobson's Farm

The arrival of the Threshing Machine was an important occasion in the farming calendar, as this meant hard work for weeks as the sheaves were put through the machine. The machine could be heard for miles as it trundled its way down the lanes from its previous job in the Tarporley area. It was a steam traction engine and behind it towed the threshing machine, like a fairground pianola on wheels. A marvellous feat of engineering if I ever saw one. There were wheels, pulleys, graders, filters arms everywhere for throwing the sheaves in all directions, string wire - you name it and it would be attached to this box of tricks.

I would stand there for hours watching as the farmers manoeuvred the monster into position parallel with the barn, where all the sheaves had been stacked ready for the great day. It would also be lined up with the steam roller traction engine which had the big main pulley for driving the belt, connecting the two machines and so bringing all the moving parts into operation. All the belts were made out of leather - some with chunks out of them where they had caught one of the arms as it sped round and round the thresher. Some of the belts needed tensioning because the wires they were connected to had started to stretch under the constant strain.

After a while, and realising I was late again, I reluctantly made my way back to school. As soon as school was over Ken and I would race back to Tom's farm and dive straight into the melee of straw and chaff, which by now was flying around everywhere as the machine was in full motion.

Looking back, these machines could be very dangerous if not treated with respect, because there were many moving parts exposed. The machine would chug on well into the night. We would be in and out, underneath, around the top - our lungs full of dust and our mouths sore with gulping in clouds of chaff. Belts and pulleys would be spinning around - mechanical arms raking, packing and throwing until at last, at the far end of the thresher, the bail would appear all tied and neatly boxed to be stored in the barn for winter fodder for the cattle. At the side, sacks were being constantly filled with grain as it ran out after being shaken free from the sheath and then tied with bailing string.

In between playing and generally being a nuisance to Tom, who tried to keep an eye on us as he threw the finished bales high up into the barn, he didn't want us to get hurt in any way and often shouted, "Mind or you will get knocked out." We would give him a hand in a small way, throwing back the sheaths that fell off the top, using a pikel (another very dangerous instrument, if not handled properly) - although Ken was very good and he managed to throw some back onto the top of the thresher.

The threshing machine made life easier for the farm workers. Prior to the invention of this machine, all the wheat had to be cut by hand using scythes and many farm workers would move across the field in formation followed by other members of the family - women and children, tying and stacking the wheat sheaves. The people of years ago would work long and hard, because they only had a few short months to reap and thresh the harvest. This would keep the community spirit going from one year to the next, through the good times and the bad. The same families have lived in the village for hundreds of years, namely - the Rutters, Dones, Dobsons, Hales, Astburies, Deans and Bratts. Even the Gooldings were in the village for a short period of its history.

Prior to the harvest, Tom would make frequent visits to the wheat and cornfields - checking, smelling and chewing the corn, testing for the ripeness that was required for the harvesting. Tom managed the farm for Sir John Egerton and it was the most central farm in the village.

Once Tom had given the approval that the corn was ready, he would take a couple of the older men from the village who had some knowledge of scything and they would cut a strip all round the outside of the field, about a binding machine's width, and this would prevent a few bushels of grain from being wasted under the hooves of the cart horses. The scythe men had perfect rhythm and could cut acres in no time at all. The fields were divided into neat rectangles of about 4 or 5 acres, easily manageable. Lots of hedgerows have been destroyed as farmers strived to produce more and more grain for the ever-increasing population of our small island.

The day of the first cut arrived and Tom was riding high on the mower-cum-binder, tugging away on his pipe full of thick twist with its unmistakable aroma, tugging on the reins as the cart horses pulled to get started, "Whoa," he shouted, holding his pipe between his teeth. As he exhaled the smoke from the pipe, he sometimes went into a daydream and his eyes became glazed as his mind went back to harvests gone by - maybe of a frolic in the corn with one of the young maidens of his youth! Whatever he was thinking about, it would always bring a wry smile to his weather beaten face before he came back to earth and reality.

Tom's two chestnut brown Shire Horses were at the front of the harvester and Tom was in position to move off, seated on the spring-loaded cast iron seat a couple of sacks underneath to keep his bottom warm. The first cut of the binder was preceded by an air of expectancy after months of repairing and maintaining the machine, and the constant oiling of all the moving parts. Now they were all being put to the test. A perfect start and we could not help but notice the look of relief on Tom's face as the binder started to pick up the corn sheaves, chewing round and then throwing it out in a neat tied up sheaf, ready for stacking. Ken and I would be stacking a few sheaves here and there ready for the cart to pick them up, but our main concern, yet again, were with the young swallows who were constantly diving and, on occasions, brushing our hair as they swooped passed on their final piece of training before they headed off for their winter breeding grounds.

During the course of the long hot day, Tom would stop for a rest and have a drink of tea out of the billycan. Eventually it would be offered to us and we would immediately drink it very rapidly in the hope of getting some more - but I'm afraid there would be no chance of that, as Tom gave us one of his looks and drained the last dregs of stewed tea from the can!

After having his smoke Tom would look around for a bit of entertainment and his eyes would fall on me and Ken.

"Who's the best scrapper out of you two then?" he would chuckle.

Ken and I would both shout simultaneously "Me!" and then we would be rolling over in the stubble, although no blows would ever be thrown. Tom would be rolling over with laughter himself, and then he would come over and lift whoever was on top at the time and would call it a draw.

Then it was time to get back onto the binder.

"Gee up," Tom would shout and off they went on their ever decreasing squares around the field.

As the binder got to the middle of the field, rabbits started to dive out of the last few remaining square yards. This would be a signal for Tom's Grandfather to burst into action. Up until this time he had either been asleep or polishing his 12 bore shotgun. Tom had noticed that the old man was about to take aim and shouted, "DUCK!" and everyone hit the ground simultaneously as buckshot started to fly everywhere, hitting sheaves which had been stacked, and trees around the field and, of course, the odd rabbit!

Once the firing had stopped, Granddad would amble across the field with a sack, put the rabbits in and walk along to the lane back to the farm. The rabbits would, of course, be made into stews and hotpots for the morrow's dinner - and very nice they were, as Tom would bring one of his billycans containing some of the stew and would give us a taste.

After spending most of our day helping Tom (or so we thought), we would wind our way home along the lanes, feeling very tired. Tom would be out until midnight most nights during the harvest, as the clocks had been altered to give maximum amount of daylight during the summer months and so help with the War effort.

Once all the harvest was safely in the barn, bales stacked ready for whatever winter came along, it was time for the Harvest Festival - another very important date in the Church calendar. All the farmers in the area would give a certain amount of their produce, whatever it might be - corn, wheat, potatoes, fruit, and many other produces to the Church. Many of the local village women would bake bread shaped like sheaves, bread rolls and many other shapes. All these different produces would be on display inside the Church, usually alongside the font or the altar. Many of the arrangements were masterpieces and so colourful. Sheaves of wheat alongside turnips, brought yellow mangolds and all the fruit grown in the village - apples, pears, plums, damsons and gooseberries all came together to complete one big wicker basket of colour - it definitely was an art.

After the Harvest Festival Service, all the produce would be given to the poor people living in the towns near to Little Budworth.

The Shire Horses were huge animals and very intelligent, and so easy to handle. At about 4 o'clock in the afternoon if Tom was busy he would say to me, "Go and shout the cattle up from yonder field." I would be delighted that Tom trusted me to do such an important job. He would lift me onto the horse - one of the biggest in the area, and off we went. I had to pass our house so I gave a shout as we clopped by and my Mother came to see what all the shouting was about. It was only the second time in my life that I had seen that look of anguish on my Mother's face, and she immediately turned and went back into the house. She thought that if she had stayed there and waved, I would probably have fallen off! I thought to myself, "Tom, it looks as though you are in for another rollicking!" Tom would only laugh at my Mother; she could not tell anyone or anything what to do, let alone give someone like Tom a rollicking.

On arrival at the field, the horse stopped knowing instinctively that this was the field. I would give a shout (learnt off Tom), "Cow up come on then," and I was overjoyed when all the cattle headed towards the gate, without a second calling. The Shire Horse had a lot more sense than the drover for, as we got behind the cattle in the narrow lanes, if one of the cows ventured towards the open gate, the horse would give a snort and the cow would think better than to head for richer pastures and would come back to the herd.

After a few trips down to the far field, I began to realise that I was not guiding the horse at all - he obviously knew the route by heart and the anguish of getting the cows back to the farm was alleviated for me.

Once back at the farm, the horse would line up with the wall outside the farmyard so that I could dismount onto the specially made rostrum. The intelligence of these fine animals was amazing. They could work all day pulling a plough with a nose bag of oats every so often as an incentive, and a bucket of water every hour from the pond, and they would still have energy for round-ups at the end of the day or any other extra chore the farmer might have around the farm on that particular day.

The Shire Horses were much more economical than the tractor, because they cost the farmer absolutely nothing to run, but, unfortunately they were a great deal slower and as the population exploded, speed became more essential for the farmer to compete.

The countryside still remains picturesque - but for how long? For ever, I hope. I think the farmer will ensure it stays more or less the same, after all, it is their environment and they have the best understanding of what makes `the countryside tick'.

As the cattle moved into the shippon, one of the cows slipped on the slurry and it's back legs caught me and I went head over heels into the cow muck and landed flat on my back. I could feel the cold stinking muck soaking through to my skin and running into my shoes. As I stood up I must have resembled the scarecrow which stood in the bottom field; maybe I would have been more effective!

Tom appeared round the corner of the shippon with a scowl on his face wondering why there was a hold-up and as he noticed me, he gave out such a burst of laughter it could be heard all over the County, and some of the cows decided to make for the stalls without any persuasion at all. Tom looked at me and was stumped for something to say; finally, he said, "Go up to the farmhouse and see Mrs Rutter," I splashed my way up to the back door where I knocked and waited for a while. After what seemed like an eternity, Mrs Rutter opened the door and immediately shut it again, saying, "Go and jump in the pond!"

"But Mrs Rutter, I can't swim," I shouted.

But Mrs Rutter wasn't concerned whether I could swim or not, she just wanted to get that stinking mess away from her doorstep. I turned to go home and there was Tom, leaning on the shippon door laughing - again! I just couldn't see the funny side of it myself and went home, only to be plonked into the freezing cold water in the sink, and Tom was in for another telling off - according to my Mother.

On one occasion we were due to go down to the `Mangold-wurzels field', as we called it, to load the flat wagon with mangold from the store which was covered in soil and straw, to protect them through the winter months from frost and snow. Tom was at the reins and Ken was riding shotgun on this occasion. We had to go along the walled perimeter of the Oulton Estate to the clove and when we arrived we loaded up as high as possible. I did notice the Shire Horse glancing around every so often to check that the wagon was not too full, and also so that he would be able to pull it up Lodge Hill.

On the journey back to the farm I was asked to run alongside and pick up and throw back on any that fell off the cart. In my enthusiasm whilst darting in and out and under the cart, I mistimed the pace of the cart and the rear wheel ran over my foot. I didn't feel anything at first, but after a few minutes my foot began to throb - a pain I had never known before; I thought my foot was going to explode. I screamed and Tom jumped off the wagon, closely followed by Ken. Tom picked me up and put me on the cart just behind the driver. The pain was getting worse so Tom cracked the reins to try and get more speed out of the horse. The horse sensed that there was something wrong and tried to increase his speed, and managed to get an extra 5 mile an hour going down the slight gradient at the Alms Houses.

Back at the farm, Tom had dashed into the house and duly returned with Mrs Rutter who was rolling her sleeves up as if she were about to perform a major operation; I didn't like the look of it at all and tried to make a move for home but my foot was completely numb. The cry went out from Mrs Rutter, "Get the goose grease and the blue unction." This was a cure for most things in the hard up days of Wartime, and then Tom, as if taking orders from a Sergeant Major, shot into the farmhouse again and reappeared with two jars - one was the colour of dripping and the other a very light blue. Mrs Rutter snatched the jars off him as if vital seconds were being lost before an amputation and she then scooped a big handful of each and started to kneed them together into one big mess. The eventual colour was similar to that of a midden in the yard.

"Off with your shoes and socks," she ordered. I obeyed immediately, for by this time the pain was unbearable and as she plastered the concoction onto my foot, it began to ease off - thank goodness!. It was then wrapped in muslin and sacking tied it with string. Tom lent me one of his Grandfather's walking sticks and off I went home to attempt to get up the steps. Luckily, my Sister spotted me and told my Mother. My Mother and Father came running down the path and lifted me into the house. My Mother unwrapped the bandage and let out such a cry when she saw my foot. My Father had one foot through the door on his way up to see poor old Tom again when I managed to sob out what had happened. Once the stuff had been removed it didn't look so bad. The wheel had cut across the top of my right foot and there was already some bruising. The next day my whole foot had turned black and the pain was still unbearable. Many remedies were tried but to no avail - nothing stopped that pain.

After a few weeks the pain and the bruising had almost disappeared, and I could move my foot quite freely, so it was back up to the farm again. Ken did let me ride shotgun for quite a while after that incident.

A lot of the machinery around the farmyard was unguarded. The mangold-wurzel slicer was a very dangerous machine if not handled properly, and it was very rare that Tom let us go anywhere near it. It was the shape of a bowl and the mangold were dropped into it and a geared wheel would be turned to start the very sharp blades rotating which sliced the mangold into small pieces to be fed to the cattle. On recollection, I would imagine that many a finger could have been lost if there had been a lapse of concentration. Pitchforks were also sometimes left around, but in general Tom was very safety conscious and stacked most of the forks, rakes and shovels against the shippon wall; in that way, everyone could see where they were.

Top of the Town Farm (Ken's Father's farm) was first farmed by Ken's Grandfather in 1892 and was a small farm in comparison to a lot of the farms in the area. It was well managed by Ken's Father, although it was hard physical work for all the family. Ken was doing his fair share of the work, even at the age of 7 and he was quite capable of doing a good job - whatever the task may be - milking, feeding the cattle or cleaning the shippons.

At a guess I would say there were about 20 to 30 head of cattle on the farm together with a few pigs and a variety of poultry; the Bantam hens being the most attractive, with their multi colours which shone in the sunlight. Two Shire Horses did a lot work around the farm and of course the dog, `Jack', who looked very much like a Border Collie, who incidentally had many a scrap with our Labrador and always came off the better.

How Ken managed to fit school into his day, I will never know, because he would be up early in the morning giving his Father a hand with the cattle etc, and would still be grafting away after his tea in the evening. I know because he would not be allowed out until he had finished his chores. To me, the whole farm was just one big adventure playground and I spent many happy hours trying to help Ken or, more often, getting in the way as usual.

At the rear of their farmhouse there was an old 1920's bread van where we would pretend to drive all around the world, or just delivering bread to various parts of the village. Ken's father used it to store most of the farm implements and, of course, the odd hen would get in there and nest sometimes.

Most farms had the traditional woodpile somewhere on the farm and Ken's farm was no exception. It was in the orchard under the pear tree - wigwam shaped stack of branches about 8 feet high with the middle left open for ventilation. This was a place to hide or check the various stages of a thrush's brood that happened to nest in there one year. There would be many different types of birds that would nest in there during the course of the nesting season. Almost every day Ken would have to chop some of the branches up for the fire in the big room downstairs in the farmhouse. Just lifting the axe was no mean feat - I know, because I tried.

The centre of the woodpile was used for hiding and also for having a quick drag on the old Woodbine when we could get our hands on one. Why I bothered, I don't know, because I was always ill afterwards, even though I didn't inhale the smoke! My Father suspected that I may have been partaking in the odd weed or two. How, I'll never know, but luckily Ken had wised me up, because my Father had been around to see Ken to give him a lecture and also to find out if I had been smoking too.... thank goodness Ken kept his mouth shut!

Although the name of Ken's farm is printed on the Ordnance Survey map as Top of the Town Farm, I always called it Pinfold

Farm, because this seemed a more appropriate name and was more countrified. After all, the Pinfold was more or less opposite the farm and this would be where all the stray cattle would be kept in years gone by, until the farmer collected them.

The main building next to the house was a two-tiered red brick building and housed most of the animals, shippons at the bottom and the loft above, where all the straw and hay would be stored for the winter. Separate to the shippons was a pigsty - a small, brick built building with a surrounding wall and a slate roof - a luxury in pigsties really! Pigs are very amusing animals and I would watch the one in Ken's pigsty for quite a while until he realised that I had no food for him, and he would move indoors giving his full repertoire of grunts. Contrary to what people think, pigs are very intelligent and can really only be bettered by the Shire Horse. The pig seemed to approve of his little shelter and appeared to be very happy and content - totally unaware that he was only being bred for his bacon; a fact of life in the countryside. I can recollect sides of bacon hung up in the annexe to the kitchen slowly maturing and curing until ready for eating.

Milking time for Ken was time consuming, as he would have to milk all the cows by hand - a task I could never learn, try as I may, I was just no good. Ken was very good at this task and also an expert marksman with the teat. Returning to the shippon with the empty pail after pouring the milk into the cooler, Ken would fire at me and hit me smack in the eye with the warm milk from the teat. My face would be running with milk - probably good for the complexion!

The living room of the house was very long with a large oak table in the middle and a large Grandfather clock in the corner chiming every hour and on the quarter - such a beautiful tone. Along the walls were prints of Scottish stags; a real model farm-house.

Hitler's V1's and V2's had started to reach the north of England, close to the end of the War in Europe - one landing on the outskirts of Tarvin which was only up the road from Little Budworth. I remember the night well. It was a clear starlit night - Christmas Eve 1944. My Mother was petrified as the buzz of the engine grew closer and closer, and I can still hear her trembling voice.

"The engine has stopped right above the house....quick, under the table!" she instructed.

My Mother was so convinced that our table was the saviour of our lives many a night. If one of those V1's had landed within half a mile, it would have blown the house and the table to Kingdom Come!

All sorts of rumours would spread relating to these rockets, and that once the engine stopped it would fall vertically to earth. Therefore, on my reckoning, that bomb should have dropped on Little Budworth, but luckily the rumours proved incorrect that night.

Early in the summer of 1945 my Mother mentioned that we would be going to the VE celebrations at my Grandparents' house at Parkside Road in Bebington on the Wirral.

The day arrived and I was very excited, not only because of the VE celebrations, but also at the thought of seeing my relatives.

It was a very hot early May morning and my Mother had hold of me on one hand, and my Sister, Susan, on the other, as we strode out to catch the bus to Chester. Once in Chester we would change there alighting onto the Birkenhead maroon bus and getting off at New Ferry - what a journey, but well worth it just to see the welcoming smiles of my Gran and Granddad, and no doubt meeting many of my cousins.

New Ferry to Parkside was a good mile and as we reached Bebington Station Bridge my Mother let us go on ahead on our own to run the rest of the journey to 106 and surprise my Gran, or so we thought.

As we raced around the corner at the top of Parkside, I could not help but notice that a brick building had been built right outside 106. Apparently it was another shelter with EWS on the side with a tank on the top full of water. Many a happy hour was spent playing in that shelter for months after the War was over.

The big day arrived and in the afternoon of VE Day the road was blocked off and all the tables and chairs were positioned right along the middle of the road, covered in various coloured table clothes which had been supplied by all the families who lived there. The tables were then laden with all varieties of "butties" one could imagine, home made cakes, scones and even jellies which had been obtained for the occasion - never seen by most of the children during the course of the War.

Fancy hats had been made by parents out of old newspapers and worn proudly by the children, although most of them resembled the Sou-wester style. Gallons of "pop" was drunk along with the orange squash which was issued by the Government for free!! Shops had sent hundreds of balloons and other decorations and, in my eyes, this was the most colourful sight I had ever seen!

After a few hours the majority of food had been consumed and many of the children were feeling a bit sick and consequently disappeared into the shelter, only to come back for more!

Eventually all the tables and chairs were moved back to the sides of the road and the old wind-up gramophone was brought out and the road was used as a dance floor. All the children and parents (mostly women, whose Husbands' were away in the Army), were dancing and singing "The Okey Kokey" and "Knees Up Mother Brown," and also, to be sung many times, "We'll Meet Again." That one must have been worn out by the end of the celebrations. Good old Vera Lynn kept the morale of the troops up during the course of the War.

Everybody was so happy, although I could not help but notice my Aunty Vera sitting with her very young Daughter with tears streaming down her face; I couldn't understand why at the time, but the fact was that her Husband was still in the middle of Germany waiting to come home after six long years, going right through the thick of the stinking Nazis War; Mr Reuben Thelwell B.E.M, a Sergeant with the 6th Airborne Division. I was very proud that he was my Uncle and no doubt he would arrive home and celebrate in his own quiet way.

Eventually I received the inevitable warning from my Mother, "We're on the move again."

"I'm not going," I said.

However, my Father altered my opinion quite rapidly, with his comment of: "We'll see."

I would like to have thought that my pals missed me, although at that age it would be doubtful and everything must carry on as normal.

It was 1946 and the Yanks had been gone a few years now - one day they were there and almost overnight they were gone;

it was as if they had never been there at all. I realised on my way to school when I could hear the crows and the rooks above me in the early morning sun, and there was no music from the camp; it was sad, I suppose, and quite eerie.

Even after leaving Little Budworth I would often return to see Ken and roam around the village for a day, call in on Tom and have a laugh and a joke.

SUSAN AND IVOR. LANGDALE RD. RUNCORN 1941

**SUSAN, IVOR, KEN AND ANN WITH JACK!
"THE MEADOW" ON KENS FARM. 1944**

AUTHOR, SIX YEARS OLD 1944 REAR "SELKIRK COTTAGE"

91

SUSAN, MOTHER, IVOR & TIBBY, SELKIRK COTTAGE 1944

OLD RUNCORN   The Transporter Bridge   COLLECTORCARD   C1821
and Manchester Ship Canal   c1929   Croydon CR0 1HW

RUNCORN 1940–43

SELKIRK COTTAGES, LITTLE BUDWORTH
ST. PETERS CHURCH IN BACKGROUND

"EGERTON ARMS" LITTLE BUDWORTH
OWNED BY JOANNE DOBSON

"THE COMMON" LITTLE BUDWORTH

LITTLE BUDWORTH POOL
DISPLAYED IN "THE EGERTON ARMS"

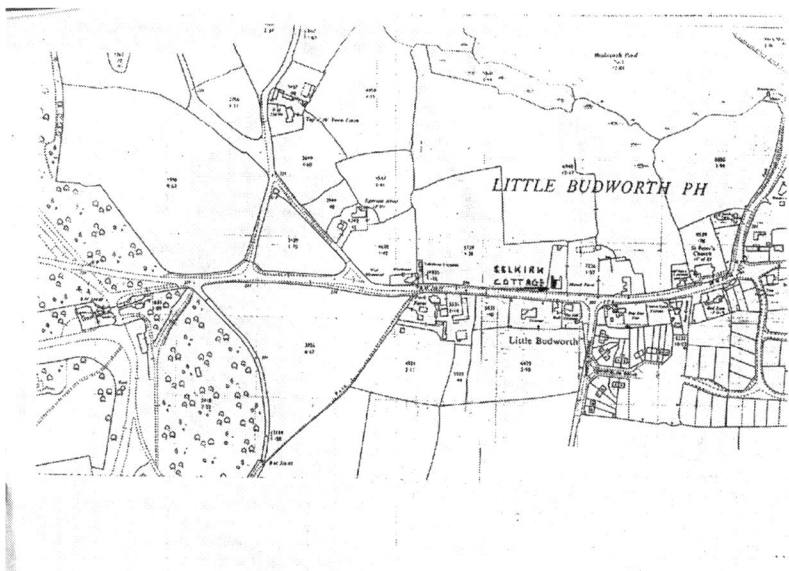

MAP OF THE VILLAGE

"THE LODGE" OULTON PARK

MILL LANE, LITTLE BUDWORTH

"RED LION" LITTLE BUDWORTH

Tug-O-War(Drinking) Team
Crewe 1953
Coached by Sgt Len Cooper

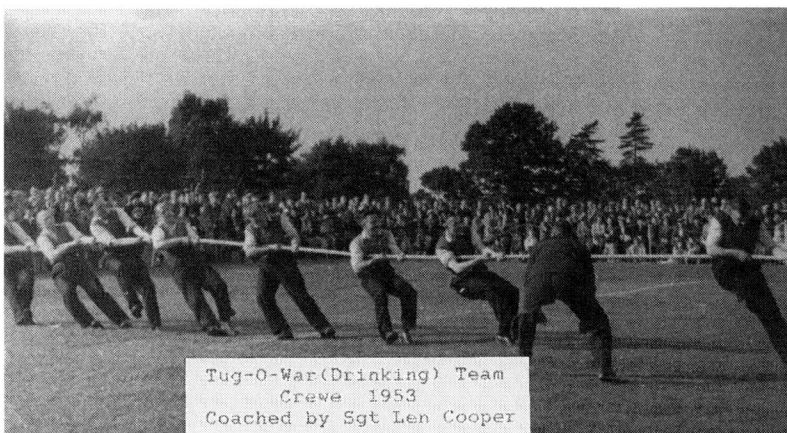

CREWE POLICE TUG-O-WAR TEAM

County Grammar School
Crewe.
E. R.
1953.

AUTHOR AND JASPER (RINGED)

CHAPTER FIFTEEN

Chestnuts and Mushrooms

A lthough not far from Little Budworth, it seemed to take a very long time to get to Stockton Heath. We were now turning into Waverley Avenue just around the corner from the Bridge Inn and arriving at No. 45 late in the afternoon. We were in North Cheshire, just across the Manchester Ship Canal from Warrington. Fortunately for us, at that time there were fields at the front and the back of the house. A tip about half a mile away called 'The Delph' at the front and at the back, the land fell away to the Bridge Water Canal. It was just after the War and a Labour Government was in power and the order had gone out to build thousands of council houses for the returning troops - a good idea at the time.

At almost the same time as we arrived, the builders moved onto the front fields and commenced clearing for the new estate of council houses. For me this created new activities such as lobbing stones into lime pits and taking odd pieces of wood left by the builders for the fire, because coal was very scarce at the time, although we were virtually living on top of a coal seam.

Again, my first outing was to see the Headmaster of several schools. The first one we visited was the newly named Council School, but understandably they wouldn't take me as I was virtually illiterate, having spent my first few years at a country school (during the War) which did not have the facilities for writing or learning the basic skills. This was no reflection at all on the teachers at the school who did their very best with the limited resources they had available. The second school I visited was St Thomas's Church of England School; I thought to myself, they must take me here because my Father's middle name was Thomas. They did take me, although I don't think my Father's middle name had any bearing on their decision.

By this time my Sister, Susan, had started school and it was my duty to take her to school every day and look after her on our daily walk down to St Thomas's in Stockton Heath, just over a mile away. The snow and the frost never let up that winter (1946-47); it lasted until the end of February and all I can remember was being permanently cold from the moment I got out of bed, right through my breakfast of Scott's porridge oats, until the time I arrived home from school again. Unfortunately the school at that time could not afford fuel to heat the boilers and I can still picture the whole class sat there in their coats and scarves right through the long cold day.

During our daily walks to school, my Sister and I would have to pass the building site which had now started at the rear of the house. It was still freezing, the sky was a very light purple, the trees were laden with frost and the snow, which had fallen days before, was still hard and brittle to touch. We were about to approach the site crane when there was this volley of bad language from the crane driver, as he leapt from the crane and landed on what only must have been the ganger. The two of them rolled over and over in the snow, their punches hitting the hard frozen ground rather than each other. As soon as my Sister saw the commotion she ran flat out back to the house, but I was literally frozen to the spot. The ganger managed to get to his feet and tried to calm the contest down.

OK," he uttered through snow covered lips, "Let's calm it down now Paddy, I only said that you were not going straight enough with that trench."

To which Paddy replied, " I've dug trenches out all over Ireland and nobody has ever said that I wasn't going straight before," and with that he aimed a slushy, wet Wellington directly at the ganger's groin, hitting the target with a crisp, frosty thud! The ganger summoned up quite a lot of strength and after that I noticed tears in his eyes - whether they were tears of anger or tears of pain, it was hard to distinguish. A much larger man than the crane driver, he dived straight at him and they both rolled over in the slush and the mud until they disappeared down a giant manhole, and after a couple of seconds there was a loud splash as they hit the bottom and then there was silence.

What seemed like hours went by, until two muddy hands grabbed the top of the manhole - it was the ganger. The crane driver had now scrambled to the top and both pairs of eyes stared at me - bleary and full of mud. As their eyes left me and turned to one another, they looked like two giant sloe worms. The ganger had lost his cap in the melee and this concerned him as he saw the cap as a sign of authority.

After spitting most of the mud out of his mouth, he spluttered, "Where's my cap?" and glanced back down the manhole mournfully, and was then dragged back down as the crane driver used him to lever himself out. I can recall learning many swear words that day, because as the ganger fell back, he shouted something that made the crane driver's parentage very doubtful. The crane driver smirked and made for the nearest hut and brazier to dry off his saturated clothes.

By this time my Mother had rushed out of the house holding my Sister's hand enquiring why she had gone back to the house in tears.

Later that day on my trudge home from school, I noticed the two men sat around the brazier warming their hands and dragging on a soggy soiled cigarette; they glanced over at me and smiled, and shouted, "Good night Son." No doubt they would be in the Bridge Inn that night downing a Guinness or two, followed by Whisky chasers. They worked hard and played hard in those far off days of hard manual labour.

St Thomas's School was a good traditional Church of England School which laid down a very good foundation for my education. The school was small but compact and the teachers, Mrs Morris and Mrs Butterworth, worked very hard with the inadequate facilities available to them. Nothing changes.

We were still using slates and chalk in some of the lessons, mainly in arithmetic. Singing tables was another thing that I remember quite well, but it always seemed to go very quiet when seven times nine came around. After several lessons at singing the tables, they were known by heart. We didn't have to think - it came automatically. I was always relieved when twelve times twelve came around because I had sung them on the one deep breath almost, so as to keep up with the rest of the class, although at the end they were all inhaling deeply.

School became interesting for me because it was a well organised and disciplined set up. At break times there would be
separate playgrounds for the boys and girls, which were traditional. The morning assembly was always a serious occasion, when hymns would be sung and prayers said for the day.
Land of Hope and Glory was the class favourite because it had
a touch of patriotism to it, and of course the British Empire was
still going strong and it would then be followed by Jerusalem,
Walk upon England's Pastures Green. Of course these songs
were written in the 19th Century when England was a mass of
green.

In the two years I spent at St Thomas's School, my 3 R's
improved 100%.

The school building itself was built of old red brick with
sandstone corners. Alongside the school was St Thomas's
Church and also built of sandstone with two rows of mature
lime trees on either side of the narrow path that ran up to the
Church entrance.

It was late 1946 and everything was still on the ration and
many things were scarce. The Manchester Ship Canal ran more
or less alongside the school and on occasions the word would
go around the school that there was a `Yanky boat coming up
the canal', and the classroom would almost empty as we moved
down to the canal.

As the ship went passed on its way up the Port of Manchester,
the American sailors would throw all sorts to us - mainly grape-
fruits, oranges, chewing gum and sweets. There would then
be a mad scramble down the embankment - a very dangerous
practice as the cobblestones were covered in wet green slime
and was very slippy. On one occasion one of the boys actually
fell into the water, but luckily we had the sense to form a chain
and pull him out and then lay him on his stomach to let the
water drain out of his lungs. Then the rest of us would carry
on with the collection of the goodies that were strewn about the
embankment.

The ship disappeared into the distance under the Latchford
high level train bridge. On arrival back at school, the Headmaster
was waiting at the school entrance with arms on hips looking
at his watch and would then give us a good telling off. What
had been our 10 minute morning break had lasted about an

hour. The unfortunate lad who had fallen into the canal had been home to change his clothes and looked quite refreshed. He was pleased with the donation that we gave him for his efforts, which was mainly chewing gum.

The school playground on the boys side backed onto the shops on London Road, and there was a wall about 10 feet high bordering, and on Monday mornings the fruiterer would throw any fruit he had left from the weekend into the playground, causing quite a rumpus as us lads dived into the scrum to try and get some fruit. After the morning break we would file back into the classrooms - some of us with bright red faces covered in pips and apple juice. Once we were in the classroom it would reek of fruit and the teacher would be sniffing the air during the course of the lesson trying to decipher the smell.

During the course of the school year there would be numerous amounts of games - mainly seasonal. Many had been played for hundreds of years; how it was ascertained when to start and finish certain games was never really worked out. However, one day we would be playing marbles and the next it would be conkers - marbles being a very serious game. A circle would be drawn with a piece of chalk about a yard in diameter and then the marbles would be placed inside and whoever had first go would try to flick marbles out of the circle, using his own individual style - of which there were many. I could never afford marbles, let alone play, and on the rare occasions that I did, I was hopeless - losing them in no time at all!

Now conkers I was not too bad at, mainly due to the endless supply I could find in the woods at Appleton. Some people would harden the conkers by baking them in the oven, but would soon be found out and after a meeting of the `Conker Committee' they were disqualified.

These games lasted for about a month as no doubt people got bored and turned to the next form of entertainment, which was usually free - as whatever we used could be either made or plucked from a tree. Jacks were made out of clay - a set of five about half an inch cube in size. To start the game they would all be thrown into the air and whatever landed on the back of the hand were deemed to have won - the rest on the floor would have to be picked up, whilst throwing one Jack into the air. Once all five had been picked up, the game would progress and there would be many variations, and the game could go on for hours - 1's, 2's and 3's, and so on.

I should imagine that the cheapest game played would be rugby league, using an empty matchbox. A pitch would be marked out, two would play and using the forefinger, the matchbox would be steadily flicked inside the rectangle which would usually be about a yard long and 18 inches wide, with a narrow strip of about 3 inches wide where the matchbox would have to settle for a try to be scored, without touching any of the lines, once agreed by the two players. Goalposts would then be made by using the thumbs and the forefingers held together at right angles and then placing the forefingers on the ground in the goal position. The taker of the kick for goal would then place the matchbox on the back of the hand and flick it with the index finger with some force, to take it over the makeshift goal.

Skipping and hopscotch were other seasonal games, although they were mainly played by the fairer sex and quite often interrupted by the unfairer sex! These games kept the youngsters fit and no doubt gave them a sense of timing, rushing in and out of the rope to try and keep the rhythm going and not stop the rope. Sometimes there would be upwards of 10 skipping together under the rope. Hopscotch was a very skilful game and cost nothing.

Although now troubled by asthma, I still managed to partake in most of the games, but during an attack I would be very short of breath and consequently sidelined. I always managed to go to school though, knowing that being amongst other children it would take my mind off it, which it did to a certain extent.

1946 was a very cold winter; the canal froze over in late December and was several inches thick, which in turn prevented the barges from moving along the canal (Bridgewater). There had been many attempts by the barges to break the ice, but to no avail. After an hour it would be frozen over again, so they gave up and went on the barges where they lit fires ready for the even colder nights. Living on these barges they would be below the waterline and therefore next to the ice that had hemmed them in for days on end - it must have been well below zero.

Most of the children would cross the canal when it was frozen and slide up and down for a while before winding their way to school. My Mother had warned me not to go near the ice, especially as my Sister was with me as well. We had to take the normal route passed the Rylands wire works, and the Bridge Inn and over London Bridge. It was all downhill from there to St Thomas's.

Going home from school one cold and misty night, I could not resist a slide on the canal. First of all I made my Sister go over the London Bridge and wait on the other side, which she did very reluctantly. I found that with a good run I could slide for miles but after about 10 minutes of this I had to go because, knowing my Mother, she would be worrying even if we were a couple of minutes late.

After a settling in period at St Thomas's and being a newcomer, and also a policeman's Son into the bargain, I was singled out as a threat to the school Nol's title. I had no option but to reluctantly go along as the Jackals had arranged the bout by break time. I can remember his name very well, an unusual Christian name - Wycliffe (Smith), renowned for his speed. I instantly thought of Joe Louis and the speed at which he could throw punches and even catch flies off the wall. No Ken (Dobson) to help me out now - how I wished I was back at Little Budworth where life was so simple.

Break time arrived and I was seriously considering throwing in the towel, so to speak, but the words of my Father echoed in my ears, "If you ever come home here with a black eye lad, you'll most likely get another one off me!" and, of course, I took those words seriously then.

The 10 o'clock bell rang - it was like a death knell to me; I felt my whole body go faint and sweat appeared on my brow - yes, it was fear. The Jackals had marked the ring behind the bike shed about 10 feet square and etched No. 1 in Wycliffe's corner. I could feel myself turning a little paler as I caught Wycliffe's glance. He was a tall, slim lad, built more for running than fighting, whereas I was stocky and plumpish in those days. Turning my back on Wycliffe I thought I would give the crowd their monies worth, so I threw in a few imaginary punches, bobbed and weaved and then turned around again to face him. He wasn't very impressed at all, as he pulled the ugliest

105

face possible in my direction. My knees buckled. Some idiot in the crowd impersonated a bell and as I turned to face Wycliffe, I wondered where he had gone, because all I could see coming towards me, was what could only be described as a windmill - arms going round and round so fast they were a blur. As he got closer I was looking for an exit, but instead, like a fool, I started bobbing and weaving, which was undoubtedly useless because as we got into close quarters, his fists just rained down on the top of my head and if I hadn't shouted, "I give in!," very quickly, I would have been driven into the ground like a tent peg. I was stunned in more senses than one.

I often pondered whether anyone had ever come up with a defence against those unusual tactics. I scanned the papers for years after to see if Wycliffe ever made the grade in the real ring, but no, he did not.

Back in the classroom my nose started to swell and turn a lovely shade of purple, and by the end of the lesson my eyes were going black. When I arrived home I told my Mother I had walked into a door - I think she believed me. I wasn't sure whether my Father believed me or not, but the very next day he was showing me the art of boxing. I nearly said, "It might be alright against doors, but not against Wycliffe."

Appleton was the next Parish to Daresbury - the place where Lewis Carroll got a lot of ideas for his classic book - Alice in Wonderland. He often stayed in the area where he befriended a Daughter of the Liddell family named Alice. On reflection, I can quite understand how he got many of his inspirations from because the house, Walton Hall, was an eerie place. I would often venture into the grounds of the hall but would never go into the then almost derelict building. Although some of my friends would dare one another to go in, they would stop at the door. There was a notice outside saying `Keep Out', and I think the property was to be sold on.

On one occasion the conker season was in full swing so we decided to go into the grounds and throw sticks up at the Horse Chestnut trees to bring the conkers down. We had just climbed the fence that had a notice fixed to it saying, `Trespassers will be prosecuted,' which we used to lever ourselves over, and were walking over the field, when we heard a shout from behind, "Hey you lot, come here!"

We turned around and there, leaning on the fence, was a big fat jovial Policeman beckoning with his hand for us to go over to him. My friends immediately dived for the nearest cover and ran away, but I went over to him because he looked like a nice copper with a smile on his face. As I arrived at the fence, his smile changed to a scowl.

"Can't you read?," he snapped.

"Yes," I proudly replied.

By this time my friends had reappeared and had strolled over - either they had decided to give me some moral support or they just felt guilty for letting me take the telling off on my own; but they immediately changed their mind as the copper took his note book out from his tunic pocket. Wetting the tip of his pencil with this tongue he said, "Names." I cringed - I didn't know what to do and not for the first time in my life either, and no doubt there would be many more occasions.

My friends gave their names and as they did the copper gave us all a lecture on walking on other people's land and destroying the property. I could not believe what I was hearing. He was throwing the book at us just for throwing at the conker trees. His eyes eventually came to rest on me.

"Name," he smiled.

"Ivor Goolding" I replied with tears in my eyes.

He then stopped writing, stared at me for a while and then stammered, "Is your Father a policeman then?"

"Yes," I cried.

"Ah well, I will let you all off this time, and don't say anything to your Dad," he smiled.

As if I would! I would never dare tell my Father about any of my escapades - even after he had retired from the Cheshire force.

Venturing into that area again several weeks later, we gave the conker trees a wide berth and walked on past the derelict house which was all boarded up with paint flaking off the walls and the window frames. Some of the glass remained but most had been knocked out by the odd stray brick thrown from the other side of the fence. We moved around to the back of the house and through the overgrown gardens, once landscaped but now more or less returned to its original state.

Once out of the garden we continued into the fields, which banked down to a stream and then on to Daresbury Church in the distance, with its beautiful stained glass window dedicated to Lewis Carroll and depicting scenes from Alice in Wonderland. It was early morning and the dew was still on the ground soaking our feet as we walked across the fields.

As we wandered around eating the chestnuts we had picked earlier, I could not help but notice the hares and the rabbits having their early morning run around, jumping and hopping in the distant mist. This brought back memories of Alice in Wonderland, although I did not read the entire book, the scene before me was reminiscent of some of the things written in the book. We sat down and peeled the rest of the chestnuts, ate them, and then watched the animals a while longer as they dived in and out of burrows, hares shadow boxing and thumping the ground with hind legs, as if stamping out messages to their mates spread around the field in circles, as if planted by the elves the night before, so neatly laid out.

"Can you eat mushrooms raw?" I asked, looking at my two friends who still had their eyes transfixed on the animals at the bottom end of the field. They turned their heads and looked at me in a mystified sort of way.

Eventually Mike replied, "I don't know, and I don't think I would like to try."

I then replied, "If you can peel the skins off the top, then they are definitely mushrooms," and with that I started to peel the skins.

"They are mushrooms," I confirmed.

I then tried a little nibble at the side of one of the bigger mushrooms. They seemed quite edible and then Tony and Mike reluctantly tried some as well, until eventually we had eaten a whole mushroom between us.

"We'd better not eat any more just in case they make us sick," I said.

We then decided to walk over to the hares and the rabbits, and as we did so I felt dizzy, and my eyes would not focus on the far side of the field - the direction in which we were heading. The three of us then slumped to the ground and lay flat on our backs, as if strapped to the wall of death as the field started to spin round. There was no pain at all in the stomach - it was as if my eyes wanted to leave my head. We were now clutching the grass as if were about to be spun off the face of the earth, as it seemed to go round faster and faster. I tried to focus on the Daresbury Church in the distance and in doing so my eyes settled on the hares at the bottom of the field once more, and they had now grown tenfold and had obtained top hats. As they looked in our direction they appeared to be laughing.

This was all very frightening, especially when the hares moved closer to us. I could not move - it was as if all my muscles had been deadened by some unknown force. The ground beneath me rumbled like an earthquake and then, as quickly as the experience started, it finished. It was as if the effects of what we had eaten had run its course through our systems. We then staggered to our feet and wobbled out of the field and then home to tell our tales - which, of course, nobody believed.

I have often wondered over the years if Charles Dodgson (Lewis Carroll) had ever tried that potion and that maybe that his how he got his inspirations for his book `Alice in Wonderland'. How were we to know that we had stumbled across an hallucination drug?

Saturday was our day for a visit to the Palace Cinema in Warrington, and the weekly serial of Roy Rogers - the famous cowboy, and his even more famous horse, Trigger. We would get the bus from Stockton Heath and alight at the Gaumont which was facing the bus depot. We would walk a couple of miles up to the Palace Cinema and pay nine old pence to go in, where we would sit right at the front and join in the cheering and booing as the goodies and the baddies raced across the Arizona Desert. Trigger would outrun any horse - even with Roy hindering him as he jumped from side to side, riding backwards, and hanging onto the poor horse's tail, with his six shooter blasting away for all they were worth. How they hit the target, no one will ever know, but the baddies went down one after another as the chase continued for tens of miles. Roy would dismount by grabbing a branch of a tree that was overhanging the trail and then proceed to cover his trail - unknown to him, watched by the baddies on the mountain above. This was all so very funny and entertaining for us.

When the lights came on at the end of a show, we would race out of the Palace smacking our backsides as if riding imaginary horses, with forefingers for six shooters. I think everyone from the cinema to the bus stop was shot at least ten times and it didn't stop there, because once on the bus it would be converted into a stage coach; much to the annoyance of the bus conductor who would be held up, and also shot dozens of times, before we arrived back at Stockton Heath. We invariably managed to get the conductor so confused that we often got away without paying the fare. The serial would usually run for about ten weeks and it was compulsive viewing, even though the main film was rubbish!

If a woman happened to appear in a film in those days, all the lads would boo - a real shame really, because there would always be a nice woman in the film smartly dressed with about 15 children and always down at the stream washing clothes and not a hair out of place.

After the ninth episode I had an idea that I passed onto my friends. Although they didn't understand at the time, I asked them to collect as many moths as they could and keep them in a jam jar. Come the following Saturday, off we all went to the Palace with jam jars under our coats. When the serial finished, we would unscrew the tops off the jars and let the moths out into the cinema, and they would obviously head for the projector beam and consequently blot out the film. The projectionist would be trying all ways to adjust the camera, not realising the real cause. In the event, the film would be stopped several times until the manager announced that there was a fault in the film.

The film would be shown again the following week and that entrance to the show would be free! So, in effect, we would see the main film and the serial free. So was it all really worth the disruption? I don't think so, really - maybe a laugh for us at the time, but not recommended.

It was at one of these weekly visits to the cinema that the full horror of War came over to me. Atomic Bombs had been dropped on Hiroshima and Nagasaki the previous year, and the film of the aftermath was now on general release. Usually there would be a free for all during the interval and the noise would be quite deafening as youngsters shouted and screamed at one another across the cinema. However, as the newsreel went on there was a deathly hush - a silence I had never witnessed before, as the horrific pictures of men, women and children, almost burnt to a cinder, went on, showing children writhing in agony with skin peeling from their bodies. We all started to cry - it was terrible.

At Stockton Heath I was given my first bike - it was slightly too large for me.

"You'll grow into it," my Father said.

"Maybe," I thought, "in about 10 years!"

I could very often be seen careering around the district at a tidy speed. The footpaths, like the roads in Waverley Avenue, were unmade and were very dusty in the Summer months. On no account was I allowed to leave Waverley Avenue, because, obviously, in my parents' view I was not very steady at all on my new bike, but on this occasion I went against their word.

Although not very far away, it was decided that we go for a bike ride to Moore, which was about 3 miles from Appleton, for the purpose of train-spotting - something I had never done before.

As we rode along the canal path in single line file, very wobbly and unsafe with the canal beckoning on one side and a hawthorn hedge on the other, I could not help but notice how low the water was in the canal, and there were old bike frames and tin kettles showing above the waterline. This was due to the very hot Summer that we were going through in 1948 - one of peace and tranquillity and never-ending sun from morn till dusk.

We had now reached the Walton Arms (a pub frequented by my Father most Sunday nights when he was off duty), joined the main Warrington to Chester Road, and eventually arrived at Daresbury. We turned right onto a cinder track which brought us to the main railway line through the district. It was a busy junction and trains were going through quite often.

I was not too keen on the idea of collecting train numbers initially, although I did become more of an enthusiast as The Coronation Scot flew past on its way to Holyhead - no doubt transporting Royalty to Anglesey. These beautiful pieces of engineering, so big and with all the moving parts visible from where we had positioned ourselves, right on the embankment, steaming past at speeds I had never imagined. The draught from the trains blew our hair and coal smoke stroked our faces as the engine strove to get more speed as she climbed the incline out of Moore. The embankment had been built with clinker from the near iron foundries at Irlam, and the coal mines of the South Lancashire coalfields and, believe me, it was very black indeed!

After an afternoon watching and noting all the engines that had passed us, we decided to head for home. I was still in short trousers and was also wearing the traditional diamond patterned pullover - the fashion of the day. It was now hard to see any colours on the pullover, and the grey trousers were now a very dark grey as a result of the constant climbing up and down of what could only be called a `slag heap'. My whole being was now starting to blend in with the surroundings, and after stuffing my little note book into my trouser pocket, putting my chain back on for the fifth time, it was time to wind our way along the lane and, hopefully, reach home in one piece (meaning me and the bike!)

Eventually upon reaching Bridgewater Canal, the water was a little deeper here, so I decided to try and remove some of the grime from my legs, using grass wetted by dipping in the canal. Unfortunately this only added to the mess, as the coal dust spread even more. In my effort to get more water onto the sheets of grass, I lost my balance and tippled over, head first, into the canal. Luckily I came back up, standing in three feet of water, gasping for air. As I had struggled to get out of the mire, I had collected a mass of green slime on top of my head from the bottom of the canal, much to the amusement of my friends, who had been watching very attentively up until then and no doubt were relieved to see me surface from the deep.

They had had enough and got on their bikes to head for home, staying well away from the smell and the mess that was me. I was soaked to the skin, my shoes were full of water and even after emptying them out they made a squelching noise as I strove to get onto my bike for the trip home.

When I eventually did arrive home, I decided to go through the back door. Mother was in the kitchen preparing tea and happened to glance up from her chore - her eyes freezing on me in disbelief - a black stinking mass at the bottom of the garden. She ran out, after recognising some of the patterns on my pullover as being her own knitting, pushed me into the house and into the bathroom before my Father cast his lawful eyes on me. Both dogs had run out of the house in disgust at the smell, only to come back hours later sniffing the air and very nearly giving the show away, as my Father was in the house then, looking very suspiciously at the dogs.

"What's up with them two hounds?" he said enquiringly.

My Mother glanced at me and then said, "I don't know, they've been like that all day."

My Father looked around, gave her one of his double frowns, thought for a moment, and then said, "It's the sign of an earthquake when dogs are uneasy all day," and smiled to himself.

My Mother screwed one side of her face up as if in a nervous twitch and said no more. She just looked at me as if to say, "You lucky so and so!"

I knew that, but I would have to give those dogs a talking to.

Stockton Heath had originally been built for the businessmen of Warrington and the surrounding districts, and consisted of solid Victorian buildings. Appleton was adjoining Stockton Heath - an area of private dwellings.

As the nights drew in and Bonfire Night approached, we were fully occupied at night collecting rubbish for the bonfire, which was sited directly opposite our house. As we were allowed to stay out for an extra hour, we would be looking around for extra games to play. Fed up with lighting other people's bonfires, it was suggested that we play `knick-knack'. I had never heard of this game before and, unfortunately for them, the houses of Higher Appleton had been chosen on this particular occasion. It was to be the first and last escapade at knocking on doors and running away.

It was a freezing cold night at the end of October and we were on our way to Higher Appleton - Mike, Tony (also policemen's sons), and I; our Fathers' maintaining the law.

The first few doors presented no problems - owners would appear at the doors peering up and down the road, muttering and then returning to their warm fires.

After a while of hiding behind hedges and then up to the next door, which was in an elevated position up a flight of steps, we knocked on the door. As we were ambling up the road, what can only be described as a `bat out of hell' - a blur jumped down the steps of the house and gave chase! Well, we slipped into top gear very sharpishly. I think this man must have been in training for the '48 Olympics, because his speed was quite phenomenal - as if he had been waiting behind the door, poised ready in starting blocks and waiting for the knock. How were we to know that there had been numerous gangs around that night doing the same thing? This man was furious. We managed to round the bend at the top of the road and our little legs gathered a bit of speed as we came onto London Road, which was downhill, right through Stockton Heath.

Mike was now in the lead by about 10 yards - him being the tallest one of us and also the quickest runner - he could outpace me and Tony by miles. I was last at the second furlong marker, rapidly running out of breath - my lungs were bursting and I thought I was going to pass out! Eventually I was about to slump against the wall, when this man ran passed me, and that was all I remembered until I came round - about 10 minutes later, ears tingling and tears running down my cheeks.

On squinting down London Road I could make out Tony - also slumped against the wall, and then further on Mike was also in the same position, wondering what had hit him. After shaking ourselves we limped home once more - but NOT to tell this tale. That man had taught me a lesson - although sometimes people do not learn by their mistakes. I will never forget the footsteps of that man as they got closer and closer, my heart going faster and faster as my legs got weaker and weaker, and turning to beg for mercy as he drew alongside me and then the lights went out. I never ever played that game again - a case of the punishment fitting the crime.

As Bonfire Night drew closer, we would busy ourselves in collecting more and more rubbish to pile on tope of the ever growing bonfire, with the usual den in the middle to guard it from other marauding gangs, who would be after easy pickings for their own bonfires. We had to be on our guard all night, because some of the more adventurous would try to light our bonfire. I saw many bonfires go up in smoke days before the event - much to the disappointment of the younger children. We would get most of our material from the Delph tip where an old decaying house had all its beams and rafters exposed ready for taking - a lot would be used for the domestic fires as there was still a shortage of solid fuel, even though the War had now been over for almost two years.

Whilst at St Thomas's School we were advised to join the church, which I did, and became a member of the choir - although I must admit this was more for the monetary gains than for the true meaning of the hymns I would be singing. Choir practice would be every Wednesday night and it was also a good reason for me to get out at night in the Winter, and earn a few pence as well. We would be paid one penny for practice and if the voice was up to standard and really tested the acoustics of the church, the individual would be selected for the choir on a Sunday. This could entail three services which would pay the princely sum of two pence per Sunday. Each choirboy would be given the money at the end of the month, from which would be deducted a percentage towards the church and other charities, leaving a lordly sum of two shillings and sixpence - which was a lot of sweets and crisps in those days. The Church Lads Brigade practice would be in the Church Hall which ran adjacent to the school and a uniform would also be provided, for a small fee.

What really attracted me to the CLB was the chance of playing the drums, and of course the trips out to different places - usually fairgrounds, and in this particular year it was to be Belle Vue. The trip would usually be in late Autumn after the Harvest Festival. An early morning start was necessary to clean and put on our uniforms - with a little help from my Mother, of course. We would run down London Road to meet the coach outside the church and away we would go - singing and shouting, and under strict orders to behave ourselves as we were representing St Thomas's Church and the CLB.

On arrival at Belle Vue we would all be lined up and inspected, ready for our march into the stadium. As all the bands struck up and we started to march into the stadium, a sense of pride did come over me and I even managed to keep in step with all the lads around me. As we marched around the stadium with the band playing `Onward Christian Soldiers', the people were clapping and cheering. I must say, it was a very colourful scene with all the different types of standards waving in the breeze.

The parade would last for about 2 hours as there were many bands to march passed the datum with the CLB Chief taking the salute. Once the afternoon's festivities were over, it was over to the fairground enbloc.

As I walked under the arched entrance with all the fairy lights flashing, I stopped and looked in awe at the sight before me, my mouth wide open at the many different things that were flying around or up and down - dodgems, caterpillars, big wheels and hundreds of stalls. My immediate thought was money - I thought to myself, "Ivor lad, that five shillings is not going to last very long." I emerged from the penny arcade winning two pence, so that went towards another ride on the dodgems. The big wheel was turning slowly and people were screaming as they reached the top, as the wheel stopped to let people get on at the bottom. It was not for me, as I was scared of heights anyway and I was convinced that my money could be spent more wisely elsewhere in the fairground.

As it began to get dark, more and more lights were switched on and it took on an entirely different appearance - no doubt to attract people from the surrounding area for a night's entertainment.

As the money disappeared and the dark descended, I decided to make my way back to the coach. The rain had caused the ground to become very muddy and my uniform was looking very shabby. Most of the CLB lads had also managed to pick a bit of the Belle Vue mud up as well, and the coach smelt a bit ripe on the way home. After a few choruses of `Ten Green Bottles' and `I've Got a Lovely Much of Coconuts,' we arrived back at Stockton Heath feeling very happy after having a marvellous day out at Belle Vue.

CHAPTER SIXTEEN

Whitsun Walks and Cruising Down the River

The church played a big part in the organising of entertainment for the young - in that they had Guild nights and many other forms of meetings for the more mature people of the parish.

The Whitsuntide Walk was another of the main events in the church calendar. This was where all the churches of the surroundings area would congregate outside St Thomas's Church with all their banners held aloft in full glory, denoting their church embroidered in six inch capitals for all to see. There would also be many bands leading the procession and as they moved off, they would start playing many tunes - usually hymns. The walk would head towards Walton Park and the footpaths would be packed tight with people - mainly parents and relatives of the children walking and they would throw money as we passed by. My Grandparents and some of my Aunties, Ethel and Bett, would be there just to see the spectacle, because in their town they did not have this sort of procession at Whit - maybe it had been forgotten about over the years. There would be many disruptions of the momentum of the march, as the children scrambled for the money thrown by parents and relatives. A lot of the money collected would be spent at Walton Hall on ice creams and lemonade once the whole procession had arrived, but a percentage again would go to the church and local charities.

I had my first taste of work while I lived in Stockton Heath at the ripe old age of 10 years. During the school holidays my Father had fixed me up with a potato picking job at a farm in Appleton. I do not recollect seeing much of my Father in those days at Appleton because he was either on duty or playing one of the seasonal games he took part in for the Police. He must have been thinking of me for him to fix me up with this job `Spud Bashing'.

I arrived at the farm at 8 o'clock one very wet Monday morning - I don't think my Mother wanted me to go because she gave me a very soulful look as she handed me some sandwiches for the tea break - if there was to be one.

It was absolutely bouncing down - typical Stockton Heath weather at the time; 1946-48 - rain, rain, and more rain. The other people who were there, the grown-ups, moved around from farm to farm picking potatoes and they were prepared for any type of weather. Their ankles would be covered with gaiters, old sacks around their shoulders, and they would sit in the barn waiting. On its return they would all shuffle out and start the back-breaking job of filling sack after sack for hours on end. The poor old horse pulling the thrower had one of those long miserable faces as if he knew he was in for a long, wet day. A nose bag was fitted to give him some incentive to carry on - although after he had a mouthful his expression showed no sign of cheering up. The steam was rising from his body as the cold rain bounced off his harness and settled on his shining coat.

After I had filled half a sack I was getting tired and on glancing around the field I noticed that most people had filled 3 or 4 bags! There could be no help from other people as they were paid by the amount of bags they had filled, so I just had to plod on the best I could. I eventually got into the hang of it as the morning dragged on and by tea break I had filled nearly 2 sacks - now realising that it was every man for himself as the potato thrower went passed.

At the morning break people brought out their own billycans with tea - some had toast and many lit their first cigarette of the morning. I was saturated through to the skin - this seemed a regular occurrence for me!

There were plenty of other children scattered around the field, but they were a lot older than me and appeared to enjoy the task. There were also many women toiling away who were no doubt trying to earn enough money just to pay the rent, as many of their Husbands' would be earning buttons in casual jobs.

One of the women must have felt sorry for me and came over and asked how I was doing. She offered me a cup of tea which

I willingly accepted. Releasing my grip on my sack, which I was guarding with my life, I drank the tea and immediately felt the benefit as the warm feeling of it hit my stomach, and sent a warm glow around my whole body.

The potato thrower was now on the move again and I scrambled to pick up the fresh mud-caked potatoes and then throw them into my sack. My fingers were still numb, but the kind woman who had given me a drink of tea, slipped a few arms-full of potatoes into my sack. My faith in human nature had been revived.

During the course of the afternoon the weather brightened up and there was even a glimpse of the sun and I was able to fill another sack. These sacks had to be filled right to the top, as that was adjudged to be a full hundred weight. Once the sacks were full a flat wagon would come along with a burly man at the reins, jumping on and off and throwing sacks up in one go - he was built like a giant and had hands like shovels. I thought I'd better keep moving or he might throw me on the wagon as well!

At the end of the first day I staggered home worn out - it didn't take me long to fall asleep that night. I did notice my Mother looking at me with a worried look as I drank my Horlicks and she enquired as to how I'd got in that state. She had obviously never been potato picking, Maybe she would have a word with my Father, but if she did it made no difference, as I was on my way again the very next day.

What few muscles I had then were aching from the previous day and as I turned into the farm gate they got worse at the thought of having to fill even more sacks.

Thursday arrived and the sun was shining brightly so I didn't mind going on that particular day. My Mother had obtained a pair of Wellington Boots from somewhere - although they were several sizes too big, they kept the wet and soil out. After a while my legs started to get chapped so I took the boots off to give more freedom of movement. I was now working in my bare feet, and enjoying it as the ground had dried out considerably.

Once the ten o'clock tea was finished one of the teenagers about 10 furrows away from me playfully lobbed a potato at one of the women close by and hit her in the middle of her back.

She didn't really notice as she strived to pick more potatoes, and fill more sacks to earn a little more bonus. A man next to her saw who had thrown the potato and retaliated by throwing two back in quite succession. Unfortunately, one of the potatoes hit the flat wagon driver on his head as he heaved another full bag onto the stack. Well, one potato missile led to another until there was a full scale battle raging and I just stood there in disbelief - mouth agape as usual.

The farmer arrived at top speed with his two collies wondering what the commotion was about and noticed two lads of the same age as me still throwing potatoes, and immediately said, "You're sacked!," pointing in my direction! I could not believe he meant me, but I'm afraid I had to go as well for looking stupid - something I didn't find too hard to do in those days. "Sacked" - I thought this word was very appropriate for the occasion, as we were knee deep in them!

Finally, the dear lady who had helped me fill my sack said, "It means that your service is no longer required."

I arrived back at the farm expecting a good telling off from the farmer.

"Get off my property!," he yelled angrily. He did not give us one halfpenny between us for the four days hard labour we had put in. I went home crying and thinking what a cruel world it was again.

Arriving home before dinner my Mother thought that I had hurt myself, but when I told her the story she was very annoyed. My Father was on the early shift that week and would not arrive home until after 2 o'clock in the afternoon. When he did arrive he hadn't even taken his boots off when my Mother told him what had happened. He immediately shot out of the house, jumped onto his bike - similar, I thought, to Roy Rogers jumping onto Trigger, and at speed and in a cloud of dust he just disappeared up Waverley Avenue. He returned 10 minutes later with ten shillings - some for me and some for my Mother. That's what I call justice and in some respects my Father was a fair man. However, I could never understand why he changed from one mood to another so quickly - it had to be the shift work, I thought.

Sunday was a day of rest. I was still not allowed out on the Sabbath. Sunday night was still the traditional walk out and this was the only time we would get out of the house on that day. It was always a set walk along the Bridgewater Canal to Walton. We now had two dogs, as my Father had persuaded my Mother to go and have a look at a Spaniel that was locked up at the Police Station and, according to my Father, she was going to be destroyed the next day. Of course, my Mother fell for her when she saw her - although my Mother had said adamantly only a few weeks before that no more dogs were coming into the house.

Of course my Father had bright ideas of breeding, but Lassie would have none of it I'm afraid. My Father was going to give her strict housetraining once she had got used to Jock. Lassie did not succumb to training very easily. He started by trying to housetrain her, but to no avail. I thought I saw signs of my Father cracking up during this period of intense training. Lassie was very moody and snappy - just like my Father I suppose, so a stalemate was definitely on the cards.

Jock, the Labrador, knew who the master was as he had received his intense training years before ....poor dog. He would slink away the moment my Father raised his voice around the house, but Lassie would always stand her ground and bare her teeth at him. My Father gave up and, in a way, admired her - a lesson I should have learnt from her. It was the same with Lassie on our Sunday night walks; she would always go in the opposite direction that my Father wanted her to go. Once off London Bridge and onto the towpath of the Bridgewater Canal, Jock would dive straight in and swim alongside as we walked, but Lassie would swim over to the other side and away through the bushes in Walton Park - she hated water. Jock would swim from London Bridge right up to the Walton Arms - he had to, whether he wanted to or not, because if he tried to get out my Father would push him back in.

"We've got to get rid of all those fleas you've collected this week," my Father would say.

In the meantime, my Mother would be impersonating Ronnie Ronalde, whistling into the bushes for Lassie. Eventually Lassie would appear wagging her little stubby tail and my Father would put her straight on her lead, and I thought I saw a hint of a smile on Lassie's face.

On arrival at the pub my Father would go in and buy four packets of crisps and a bottle of pop. He would give them to my Mother and then return to the pub for the night. We would then wend our way home, and that would be our regular Sunday night out.

About 100 yards from our back gates ran the Bridgewater Canal where the barges would ply up and down all day from dawn until dusk. They would be carrying coal or chemicals up to Manchester from Runcorn, and visa versa, and some of the barges were still being pulled by Shire Horses along the towpath. These barge horses were big and strong animals and would go for miles on one full nose bag of oats, and would automatically stop at the bridges - knowing that they would have to go over the bridge to change towpaths. I remember those barge trips from London Bridge up to Lymm so clearly. The barges were motorised with a little putt-putt engine at the rear.

The barge would pull away early on a Sunday afternoon with a full load of people and children. There would be an accordion player on board and the singing would go on for the duration of the trip. People would start singing the hit of the day and, very appropriate for the occasion, `Cruising down the River.' My Father would usually be on duty so my Mother would take us - we laughed and sang until our throats were sore. After a few choruses of songs we came to the Grappenhall Bridge which was about halfway. The scenery along the route was breath-taking with the willow trees hanging down towards the water in some parts, with the swallows skimming over the water catching flies. The sun's reflection on the water would scatter into a million ripples as the bow of the barge cut through.

The trip would take about an hour and once at Lymm everyone went down the gang plank and headed for Mr Dellucci, the ice cream man, who would have many cornets ready for the thirsty people. The return trip was just as enjoyable as the singing got louder, tonsils having now been oiled with pop and ice cream. The barge would sway from side to side as the people rocked from side to side, in time with the music. I can recollect the bargee or, dare I say it, the pilot, being slightly under the influence of alcohol, and the barge was now on automatic pilot and it was veering from bank to bank. My Mother started to look a little but concerned as she joined in the singing of one of her favourite hymns, as the barge bumped into the bank. The choir would sing an octave higher and the barge would then settle back into the middle. On arrival back at London Bridge, I could see the look of relief on my Mother's face as the barge anchored up and we all jumped off - the bargee waving and laughing, still singing. Once off the barge my Mother would say, "Of course it didn't worry me, because I am still a very good swimmer." We would then walk home laughing all the way at the events of the afternoon. My Mother was still talking about these trips 40 years later.

CHAPTER SEVENTEEN

Keeping the Home Fires Burning

On many occasion in the depths of Winter with snow and ice lingering on and on through January and February, my Mother, although a policeman's Wife, was obliged to take any bits of wood that were lying around outside the house, usually on the building site, whilst my Father was on duty. One day the builders had moved half a railway sleeper into position in front of the brazier to keep it thawed out ready for the morning fire. My Mother had noticed this through the lace curtains in the back kitchen. I arrived home from school and it was already thick freezing fog. "Could you give me a lift with a piece of wood just outside the back gate?," my Mother asked. I instantly thought it would be a small tree branch, and as I squinted through the swirling mist, standing on what I thought was a pile of bricks, I said, "Where is it?"

My Mother smiled and said, "You're standing on it."

As I looked down I realised that it was a railway sleeper.

"How the heck are we going to drag that back to the house?" I asked.

I had my balaclava on together with several pullovers and a lumber jacket, and as I breathed through the balaclava, my breath froze immediately on the outside. It was the thought of the cold that I managed to muster up some extra strength from somewhere, and we managed to get the sleeper through the gate and into the backyard. Apparently, half the neighbourhood had been waiting for darkness for the same reason.

The following morning, on leaving for school, I noticed a lot of sawdust strewn around the garden, as my Mother had been cutting the wood during the night - bless her. My Father never queried where the wood had appeared from - as long as there was a roaring fire in the hearth for him to warm himself before he went on duty at 10 o'clock at night.

A lot of my time was spent watching and waiting during that Winter (one of the coldest on record - 1946-47), for the builders to finish work. They finished early in the fog, supposedly giving them time to get home whilst there was still a bit of light. When they had all left and just before the cocky watchman arrived, I would nip out sharpish, scraping around all the braziers for any coke that was lying around - some of it still hot; it all went in my bucket - just enough to keep the fire going in our house for the night. Some of the pieces were still glowing and I had to douse them in the snow so that I could pick them up. There would be many holes in my gloves after a night's mission. The weather hampered progress of the builders, and how they managed to complete the site on schedule and make such a good job of the brickwork, I will never know, because every morning the first two hours would be spent clearing up the previous night's snowfall from the brick piles and lime pits.

The Summer that followed was very hot and in the end was declared to be a drought. The Bridgewater Canal was almost empty and, again, barges could not move along its waterways. Under the London Road Bridge it was like a scrap metal yard where people had thrown old bikes, dolly tubs and even rusty old gas ovens - all revealed as the water was barely a foot deep. It was possible to walk across the canal again, not over ice but over mud this time. It had only been a few weeks before that people had been diving into the canal off the bridge, now realising how lucky they had been not to have killed themselves, as all the rubbish was revealed.

The local fisherman were extremely upset for they had been denied drowning worms in the Winter due to ice, and now it was as a result of the lack of water. Where would all the fish be anyway - basking in the muddy water that was left? Maybe.

The fishermen all moved up to the dam at Lymm, but were immediately stopped by the police with the stern warning, "No fishing until the drought is over." There was plenty of water within 2 square miles of Appleton, in that there was the Manchester Ship Canal, the Bridgewater Canal and the River Mersey - now, alas they are all redundant; except for the River Mersey. She goes on forever, even after the industrialists over the centuries have tried to kill her with the constant oozing of waste and acids from the numerous chemical works spread long her banks, as she meanders from the Peaks in Derbyshire, to the Irish Sea off Liverpool. I hope people will eventually realise what is happening to their environment and do something about it.

CHAPTER EIGHTEEN

Harry Bath and Brian Bevan

Warrington was the Mecca of Rugby League and some of the greatest players to have played the game were at Wilderspool at this time. Names like Harry Bath, Brian Bevan and, of course, the brilliant scrum half Gerry Helme, come to mind.

My Father would take me to the game when he was off on a Saturday. The Wilderspool Causeway would be a mass of bodies as they headed for The Wires (their nickname) ground. It would be a capacity crowd at almost every home game - especially if they were playing Wigan or Widnes, two of the other top teams in 1947 - 1948. Brian Bevan was reputed to have been faster than any of the local coalminers' whippets, as he flashed down the right wing - a blur, his bald head glistening in the Winter sunshine. Once in full flight and heading for the corner he would launch himself horizontally through the air for 5 yards and then hit the turf and slide for another 5 yards, touch down, and then hit the billboards, before coming up smiling, with many of the crowd patting his bald head with delight. Most of the Brian Bevan tries were spectacular and this was one of the many hundreds he scored throughout his career - of course, he was always well supported by Big Harry and the nippy Gerry.

During those halcyon years they were always winning the league or appearing in Cup Finals at Wembley; mainly against their old rivals, Wigan. Years later I had the privilege of meeting Harry Bath - a giant of a man, holding the Challenge Cup they had won the previous season. He had hands as big as navvy's shovels and a smile as wide as the Ship Canal. He was making a guest appearance at the Hoole Carnival in Canadian Avenue.

Back at Waverley Avenue we had our own pitch marked and it was also called 'Wilderspool', and many a cup final was fought there. My asthma was gradually getting worse but I still made the best of the good days, and on bad days after running for a while with the oval ball, I would lie down and gasp for air for a good 5 minutes. The lads playing would jokingly call me, 'Old Wheezer', and told me to lay off the Woodies. I was just over 10 years old and I thought I would suffer with this lack of breath for the rest of my life. Moving into a more industrialised area didn't help any, and I just resigned myself to the fact that I would have really bad attacks in the Winter, when I would be laid low for days on end, finding it difficult to even breathe, let alone run - although I did try to join in most of the games.

It was during our stay at Stockton Heath that the National Health Service was inaugurated. It was the greatest scheme ever brought out by any Government and meant that the working class could now have free medical treatment for the first time - it was 1948. My Mother was determined to rid me of this lack of breath, as she called it. We sat in the surgery for about half an hour and, glancing at my Mother, I wondered who was the most nervous - me or her. It was like waiting for an operation but eventually the cry went out "Next," and I made a move towards the door, but my Mother took me by the hand and whisked me into the Doctor's surgery. On entering the room we were confronted by a pipe-smoking Doctor in a tweedy jacket with a stethoscope draped around his neck.

"Take your shirt off lad," the Doctor ordered. My Mother sprung into action and my vest and shirt came off in the one movement, and if I hadn't been quick, I think my head would have come off too! She was only trying to oblige, I suppose.

The Doctor unravelled his stethoscope and said, "Deep breath," all at the same time.

As I drew my first breath it must have sounded like the Bagpipe section of the Scots Guards, and even louder as I exhaled. The coldness of the stethoscope as it was placed on my ribs forced me into taking another extra deep breath, and the Doctor snapped, "I'll tell you when to breath in and out lad!." My Mother nodded in approval at the Doctor's words.

The Doctor tried very hard for me, even with his limited knowledge of the complaint, and gave my Mother a prescription to take to the chemist which was situated opposite the Police Station in London Road. This was all new territory for my Mother and I sensed that she was enjoying her little trip, to both the Doctor's Surgery and the Chemist, all in one night; I also think she was pleased that finally something was going to be done about my asthma.

We had been waiting in the Chemist awhile before the Chemist re-emerged from behind a stack of coloured bottles and gave my Mother a sealed parcel. We then had to walk up London Road, a very steep hill, and I had a struggle keeping up with my Mother as she increased her step in her eagerness to open the little parcel that the Chemist had given to her. Once opened, my Mother unravelled what looked like pink cotton wool - this was known as Thermogene, and was placed on the chest to draw the asthma out, as the Doctor had explained. I must say it was hot - it would almost burn a hole in my chest once applied and force me to hold my breath for quite a while. In the other package were some cough sweets and these were taken quite often during the day - they eased the asthma a bit, as well as tasting very sweet and moreish.

I must say that I did enjoy our far too short stay in Appleton, although everything seemed to be so grey and dreary with the never-ending rain. During the rainy days my Father would sometimes take it upon himself to play with me and my Sister for a while, before going onto his next shift. We hardly every saw my Father. Hours before he was due to go on duty, he would spend an awful lot of time getting ready - cleaning his boots, putting his collar studs in his shirt, making sure his tie was neat and at the right length, and spending at least 10 minutes brushing his police hat. Then, finally, with all his regulatory uniform on he would ask my Mother to give him a final brush down whilst standing in front of the mirror. Smartness was a top priority for my Father - although he did not have the back of a guardsman, ramrod straight, but more of a rounded and strong back, "A Cheshire back," he would proudly announce, if he saw me watching him brushing his tunic. I did hear a rhyme about the Cheshire man but would never dare repeat it in front of my Father, but I don't suppose he would mind now.

Cheshire born, Cheshire bred,
Strong in the back,
Weak in the head. Anon.

CHAPTER NINETEEN

A Brush With Authority

Throughout his career, my Father foolishly thought that no man was better than he - whether he were an Inspector or a Superintendent; he would not liken to orders readily - something that was going to rub off onto me in later years, unfortunately.

Consequently, whilst my Father was stationed at Stockton Heath he had a few scrapes with the police hierarchy, a Superintendent alas, and from what parts of the story I have learnt from my Mother and some of the Constables that knew him, he was very lucky not to have been fired.

The Superintendent had wrongly accused my Father of doing something or other, against his orders and, according to my Father it was all fabricated. My Father was the sort of copper to clip a youngster around the ears for minor offences, instead of booking them and this, unfortunately, was the sort of action this Chief was trying to stamp out, in order to give the police a new image.

My Mother said that my Father was summoned to appear at a hearing and was escorted by two Officers. While the Officers were waiting outside, the Superintendent concerned walked passed and my Father went to confront him about the ridiculous situation that had arisen. However, before he could set out of line the two Constables on escort restrained my Father, luckily. My Father would never have thought, let alone do anything detrimental to the Police Force or his own name, and he must have been incensed at the accusations to have acted in this way.

My Father's case was admonished and I suppose, in a way, he had the two Officers escorting him to thank, for restraining him in that moment of fury, whilst waiting for the case to be heard.

The following day my Mother took me to one side and said, "I don' think it will be long before we're on the move again, Son."

Obviously my Father had told her a lot more than she had told me, which was fair enough. What a shame though, as I had settled nicely into my school and even managed to get a girl-friend called Beryl, although we rarely saw one another. I can recall she had raven black hair and lived in Grappenhall, which was out of bounds to me, but I went to see her a few times - we were both 10 years old at this time. It was a case of "hello," throwing a few skimmers across the lake alongside her house and then off to the Delph with my friends from Appleton, who had acquired a box of matches and 5 Woodies. A cigarette was lit and passed around - some inhaled the smoke whilst others just drew and blew it out straight away - yours truly inhaled and couldn't stop coughing and spluttering for ages afterwards - no good for my asthma at all, I'm afraid.

Once we got bored with that, we set a bicycle tyre alight and dragged it around the dry bracken and in no time at all the area was ablaze. We disappeared behind the old barn on the tip as the fire engines arrived, sprayed the fire and saw us in the distance watching, and gave us a good soaking into the bargain.

This sort of behaviour was unforgivable really, but at 10 years old we were not aware of the dangers that we were creating for ourselves.

The following day my Mother shouted to me in the avenue, "Ivor - here for a minute!"

"Oh no," I thought, "She knows about the small fire at the Delph yesterday."

I walked over slowly to the front gate and was about to make an excuse when she said,

"Guess what? We're on the move again."

"Where to?" I asked.

"Hoole," she replied.

I thought to myself, "Great - that's France!"

"Where's that?" I asked.

"Near Chester," my Mother said proudly.

"That's only up the road from here isn't it?" I enquired again.

"Yes, Hoole is not far from here," she confirmed.

And she really emphasised the `H' in Hoole. So it was farewell to Appleton, Waverley Avenue and The Delph where I had enjoyed two years there. Although it was just after the War and everything was still rationed, as children we made the best of what little we had, or else!!

CHAPTER TWENTY

Asthma and The Apple

On arrival at Hoole, my Mother took me to my new school and to meet Mr Hewitt, the Headmaster. I can recall Mr Hewitt looking over the top of his horn-rimmed glasses as he talked to my Mother about the school, and enquiring about the education I had received up until then. I didn't utter a word. I must have passed the weighing up and down test, because Mr Hewitt accepted me into the school - Hoole and Newton Council School, Canadian Avenue.

Our new house was at 43 Sandileigh. It was quite a large semi-detached house and, according to my Mother, one of the nicest houses they had ever lived in until then. It was located about a mile from the centre of Chester and had a small garden at the front and a long garden at the rear.

After being in our new home for a few days, Jock went missing and didn't return for at least 2 days. We thought he had made his way back to Appleton, but he turned up looking a lot thinner and what I thought looked like a smile on his face. My Mother took him into the house and gave him a big bowl of scrap meat - it was no wonder he came home, and it's a wonder he hadn't bought his girlfriend as well.

By this time I was around 11 years old, and my Mother's top priority when we arrived anywhere new was to register with the new Doctor, as the National Health was going strong. Dr Martin was the Doctor we were advised to see - he was young and straight out of training with lots of new ideas and theories. My Mother gave him a rundown on my asthma and told him how much worse the attacks were becoming. He just listened and smiled. He then asked, "Do you have any pets in the house?"

"Yes," my Mother replied, with a tone in her voice as if to say, "what's that got to do with anything?"

Dr Martin immediately followed up with a very brief statement, "Get rid of them."

My Mother was lost for words. She looked at the Doctor and explained to him that they were part of the family and that she could not part with them just like that. It was now widely believed that certain types of asthma could be triggered off by the fur and the mites that lived on dogs - whether that was so in my case I do not know, but it did become obvious in later years as Jock stayed with us until I was 19 years old. Dr Martin gave my Mother the usual prescription for a box of tablets and another larger box of thermogene. This stuff kept my chest warm alright, and many a time nearly burnt a hole through, if on one of those rare occasions I actually sweated. The attacks didn't ease off. They were now definitely getting worse, but I tried to ignore them and went to school - walking the whole way because in-between attacks I was as fit as anyone, except, maybe, suffering from lack of wind on occasions.

I settled quickly into my new school, and although I was well behind the standard of some of the children, I strove to catch up. In the hall at Hoole and Newton there was a solid oak honours board beautifully carved around the outside with all the names of previous pupils who had passed for the Grammar Schools, all etched with the date of entry. I thought to myself, "If only my name would appear there one day."

After my first term, my Father must have realised that I was way behind and deemed it upon himself to give me extra work, especially in Mathematics which, until then, was my weak subject together with English of course. These lessons went on every night and I hated them, but they give my Father credit, because he brought my standard up to a compatibility with most of the other pupils in my class, and I was thankful to him for that.

However, unfortunately I failed my 11+ and I did denote a great disappointment in my Father's ways towards me following this, instead of saying, "Hard luck - maybe next time," but I suppose this was not in his character.

I did pass the second time at 12 years old but we had moved to new pastures by then and I never did find out if my name had been etched onto that honours board.

My daily route from Sandileigh took me along Kilmorey Park, Hamilton Street, Panton Road and, eventually Clare Avenue. At the rear of the big Victorian houses along Kilmorey Park there was an entry which I would go along, cutting about 5 minutes off the journey. As with all routes to school, it became a door and tree counting exercise, as I memorised the position of most things along the route.

During the seasons of the year, apple trees in the entry would hang over the high walls and on many a morning there would be windfalls to pick and take to school. I noted the many shades of green changing as the Spring and Summer seasons progressed until Autumn arrived. The trees, especially the limes, in Kilmorey would change to a brilliant gold and light brown, and then fall to give a carpet of dark brown leaves, to be blown away by the first gales of mid Autumn. After a week-end of storms I was going along the entry and drawing level with the apple tree, looking up, when I discovered all the leaves and apples had gone, except for one very red apple hanging just over the wall. That one apple stayed on the tree through the frost and gales, all through the Winter and early Spring. I got so obsessed with that darned apple - I would wake up in the morning and think, "I wonder if that apple is still hanging on the tree?" It continued to hang there, changing from bright red to brown and then a pickled brown until, one mid-February morning it had gone and left no trace on the entry floor. I was very sad and thought, "If only it could have hung on another few weeks, it would have been rejuvenated for another year." However, it was not to be. There has got to be a moral in this somewhere. I arrived at school to tell everyone that the apple had fallen. Again, I received some strange looks.

My form teacher, I recall, was a Mr Wainwright - a tall, bald headed man with a very cheerful face and he would often add his own little joke into the lesson, making history very interesting.

In my early days at school, in my enthusiasm to learn, I often made a fool of myself with some of my answers. I can remember one such incident in a history lesson when Mr Wainwright had stood back, proud of himself after spending the best part of an hour telling us all about the Vikings. He asked at the end, "Where did we originate from?" His eyes were flashing up and down the rows of seats, looking for a hand held aloft. My hand was high above my head waving to attract his attention, and he immediately must have thought, "The new boy is showing plenty of keenness."

"Yes Goolding," he said with a smile.

"From apes," I said positively.

This reply was followed by a deathly hush from the rest of the class and a look of anguish appeared on Mr Wainwright's face. His reply was very hurtful at the time, but understandable now.

"You might have been," he said, in a very angry tone, his eyes squinting, and immediately the whole class burst out laughing.

That was a time I really did feel embarrassed and I felt my face going red as I blushed in shame, and wished that the floor would open up and let me through.

After that eventful day I really did try to concentrate more, because I knew my mind did tend to wander a lot; come to think of it, it still does. Being able to concentrate at all times must be a marvellous gift. I kept my mouth firmly closed after that lesson, much to the relief of Mr Wainwright - especially as the school inspectors were due to make an appearance at the school and assess some of the pupils. Reading was always a weak part of my education because I had never read any books.

Mr Wainwright had a very good system going whereby everyone in the class would get a chance to read - much to my horror! I always managed to get out of reading a passage from the book out loud to other members of the class for I, literally, could not pronounce the words, let alone read them out. I would mutter for a couple of minutes and then Mr Wainwright would say, "Sit down for goodness sake." In theory it was a good idea for those who could read. After a period of time I did manage to stand up and read without embarrassment and sometimes volunteered. I had a short memory.

The first book we read and studied was Scrooge followed by A Tale of Two Cities. I found that Scrooge was more to my liking because with living so close to the Medieval and Victorian Buildings of Chester, I could relate to the period more easily, imagining that Chester was actually the place where the events took place - especially on a cold and foggy December night. This was the first book that I had read until now and I found it very interesting.

CHAPTER TWENTY ONE

Learning to Swim and
"The Long Plunge"

Cheshire Education Department had also given schools permission to take classes to the baths for swimming instruction - something else that I didn't take too readily to. We would walk from Hoole to Newton to the Roman Baths in Grosvenor Street - a sort of loosening up period before we got to the baths. I was absolutely petrified of water and had no intention of ever learning to swim, because my Mother had a theory that water was no good at all for my asthma, and went as far as to say that it brought attacks on. If my Father had been aware of some of the things that my Mother used to say to us, he would have gone mad or should I say, "madder." She meant well in everything she said - bless her.

As our little procession got closer to the baths, my chest gradually got tighter and tighter and I more or less induced an asthma attack through anxiety. The instructor had his own ideas on getting youngsters to go into the water. He would line the whole class up kneeling along the edge of the baths with our hands raised above our heads and then leaning forward into the water. I could not do this for the life of me, so to speak, because I would not even put my head under the water in our bath at home.

After many weeks I did, eventually, drop into the water with a little nudge from the instructor, and when I did eventually surface, gasping for breath, I noticed a look of relief on his face, because I had obviously been both a challenge and a nuisance to the progress of the class.

Once you've tried the water, like everything else, you begin to enjoy a whole new world of exercise and fun.

My fear of water had now ended, and I often wondered why parents did not make more of an effort to teach their offspring to swim, instead of warning them to keep away from the water; especially since my own Mother was a very good swimmer and proud to be a member of the New Ferry Swimming Club on the Wirral. Of course, my Father was an advanced swimmer, as this was taught in the police, and they were able to win all sorts of medals for lifesaving etc.

After a few more lessons I had plucked up enough courage to dive off the side. After swimming a width and being given a certificate by Mr Wainwright, I proudly took it home. My Father must have thought I was ready to swim the English Channel because he entered me for the Police Swimming Gala, which, luckily, was to be held in Chester Baths that year - 1949.

My Father usually entered for the long plunge, him not being a sprinter in the water. My Mother would always enjoy watching the events, especially as both myself and my Father were in the events on this particular occasion. She was also able to meet old friends; mainly the wives of policemen she had known through moving around the County. By normal events, my Mother never went anywhere.

The long plunge was an event for men with big lungs. Each contestant would take a deep breath - some would almost drag all the air in from inside the baths. They then had to dive into the pool and go as far as possible, without moving a muscle or without taking another breath. My Father's turn came and he took a deep dive in, which seemed like hours, before he finally surfaced. Some would almost float a full length. My Father's theory was that diving deep gave him more propulsion as he came to the surface and therefore he would go further. This was not my view, I'm afraid, because as he broke water (so to speak) he seemed to stop dead, except for a slight roll from side to side which tended to move him more to the side of the baths, unknown to him. He lay there like a basking whale motionless, for what seemed like hours (I thought I saw a slight wiggle of his toes, but luckily the judges did not notice or he would have been disqualified). A worried look came across my Mother's face and she moved as if she was going to dive in and drag him out. At last her face changed to one of relief as my Father was forced to turn over and in so doing took in great gulps of water and air, and the noise was quite deafening and, no doubt, frightening for some - namely my Mother. The whole of his bald head was bright red and his eyes were nearly popping out as he swam the few strokes to the side. He made two or three attempts to get one leg onto the side and then, pulling his whole body onto the side, lying there for a couple of seconds in complete exhaustion, at last tottering to his feet, he walked passed the judges and gave them a wry smile. As he walked along the side of the pool, he was swaying from side to side as if under the influence of alcohol, rolling his head from side to side, as if trying to bring some feeling back into his brain. "Luckily he didn't pass out altogether - holding his breath that long….the silly old fool!" my Mother said in disgust. I can't recollect him ever entering for the long plunge again.

It was now the turn of the police children. My event was the one length - any stroke. Bang went the starters gun! I took a deep breath and dived, very deep, and when I finally broke water, there, about to touch the other end was a streamlined shape - legs and arms being propelled in prefect unison and water being thrashed to give maximum speed. This blurr was only to be a friend of mine later in life - a true character. Why he didn't keep swimming up, I will never understand. His name was Tony Blackwell and he said that he was a bit younger than me and got a couple of yards start. It would have made no difference if I had had twenty yards start on him! I came third out of four and proudly showed Mr Wainwright my certificate. I did see a hint of a smile on his face as if to say, "There can be some results in teaching, even from the most difficult cases."

CHAPTER TWENTY TWO

Football, Cricket and Tug-o-War

The football season had once again come around, and I found myself on the right wing of the school junior team wearing a dark brown jersey with a bright yellow "V" at the front - maybe it was to intimidate the opposition, but if it was, it never worked! We all followed the ball wherever it might go, both teams ending up surrounding the ball and kicking and elbowing for all we were worth. The game, if played away, was always on a pitch in the middle of Chester racecourse, absolutely freezing cold and blowing a gale across the Welsh Hills. It would take a week for us to thaw out ready for the next game.

Many a Saturday I would walk to Sealand Road to watch Chester City - sometimes with my Father and on odd occasions on my own. We would usually stand behind the goal at the Sealand Road end and I would lean on the barrier, just being able to see over, almost at pitch level and I could see all the playing area.

In those days, Chester had some good players, namely - Billy Foulkes, who went to Newcastle and played for Wales. Threadgold who went to Sunderland and who was a very good goalkeeper and, of course, there was Tommy Astbury, who was Captain and a very versatile player who kept on running forever - for five pound a week. Most players were on a maximum wage of ten pound in the First Division. All the team gave value for money paid at the turnstile.

The ball was all leather and on wet days would become very heavy as the water soaked through. How they managed to kick that ball I will never know, because it must have weighed at least ten pound by the end of the game. I attempted to kick one of the match balls when it flew into the crowd - I only managed to move it two feet and nearly broke my foot in the process.

Our centre forward, on one of his rare occasions, managed to hit one first time but, as usual, it sailed into the crowd and unfortunately hit a spectator, who had not been concentrating on the game, smack on the side of the head. He was knocked out, instantly lifting him off his feet and knocking him onto his back, and there he lay - mouth opening and shutting like a fish out of water, until the good old St John's Ambulance Brigade arrived shouting, "Make Way Please!," with the stretcher at the ready. They did such a proficient job, especially when they put a little bottle under the patient's noise and as he came round he said, "What's the score?" Now that's dedication for you.

My Father was a good player in his younger days and if on holiday I would often be taken on the team coach to watch them when they played against other divisions. After playing at centre forward for most of his career, he had now reverted to stopper centre half, and when I say `stopper', I mean just that! Nothing got passed my Father in one piece. His bald head would be like a magnet to the ball. Every ball that came into the penalty area he managed to get his head on it, whether it was head height, knee height or even ground level, his head would be amongst the flying boots. He head acted as a battering ram and had no doubt been used on many occasions in the course of duty, whilst plodding the beats of Cheshire. Policemen had to be over 6 feet tall in those days to join the force, and when there were 20 coppers of that size running around a field; it was like watching a herd of migrating buffalo stampeding across the prairie, having scented a watering hole. Come to think of it, they made the same sounds as well!

In most of the divisions that my Father was transferred to, he seemed to end up with the same coppers - mainly footballers, cricketers and drinkers. Names which I can recall were Harry Fitton, Jack Gallagher, Len Cooper and Bob Bullock - a mere youngster then. If they were not playing the regular games, then they would be out practising Tug-o-War ready for the police sports next to some pub in the middle of Cheshire somewhere. My Father must have had dozens of pewter mugs won for various competitions - he was forever coming home with one; I think the other policeman would give him theirs to look after and then forget all about them.

Inspector Harry Fitton had been a lifelong friend of my Father's more or less since they had joined up in 1934. Harry was the tallest man on the force standing at 6 feet 6 inches and was just as broad. He and my Father would have many celebrations, as they appropriately called them, after victory in some game or other - my Mother called them 'Booze-Ups'. They always seemed to end up at our house with my Mother making sandwiches and a big bowl of onions in vinegar which would go in no time at all - according to my Mother. She said that my Father would complain of indigestion for days afterwards. I'm not surprised with all that raw vinegar!

The day of the Police Sports at The Oval in Port Sunlight was one of their highlights in the police calendar. I will never forget my Father's Tug-o-War team marching out carrying rope under their left arms. I think my Father was the shortest at 6 foot 1 inch and weighing in at 16 stone. Harry Jacobs was the anchorman and he must have been around 20 stone, and I thought to myself, "They can't possibly be beaten!" They won on this occasion but there were times when they were beaten and by a much lighter side. So really, weight does not always apply in this game and it is often a matter of timing and the pull on the rope to catch the opposition off guard. Therefore, on this occasion, all the practice and building up of weight over the previous months had paid off.

They would usually practice next to a pub with the rope draped over the branch of an old oak tree, pulling the shell of an old car laden with weights up and down for hours. The sturdy Cheshire oak would sometimes bend with all the men on the rope. I would not have been surprised if the branch had snapped and collapsed on top of them, but there again, the Cheshire Oaks are the strongest in the world. When they all descended into the local pub afterwards, there would be hardly any room to manoeuvre at all, as they downed gallons of the Landlord's best bitter and on many a night drink the bar dry. My Mother often said, "I bet that Landlord was glad when the Tug-o-War season was over." But I had my doubts about that.

CHAPTER TWENTY THREE

Father's Weak Heart!

My Father always insisted that I attend Sunday School wherever we were stationed. At Hoole I attended All Saints and most of my Sundays would be spent there singing in the choir until there was a slight quiver in my voice, and then I was given the job of Acolyte. This involved carrying an extremely heavy cross whilst leading the choir up to the front of the church. I was always relieved when we arrived at the altar, because the cross would have to be placed into a holder until the end of the service. The Vicar had informed me that the cross was very valuable and should be handled with care.

The Vicar had started the evening prayers and in doing so would glance over in my direction as I nervously strove to lift the cross into its holder. I would glance up at him angelically and give him a wry smile, but I don't think that reassured him at all. I did wonder afterwards as to the reason I was given the job of Acolyte; maybe it was because my voice was breaking or it could have been due to my stocky build and therefore I was an ideal candidate for carrying crosses - either way, I didn't mind.

I did enjoy attending church because as far as I was concerned, it was an excuse to get out of the house for a few hours and it also gave me a sense of belonging. The church would be packed every Sunday and the congregation would sing their hearts out and on many occasions my parents and Sister would attend.

Not only would I be at the church on Sunday mornings and evenings, but I would also attend in the afternoons as well, attending Sunday School for two hours. We would have our little stamp put into our book, and at the end of the Whit the number of stamps would be counted and if there was enough, then we would be allowed on the Sunday School trip - either to Rhyl or New Brighton.

Television was now operational in the North West and the congregation started to dwindle and people, in the Winter, were very reluctant to leave the warmth of a cosy fire and trudge 2 or 3 miles through 6 inches of snow to the nearest church, when they could join in with a service on the television.

After settling in at 43 Sandileigh and meeting new friends, I started to venture around the countryside with them. I didn't seem to take to the countryside quite as well here as it took quite a while to get out of the suburban district. I had no doubt I had been spoilt having spent my younger years in Little Budworth. It was now 1949 and, unbeknownst to me, a tune called `Teddy Bears Picnic' was the number hit in the first pop charts.

One day George and Jim Lacey, also coppers Sons, and I were winding our way around the lanes of Upton and as we arrived close to a copse in the middle of a field, George started to sing, "If you go down to the woods today you're sure of a big surprise." I just could not believe that tune was the number one song of the day, although there would be plenty more just as bad! Needless to say, I did keep away from that wooded copse for a few weeks.

My Mother had managed to keep off the cigarettes even through the very stressful years of the second World War, but I'm afraid that whilst we were at Hoole, she succumbed to the dreaded weed once more - through boredom and the monotonous routine of housework. She was rarely leaving the house, except, maybe, to the shops once a week. My Mother would love to have gone out to work just to bring in a bit of much needed extra money, but my Father had his own principals and, whether they were right or wrong, they were obeyed. He would say, "My wage is enough to keep my family." It did just about that - but we all longed to be able to afford a few of the luxuries in life - having a perm was about the only exciting part of my Mother's year. She would have this done once a year and then, on arrival home, she would moan she had a headache due to being under the dryer for so long. It was as if she felt guilty about spending money on herself. I must admit, she did look very nice after the perm.

My Father did relent at Christmas and would allow my Mother to work at the Post Office sorting letters. She really enjoyed that job and would talk about it for weeks after she had finished there. She would talk about the people she had met and the laughs they had - mind you, this was only for my own and my Sister's ears! If Father had known she was enjoying it, he would probably have stopped her going.

Every place we were transferred to, my Mother would volunteer to help with the mail sorting at Christmas. The extra money would be an added bonus and we usually had a good Christmas.

Not long after we had arrived in Hoole, my Father had gone to see the Doctor for some medicine for his indigestion, but while he was there the Doctor gave him a thorough examination and told him he had a weak heart. Well, his whole world collapsed and it was absolute hell in our house because he was advised to stop smoking - which was not a bad thing really, although it was unknown to people then that smoking kills. My Mother tried to console him but with little effect. "It's not your heart, is it?" he would say. He did plod on at his job not mentioning it to anyone and physically he did not feel weak. Incidentally, when we eventually moved from Hoole to Crewe the Doctor there told him that there was absolutely nothing wrong with my Father's heart.

During this period of my Father's `Weak Heart' many a day I would turn the corner at the top of Sandileigh only to see all the windows open upstairs. It was a freezing January afternoon and on arrival outside the house, there would be my Mother wafting a paper through the window - I was mystified. Running into the house, thinking that it was on fire, I dashed up to the bedroom and my Mother said, "Get a paper quick - your Dad will be home soon!." I nipped downstairs and when I arrived back Mother said, "Waft some of this cigarette smoke out of the windows will you please?" I realised that she had been smoking as she cleaned the bedrooms. I had smelt the smoke even downstairs as I entered the house so we had a lot of wafting to do. It was quite comical really, that she should be so frightened of my Father in this way, because she hadn't started smoking heavy until my Father had been advised to stop, and then it would be because she was under so much stress trying to cope with his many moods.

"Can you smell anything?" she would ask after about 10 minutes of wafting. I would sniff for a couple of minutes, my

Mother waiting anxiously for an answer, and I would jokingly say, "Yes." She would look at me horrified and I would quickly say, "No...I'm only joking."

My Father would be due home anytime now and no doubt wouldn't be in the best of moods. Once in the house he would glance at us, say nothing and then sit at the dinner table. He would then start sniffing the air and say, "Can I smell cigarette smoke?" My Mother, Sister and I would all join in the sniffing ritual and would all say, together, "I can't." As all ex-smokers know, cigarette smoke can be detected 10 miles away by an enforced non-smoker. It was like a pantomime - Jack and the Beanstalk Springs to mind where the Giant says, "Fee, Fi, Fo, Fum, I smell the smoke of an Englishwoman!" My Mother quickly followed her last remark with, "It must have been the insurance man." Even I knew that the insurance man came on a Thursday and today was Monday. I edged towards the door; fortunately it didn't register with my Father, or did it? I will never know because his expressions never changed.

I could never bring myself to ask him about all the incidences and the misery he brought upon the household, even after I had left home years later. I just don't think he could have possibly realised what anxiety he brought on my Sister and I over the years of our childhood. Maybe he knew more than he let on, but as far as I was concerned, he was always the strict disciplinarian and I never ever understood him.

CHAPTER TWENTY FOUR

Mother's Dreams

My Mother would always be pottering around the house - dusting, washing, brushing (there were no vacuum cleaners in those days). The house was spotless. The washday ritual was a sight to behold. My Mother would drag an old dolly tub out every Monday along with the wooden dolly with the three pronged legs, and she would attack the washing with it. It would take about an hour to fill it with boiling water which she got from the gas stove - this was a very dangerous practice in itself and she would often get burns on her arms as she emptied the scalding hot water into the dolly tub. After dunking each individual item of clothing she would lift them onto the draining board ready for the mangle, at which time either myself or my Sister would turn the mangle as she passed each piece of clothing through the rollers. On most Mondays she would have to do this task on her own - we could only help when we were on school holidays.

My Sister loved to help my Mother cleaning around the house - whether it needed it or not! However, my Father, on the other hand, did not lift a finger around the house - even to wash a dish. Apparently, his excuse stemmed back a few years when he used to do the dishes and he cut his thumb on a glass, at which time he said, "Never again." He had some strange priorities. However, my Mother didn't mind, as she said she could do them quicker on her own.

The mangle and the dolly tub remained with us for many years after. A sort of monument to the chores of the past.

At the end of a washday my Mother would collapse into the armchair, light a fag and stare through the window at the clothes-line laden with washing - the weight of it brought the line down and the clothes nearly touched the floor! As she dragged on her cigarettes a smile would appear on her face as she dreamt of times gone by. She would then talk about the happy times she had when employed at Levers in Port Sunlight and how proud she was to have been part of that Company, who always treated their employees so well. She would also recall how a relative from the Belgium plant would stand and talk to her at her workplace when he visited the site, asking how her Mother and Father were keeping. He was a Manager over there but, alas, I never found out his name.

My Mother's main claim to fame was that she was related to the legendary `Dixie Dean'.  My Gran always insisted on calling him `William Ralph'. His Mother and my Gran were Sisters and their maiden names were Brett. My Mother would also talk about Aunt Annie with the one eye; she must have been another Sister of my Gran's - another Brett no doubt.

At this time my Mother said she was courting a man named Tommy Griffiths who had had a few games for Everton and was a friend of Dixie's, so this was probably how she met him. She was going to get engaged to him, but along came my Father and, as they say, the rest is history.

"Ah well," she would say, as she came out of her dreams and tugged a last drag out of a very soggy cigarette, "I'll have to get your Dad's tea ready now."

Why she had to marry a policeman and live a life of misery and hardship, when she could have had a much better life, I could never understand. She stood up and walked into the kitchen brushing a tear from her eye with her hanky. My Mother was very prone to bursting out crying for no reason at all, and when asked why, she would reply, "Oh, it's nothing." It was still an out and out man's world.

My Father was not a very understanding person - maybe that is hereditary as well. Often, the washing she had hung on the line would fall onto the garden and had to be washed again. She would dash out to remove the washing that was dragging on the ground, stuff the pegs into her mouth and run into the house again before the rain soaked her. My Father's police shirts were top priority and if one of them fell into the mud, that would be the end of the world for her, because those shirts had to be gleaming white. These shirts had detachable collars held in position by small brass studs - this was to make the shirts last longer. Putting the studs into the collar and shirt was a work of art. My Father's fingers were too thick to hold the studs and push them through the collar, so my Mother had to stand on a chair and fit them in - what a performance - every time he went on duty!   Jock was frightened to look because he knew if things didn't go right, he would be the first to get shouted at. Lassie would be playing with my Father's highly polished size tens, tossing them in the air and scratching them until my Father shouted at her. She would bare her teeth at him, but my Father just smiled. My Father was still trying to train Lassie to do as she was told, but I'm afraid he was wasting his time because she wasn't really frightened of him like Jock was, so I think in the end my Father would crack up.

It would take my Father a good hour to get ready for duty and when he went out of the door he was immaculate - boots gleaming, peak of his cap shining in the light. Looking back, being clean and tidy was one of his outstanding priorities. My Mother would brush him down with the clothes brush before he left the house and often stand looking at him as he went through the door, thinking how nice the shirt looked. Susan Hopwood, born at Woodhead Street, New Ferry on the Wirral - a very beautiful woman in her younger days.

CHAPTER TWENTY FIVE

The Thunder Storm

My Mother, in her innocence (although that was sometimes debatable!), would throw her advice around as a thunderstorm approached, not realising that she was putting the fear of God into me. This advice had no doubt been passed down by her parents and so on.

"Don't stand under trees in a thunderstorm."

"I think it's going to thunder - I've got a pounding headache."

"Never walk through an open field."

"Hide anything shiny." I would be alright there because it was very rare that I saw anything shiny.

"When near a tree and the lightening hits it. you will be struck deaf and dumb for life."

There was nowhere for me to go - I might just as well lie down and wait; it was like waiting for the hangman to pull the lever. With all the things I had to remember, it was no wonder I was petrified of a thunderstorm, and at the first rumble, which was probably about 50 miles away, my little heart would start racing.

In the late 40s in Hoole, the thunderstorms were very long and extremely violent. It would be about 4 o'clock in the afternoon and it was already pitch black on this mid-August afternoon, and the house was beginning to shake as the thunder rolled in the distance. "Where can I hide," I thought. I was 10 years old.

My Mother's first move was to open windows upstairs and downstairs - her theory being that if the lightening headed our way, it would pass straight through the windows and out again. I wanted to believe her. "Anyway, the chances of being hit by lightening are 10,000 to 1," she said, quite adamantly.

157

Now having been at my new school (Hoole and Newton in Canadian Avenue), for 12 months, I had now become very good at mental arithmetic - something the school held in high esteem. On quick calculation I reckoned that there were about 50,000 people in and around the Chester area. That meant that 5 people were going to die during the course of this storm, and I could be one of them! My Sister, Susan, like my Mother, held no fear whatsoever. My Mother then came out with another gem, "I hope it starts to rain soon, because dry storms cause the most damage."

As the storm grew closer and closer, the bangs became louder and louder, and I had not heard bangs like it since the War, when I stayed at my Gran's in Parkside Road. "Please God, make it rain," was my plea. That prayer was soon to be answered, because it came down like a monsoon and very soon Sandileigh was like a river. Jock had already made his own arrangements and dived under the stairs. Lassie had no fear either - it would appear that the female species had no fear of natural catastrophes. Jock must have picked a few hints up off my Mother whenever she talked about the War. She would say that the safest place was under the stairs. She would no doubt be reminiscing about going over to Liverpool the day after an air raid and noting that the staircases were still standing.

By this time it was very dark indeed and to me it seemed like the end of the world. My Mother was still trying to keep the morale high, (Did I note a hint of a smile on my Sister's face? Yes - they were enjoying this!) by saying, "Of course, fork lightening is the worst, because anyone struck by that and there would be no trace of them afterwards."

"I'm never going to reach 11," I thought to myself.

By this time I had had enough of my Mother's morale boosting remarks and had squeezed in with Jock under the staircase - much to his annoyance. He Growled and bared his teeth, and then squealed as I accidentally kicked him in the ribs. He was shaking and whimpering and all that I could see in the confined space were two eyes staring at me like a werewolf; it was quite frightening and the smell was unbearable!

Even under the stairs with my eyes closed tight I could still detect the lightening and hear the inevitable clap of thunder. Fear had now instilled fear under the stairs and we had both decided to get out as quickly as we could and, in the melee, Jock scratched my face and drew blood. Outside again, Jock was still wandering around the house howling and whimpering for all he was worth.

My Father had now arrived home after plodding around Chester for 8 hours, so I did feel a little safer - although I did detect that he was a bit on edge. He was moaning about the pedal on his bike slipping as he strove to get home without getting wet. My Mother, in the meantime, had said that there was about one second for every mile distance from the lightening flash and the thunderstorm clap. After the last flash I calculated that the storm was about 2 miles off and closing. The storm cheated, according to my Mother's calculations, because the next bang and flash was directly overhead. My Father jumped clean out of his armchair and shouted, "That was close," or something like that.

"Oh no, he's frightened too!" I thought, and he was my only hope for moral support. I could not believe that a big strapping copper like him who held no fear of any man could be scared of thunder. It must be hereditary, I thought.

My Mother was still messing - turning mirrors around to face the wall. This was to stop the lightening rebounding and hitting someone. She would also put all the shiny cutlery away, and thus make sure that the lightening did not have anything to attract it. She would then announce, "No lightening will hit our house." God, I so wanted to believe her. I think my Father did as well.

I was now under the table again remembering the War when we used to get under the table for protection from the `Gerry Bombers'.

The next thunder clap was the loudest yet and the whole house was shaking. My Father, although his reactions were a bit slow, nearly hit the ceiling as he jumped out of the seat again and shouted, "Eh Bah Gum," - a saying only reserved for when he was very frightened.

A nearby tree had been split in half by the lightening and the resulting fall of the trunk and the clap of thunder that followed was deafening. Jock was still howling and had now reached `Top C', and the house shook, registering 8 on the Richter Scale. My Mother suggested opening the front and back doors and stared straight at my Father for approval, but at that particular moment my Father was, shall we say, under the weather and trying to recover from the last crack of thunder, and was now accepting any suggestions my Mother made. She was now enjoying this because she realised it was her one and only chance for power and she started to throw her own little mannerisms into the fray. For instance, she would drop things, mainly pans, onto the kitchen floor. Why wasn't she frightened?

My Sister was now trying to console Jock, who was shivering like a jelly and whose ears went up and down in time with the thunder claps. My Father was right out of suggestions as he stared straight through the window at the mature Beech Trees at the bottom of the garden. My Mother then said, "If you actually saw the lightening hit the tree, then your face would stay in the same fixed position forever." My Father's eyes widened as his head turned slowly and his face contorted as his eyes settled on the back of my Mothers head as she disappeared into the hall, realising that she had taken it a bit too far and that the thunderstorm would eventually go away.

The storm seemed to go on forever - lightening flashing around the whole district, and there were pieces of tiles falling off the roof onto the concrete path which added more noise to the event. My Mother, who was now wandering around upstairs, suddenly shouted, "The chimney has been hit!" I made a move for under the stairs again. My Father was now in an apathetic mood and couldn't have cared if the whole house collapsed - he'd had enough.

The storm gradually moved away. "I hope it doesn't come back," my Mother said.

"So do I," I prayed, and luckily it didn't.

Jock was still very edgy, slinking behind chairs and hiding under the sideboard as the distant rolls of thunder seemed to last forever. My Father now showed a bit of bravery after the event by venturing outside to assess the damage. My Mother was in the kitchen preparing tea as if the storm had never occurred - that day in August 1949.

CHAPTER TWENTY SIX

A Night Out at the Cinema

The City of Chester was right on our doorstep. It was steeped in history, and I would spend many a night walking around the walls in the Summer. The walls are about 3 miles and it would take 2 hours - stopping here and there - to look at the many sites along the route. The Clock Tower, the Race Course, the Grosvenor Bridge and the Roman Amphitheatre, finally ending at the Northgate.

My Mother told us all about an Uncle Frank Wright before we arrived at Hoole. He was a Labour Councillor for Chester and had been for many years. He was a very distant relative whom we would call `Uncle' and he would keep us entertained for hours with his impersonations of a drunken man, although sometimes I thought he wasn't actually impersonating, as it seemed too realistic! He even made my Father laugh - so that was good. He did eventually become Mayor of Chester and that was an honour in itself. My Mother was over the moon.

Once a fortnight on a Thursday, if my Father was not on duty, we would all go to the local picture house, The Majestic. It was also the only time my Mother went out. My shoes would be highly polished by my Mother - my best tie and that horrible cap! My Father would give me a final inspection and off we would go - anyone would think we were going to a Royal Premiere. All the way to the cinema my Father would say, "Put that cap straight, or "Pull your socks up." He knew no better I suppose - appearance was his top priority and would be for his entire life. It was his way of teaching discipline, although it was a little harsh at times. Why he didn't show any affection for me and my Sister, I will never know.

After the film was over my Mother, Sister and I would make our way home and Father would head for the Liberal Club - the nearest watering hole to our house.

It was now Spring of 1950 and a lot of things were still on ration. The Government had made several attempts to end sweet rationing, but each time they did, people would queue and buy more than they needed and, consequently, the shops would run out very quickly, thus forcing the Government to bring back rationing once more.

CHAPTER TWENTY SEVEN

Crewe - A Grammar School Boy?

My Father's next tour of duty was at Crewe, and we arrived at our new house in Stamford Avenue on a hot July afternoon in 1950. I was not at all impressed with the rows and rows of terraced houses, because I had been used to open spaces all my life so far, and I knew my Mother did not like it either as the furniture van pulled up outside No. 11. "Your Father said that I would like it here," she said. "But I'm afraid he's wrong."

In my opinion, I thought it was a claustrophobic concrete jungle, but no doubt I would adjust - it was just a case of having to!

Crewe was the railway capital of England, where all the main lines converged from all over the Country. Most of the people living in Crewe were employed in the engine sheds - either making parts or repairing the rolling stock.

My Sister and I went along to visit our new Headmaster at Bedford Street School - a secondary modern and reputedly a very good school. I was only at the school for about three months because, unbeknown to me, I had passed for the Grammar School, but the letter informing me of such had lain in the hall of the empty house at Sandileigh in Hoole until the new policeman had moved in.

I had settled in well at Bedford Street because the school was very keen on sports and I had managed to get into the school football team, together with lads such as Johnny Morris and Richie Hancock who were destined to play for the Crewe schoolboys team - both very good players at that age.

In my first test, just before Christmas, I came 6th in the class. Obviously that meant there were 5 pupils in that class who should have been going to the Grammar School as well, but I suppose it is like everything else in the system - if you are not at your best on the day of the 11+ exam, then you fail. So in a way, we could say that Crewe Grammar was lucky to get me!

So, it was off to Crewe Grammar to meet yet another Headmaster. My Mother always accompanied me on these occasions; as my Father shunned meeting people and would usually only mix with his police colleagues.

Crewe Grammar in Ruskin Road was built in 1909 and from the outside it looked very impressive, with its neat brickwork and buttresses protruding out at regular intervals around its bulk. The main entrance was in the centre of the building and the path up to the main door was lined on either side by variegated shrubs. As we walked up to the door, I wondered who was the more nervous - my Mother or me! We pushed the large oaken doors open and were met by the school secretary who gestured for us to sit down on the chairs outside the Headmaster's study.

After what seemed an awful long time, the secretary then reappeared and said, "The Headmaster will see you now, Mrs Goolding." I looked at my Mother and her back at me, very nervously. Anyone would have thought she was starting school instead of me.

The study was of the traditional style with a large table with books spread around ready for marking and the inkwell with an old quill pen stuck in it - I don't suppose it had been used for many years. There were shelves all around the walls which were cluttered with books stacked at varying angles; the room generally resembled a library. Mr Dowling looked at me. I was short and stocky with a fat face and hair plastered down with water, neatly parted to on the left hand side. I didn't really look the part of a Grammar School boy at all, but my Mother was proud of me and I think my Father was too, but he didn't show it.

Eventually the Headmaster spoke. "How are you Ivor? Are you looking forward to joining us at Crewe Grammar?" My Mother started to answer for me but Mr Dowling raised his hand in gesture as if to say, "Let him answer for himself." He looked at me in anticipation but all I could utter was a feeble, "Yes." In my short life I had not had any opportunity to say much at home; conversation with my Father at home was virtually non-existent and he usually only spoke to me to tell me off

164

for some minor misdemeanour. Consequently I receded into a shell and very rarely came out to talk to anyone, because I didn't know how to converse. I could never pluck up enough courage to argue with my Father - even if I was in the right, because there would be a quick clip around the ear if I ever attempted to speak my mind.

Mr Dowling went on to say what a good reputation the school had and described its strict code of discipline, (I thought to myself, "That won't worry me.") He then quoted the school motto : "Mod-Mid-Are." My Mother gave one of her smiles as if she understood Latin fluently - a smile reserved only for the occasion when she didn't understand at all! We were both in the same boat.

Mr Dowling had a few pieces of paper in front of him. He picked them up, shuffled them, tapped them on the table and said, "I'm going to put you in 2c to start with, Ivor." Having passed the 11+ at the second attempt, I had missed the first year of Grammar School and it was envisaged by Mr Dowling that I would have to put a lot of hard work in to catch up.

I took my place in 2c and met all my new classmates the very next day. It would be an understatement to say that I was lost - I was absolutely dumbfounded by the new methods I had to learn and it took me a few months to get into my stride, and a lot of patience was needed by most of the teachers. I had to stay behind for extra French and Maths lessons together with another lad named Peter Bailey, but it was all to no avail for me, because I could not take in French - and as for Algebra, that might as well have been another foreign language for what it meant to me! I never did understand it until later in life and then it was very limited. "Algebra - who invented it?" I had left Little Budworth just over three years earlier and in those three years I had come along way - both in distance and in my education, and I was still very bemused by it all.

Our house in Stamford Avenue had been built in the last century. The houses had been purpose-built for the many thousands of people who had come to the area to work in the new railway industry. It had coal fires downstairs and in the bedrooms - although the latter were very rarely lit unless a member of the family was stricken down with flu and had to stay in bed for a few weeks.

Another luxury was an upstairs bath - but no toilet. Again, the toilet was outside - something which must have been insisted upon in the last century. My Mother was unhappy with the 8 foot wall that divided the two houses. Although this provided privacy, it made the living room very dark, even on the sunniest of days.

Our next door neighbours were Mr and Mrs Nicholson. Mr Nicholson worked in the Crewe Works all his life and was due for retirement, and Mrs Nicholson became a very good friend of my Mother's, because she, like my Mother, was locked into the drudgery of housework and preparing meals for their Husband's - remember, in those days there would be three large meals a day for a working man, and it was mostly manual labour so the men would burn up all the calories which they consumed - either sweating or using physical energy in the blacksmiths or the forging shops of Crewe Works. It was also very understandable that many of the men also consumed large amounts of beer. My Mother was amused by Mrs Nicholson's dialect - a distinct Crewe one where she would say, "Our Dad" or "Our Reg." Everyone in Crewe was known as "Our Dad" or "Our Mam." "I will have to ask Our Dad," Mrs Nicholson would say in conversation.

CHAPTER TWENTY EIGHT

Cockroaches and
My Father's New Local

My first Winter at Stamford Avenue was literally an eye opener on a cold and snowy morning. As I walked into the living room to eat my breakfast before starting my paper round, I would switch the light on and there, on the hearth and on the lino, was a black mass of cockroaches milling around, eating anything they could get their crab-like jaws into. As the light hit them, they would scurry back to the fireplace through cracks in the cement, into holes in the plaster that had been eaten away the previous night, and down holes in the floorboards to settle there until the following night. They would then reappear to eat any crumbs that had been left around during the course of the day. What a horrible sight first thing in the morning!

Crewe Tip was often blamed for the plague of cockroaches that descended on most households during the Winter, but many knew it was the warmth of the fireplaces that attracted them. They would just move from house to house and back again, before eventually becoming immune to the poison that the Council had put down, and in the end they actually loved it and thrived on it. They could breed and produce offspring tenfold in a couple of days, so it was a hopeless task really.

Jock became an expert at catching the cockroaches, although he could never bring himself to kill one. He would pick them up in his mouth and toss them in the air, and trap them under his paw, but very rarely squashed them.

My Father had other ideas. He would come along and put his size tens on them, squash about 50 of them, and scoop them up and lob them up the garden. He would return shaking his head as if he had a bitter taste in his mouth.

My Mother could not stand them either and had tried all sorts to get rid of them, but they seemed to thrive on whatever she put down, so she eventually gave up and resorted to using the back of the shovel. As soon as Winter was over, they seemed to disappear altogether - much to my relief. I will never forget that awful sight first thing in the morning as I entered the living room - it was like a moving black carpet. Yuck!

At more or less the same time that I started my new school, my Father found himself a new local, 'The Hop Pole.' This was no doubt recommended to him by his police friends because they were already regulars there anyway. The pub was in walking distance of our house - just up past the baths on the way into Crewe centre. On his days off, if he was not playing one of his seasonal sports, he would invariably visit this watering hole in the evening. I suppose it was an outlet from the daily stresses of either telling people off for minor things, or dealing with the local villains.

On these nights my Father would get absolutely rotten drunk, together with the other giants, and they always seemed to end up back at our house. My Mother would make sandwiches - although very reluctantly, as she was usually on her way to bed when they rolled in. I could hear them talking and laughing for hours on end, until my Mother would stretch herself to her full height of 5ft 5inches and tell them all to go home - much to my Father's amazement! Attack was the best means of defence for my Father and fortunately it always worked when my Mother got annoyed, which usually was very rare.

The front door would slam shut and the coppers would disappear into the swirling fog singing and laughing - no doubt at the sight of my Mother telling my Father off! Some nights he would manage to get home on his own - how though, I will never know. My Mother would have to try and help him upstairs, and sometimes she would wake me up and I would try to assist her. My Father would be singing and laughing and his legs were like jelly, and his arms would be slung around my Mother's shoulders. The weight of his 17 stone would gradually bring my Mother to her knees - which would not help one little bit in our collective effort to get him into bed. Once on the bed he would be left, still fully clothed, until the next day when everyone would keep out of his way. The two dogs would be missing all day. I would be in from school and, as quickly as I could make a jam butty, I would be out again - just in case I happened to catch his glance. I did try smiling in his direction once after of his binges - but this had no effect whatsoever!

On one particular occasion the day after one of my Father's `Booze-Ups', he said, "Nip down the Hop Pole there's a good lad, and see if they've got my teeth." I went very reluctantly taking Jock with me for a walk. Arriving at the Hop Pole I knocked on the front door of the closed pub (it was 9am), and my timid knock was answered by what I presumed was the Landlord's Wife, who looked as if she had been joining in the merriment of the previous night. She stood there with half a smoked woody dangling from her lips, her eyes watering with the smoke constantly spiralling up her nostrils, and into her eyes. "What do you want?" she screeched.

"I've come for my Dad's teeth," I muttered, shame faced.

"Are you P C Goolding's Son?" she asked, with a wry smile on her face, as she pulled the butt end of the cigarette out of her mouth as it burnt her lip and invited me in. I hated the idea of going into pubs then, because the place stank of stale ale that had been spilt the previous night and, even worse, the smell of stale smoke that often triggered off my asthma.

Apparently my Father had been quite sick and his teeth had gone down the toilet pan. Luckily everyone in the pub had been forewarned that my Father had lost his teeth, and that they were lurking in the toilet somewhere. Consequently, no one went into the gents and the Landlord gave permission for them to use the ladies. The teeth had been in the toilet all night effervescing. The Landlord had been acclaimed somewhat of a hero, as he had gone into the toilet and netted the teeth from the base of the toilet pan at the end of the night, and placed them on the bar in exactly the same position as they would have been in my Father's mouth. They said they'd had a bit of fun with them as they cleaned the pub out - I can't think how? The Landlord had given them a good swilling under the bitter tap and proclaimed them `Brand New'.

The Landlord put the teeth in a paper bag for me, and I went on my way. Jock was still waiting for me as I went into the street; wagging his tail as if I had been gone for years. He spotted the bag and instantly thought I had food or sweets in it. Consequently he started to sniff the bag very excitedly, wagging his tail in anticipation. I then took the teeth out of the bag behind my back, and brought them right up to Jock's face - his expression changed immediately to one of fear. He gave them one look and then, as if possessed by something, he shot off down the road yelping. Poor Jock recognised those teeth and just could not understand why they were out of my Father's mouth.

Arriving back at Stamford Avenue, Jock was waiting at the front door begging my Mother to let him in. He was still shaking and whimpering. I teasingly went to open the bag again and Jock was off like a greyhound, not to return for a couple of hours.

After that incident Jock gradually got used to my Father's teeth, because when he was on nights and I felt like a bit of fun, I would sneak into the bathroom and bring them down and place them on the floor. Jock would run away at the first sighting, but would gradually pluck up the courage, once Lassie started to snap at them, growling for all she was worth. After patrolling around them for a couple of minutes, Lassie would then jump on them and start chewing them. One of the funniest sights I had ever seen - teeth chewing teeth!

My Father's teeth, although out of his mouth, would put up a brave fight against Lassie and on several occasions bit back at her. My sides were aching with laughing so much, and when my Mother returned from the shops, she couldn't help but laugh also, until there was a loud bang on the ceiling from my Father who had unfortunately been woken up by the commotion after his night shift. The teeth were hastily picked up and put back into the cup.

The errand was the first of many to the pub to collect my Father's teeth. Sometimes my Father would be sat at the table waiting for me to return from the pub and my Mother would be waiting anxiously at the front door. "Have you got them?" she would enquire hopefully, and when I answered, "Yes," she'd say, "Quick! Give them here!."

She would give them a quick rub with her pinny. My Mother said my Father usually tried a few vegetables while he was waiting, but the meat was another matter and he would almost always blame my Mother's cooking. Seeing his teeth, my Father would give a toothless grin and take them into the kitchen to give them a good washing down under the cold water tap before putting them in. Then he would try them up and down to confirm that they were his and would then return to the table with a big smile.

My Father wasn't a very pretty sight the day after a night on the booze, especially with no teeth. As soon as he had finished his rice pudding and picked his teeth for about 5 minutes with a match, he glanced across the table at me and raised his hand. I immediately went for the defensive position putting both my arms and hands around my head. However, to my amazement, he patted me on the head lightly and gave me a tanner. As soon as that sixpence hit my palm I was out of the house and heading for the sweet shop before he could say, "Don't forget the change." Sometimes my Father could be generous.

CHAPTER TWENTY NINE

A Paper Round

My Mother had taken me to enlist with the local Doctor about a mile away and with my asthma gradually getting worse and the attacks becoming more frequent, the Doctor would very soon be sick of the sight of me! On one occasion he gave me a glimmer of hope when he said that he was going to try me on a new spray that had just come out, and had been successful with other sufferers. It had a rubber ball attached to a canister and, when pressed, it would release a bitter tasting chemical into the back of the throat. It did ease an attack for about an hour, so it did bring some relief, but like a cold, it was generally believed that an attack had to run its course - which was about 7 days as a rule. I would often fill the canister with water and use it as a water pistol, aiming at Jock, while he sniffed about in the back garden. When the water hit him he would jump and run straight at next door's fence and bark at their dog - a dog he had hated since we moved to Stamford Avenue.

Crewe was the railway centre of England, and at that time in the early 50s, it seemed to be the fog centre as well. It could be guaranteed that from early November until late January, there would be a thick smog hanging around - inevitably made worse by the heavy engineering factories and thousands of trains belching out their thick, acrid smoke.

It was one of these foggy mornings that I was woken up by my Mother to start my paper round, delivering the News of the World to the people of Crewe - it was 6 o'clock in the morning.

I had been given a new bike for passing the 11+ so my Father thought it a good idea to tie the two together and thoughtfully got me a paper round with the paper shop at the end of Stamford Avenue.

On arrival at the shop I was laden down with two large bags of papers - one strapped to each shoulder. It felt like there were a thousand papers in those bags. Why I took my new bike, I will never know, because I was more off it than on it, as I delivered along the never ending Gainsborough Road. There would be about 10 side roads the same length as Stamford Avenue and I would have to deliver there too. It was an achievement just finding my way through the fog that morning, let alone finding the names and numbers of the houses!

After a few stops the bag did seem to get a little lighter, and I was thankfully able to jump back onto my bike. My new bike was well christened that morning with the constant bangs against the wall and dropping it onto the pavement as I dashed up and down the paths - the chrome soon wore off the handle bars.

On occasions it would be raining very heavily and I would be somewhat reluctant to do my paper round. I could see that my Mother felt sorry for me, but we needed the money (Police pay was still very poor). In a way though, the paper round did get me started in the mornings and many a time I would have asthma it would not stop me going to school after finishing the round.

On these rainy mornings I would load up but within a few minutes the bag would start to fill with water and I would have to stop every so often to empty it out. My fingers would be numb, even with my woolly gloves on, as they became sodden with the rain. My fingers often froze to the shape of the handlebar grips and it would take ages to thaw them out, and bring them back, painfully, to their normal position. Gradually every paper that I extracted from the bag was soaked, and pieces would tear off as I tried to fold them neatly to put them through the letter boxes. Many of the letter boxes were heavily Spring-loaded and sometimes this made it very difficult to prise them open with my frozen fingers. After squeezing them through, they would barely be readable, and on rainy mornings there would be many complaints at the shop.

The houses I dreaded delivering to were the ones with dogs standing in the drive baring their teeth and daring me to put one foot on their territory. I would test them out first with a gingerly "Hello nice doggy," or words to that effect, but often the dog would fly at the gate, much to the amusement of the owner.

Some of the dogs, when standing in their hind legs with their front paws on the gate were taller than me. That would be enough for me, and away I would go, only to creep back later on and throw the paper at the door, in the hope that the dog wouldn't chew it up before the owner got it. More often than not, my aim was not all that good, and the paper would bounce back into the rain and when the owner came to pick it up, he would clout the dog around the ears into the bargain - it was no wonder the dog went for me, if that was the treatment he got for guarding the path.

Most of the houses on my patch were terraced and had lace curtains in the windows. At that time of the morning there would be all sorts of faces peering through the windows - scratching their heads (as well as other parts of their anatomy), eyes not properly open, some bleary and on a Sunday morning and others bloodshot after a Saturday night at the local. Some would be standing there with their arms folded, waiting to tell me off because of the state of the paper the previous day.

Seeing them through the window, I would be up the path in a shot - paper through the letterbox and away, before they could get to the gate.

On many a morning there would be woman in various states of dress still with their hairnets holding tatty hair in place, and headscarves to hide the hair that hadn't yet been combed.

Now and then, a younger woman would have a laugh at me and beckon me into the house, curling her index finger back and saying, "Come on in for a cup of tea love, my Husband's gone to work." I would run up the path, put the paper through the door and back down, before she could open the door. I always approached that house very warily. One morning there was no sign of her at all in the window, so I crept up and pushed the paper through the letterbox as quietly as possible. However, just as I was about to turn, the door opened and a hand was placed on my shoulder. "Come and `av a cup of tea luvvy," she crooned.

"No thanks very much Mrs," I nervously uttered. I then went on my way with legs like jelly trying to whistle nonchalantly. Mind you, looking back, some mornings it was that cold I often felt like a nice hot cup of tea somewhere along my route.

I would get paid for my paper round on a Friday morning - the princely sum of five shillings (25p) and it all went to my

Mother to help with the housekeeping. I didn't ever begrudge my Mother having the money, because I knew how she struggled to keep me in clothing for the Grammar School. I kept that paper round right up until the time we left Stamford Avenue - even though I absolutely hated getting out bed on those cold mornings, and then having to dry my clothes out on some days in preparation for school.

The Backs Olympics

To the rear of the terraced houses there was an entry running the full length of the Avenue which was laid in concrete with a rain gulley down the middle. This was where `Backs Olympics' would take place almost every night during the Summer months. I can hardly ever recollect going out of the front door. "Don't you get going out of the `Backs,' my Mother would say.

Teams would be picked, and there was sufficient room between the 8 foot high walls for two teams to run up and down the length of the backs. Games such as running, relays, football, cricket and even rounders in the 10 foot wide alley would take place. The teams were always mixed with an equal amount of boys and girls in each team. Obviously there would be arguments, especially on the turn in the relays, because it was by hand-touch at the top and bottom of the entry - a slap on the hand and the next runner would be away. Some would move off before being touched and, consequently, more arguments would break out. Although these disagreements would be sorted out, there were many angry stares passed between teams. With the confined space and people running flat out to the bottom of the backs, some would not be able top stop and would hit the wall, resulting in some very nasty grazes and bruising.

Time would be forgotten whilst we were involved in the games, until our parents slowly began drifting out shouting the names of their offspring in the still night air - Geoff, Mike, Anne, Barbara, Susan and Ivor. My Mother would come out several times and eventually she would threaten to send my Father out the next time - so that was good enough for me, and in I went.

My Father had the same routine as we had at Hoole, in that we would all go to the pictures once a fortnight on a Thursday which was payday. We would go to the nearest cinema on the corner of Edleston Road and Alton Street called The Palace.

Again, once the film was over, my Father would give my Mother some money for sweets or chips, and he would head for the Hop Pole pub to meet his police friends for a few pints - more like a few gallons!!

During the last century, when the railways were being laid, the elder statesman of Crewe decided that they needed a park. A large area of land to the west of Crewe was cleared and landscaped to form `Queen's Park,' in honour of their Queen, `Victoria.'

When the park was completed, it was one of the largest public parks in Cheshire, but not readily publicised the same as other parks. For what reason, I do not know.

People would spend most of their Sunday afternoons at the park, just walking (but, of course, this was before the advent of the motor cars on the scene, and this was the early fifties). It was a very pleasant way to spend a Sunday afternoon, eyeing up all the local talent and on many occasions, having a go on the rowing boats around the island in the middle of the lake, for a tanner a go. The lake was filled by the Valley Brook from the east near Alsager. After leaving the lake, it would head west to Nantwich, where it joined the River Weaver. The river was well stocked with fresh water fish.

CHAPTER THIRTY

Jasper, The Javelin and The Judgement

The Christmas holidays were over and it was back to school. The internal structure of the school was built around the main assembly hall, with the classrooms on the ground floor facing the rostrum in the hall, and the Headmaster's study in a central position adjoining them. The second floor was of the same design but this had a balcony running along three sides, so that when we came out of the classrooms, we would be looking down into the main hall, through a cast iron balustrade.

Mr Dowling was an extremely punctual man and would appear through the swing doors into the hall at the same time every morning - robes flowing behind him, Bible in one hand and notes for his sermon in the other. Assembly would usually last about 10 minutes, and then all the classes would file out into their respective classrooms for their first lesson of the day.

The third floor of the building consisted of just one room - the lecture room, and then out to the bell tower - a strictly forbidden place. Anyone daring to go up to the bell tower would do so at their own risk of being expelled. However, I never did hear the bell ring the whole time I was there - but there were a few signatures inside!

After moving through the first two years and ending up in class 4T, it was now 1953. For some reason there always appeared to be twice as many girls as boys in our class - although there were no complaints from the boys! As we all started to get taller and fatter (in my case!), some of the lads would manage to jam their legs in the desks, and the desks would rattle up and down - much to the annoyance of the master in charge. However, I never had that problem, as my legs were still short and fat.

Mr Worgan was our new form master in 4T. Mr Dowling obviously knew what he was doing when he put me in the `C' stream, because, try as I may, I could never catch up on the first year I had lost. Although 4T had a better ring to it than 4C, I was proud to be in a technical class.

By this time I had perfected a whistle whilst not opening my mouth. Most teachers would look straight at me, but could not detect that I was making the noise, because when I stopped, my expression would not change. Most members of the class knew it was me though!

In general, if a pupil did not understand the lesson, he or she would generally fool about and distract the other pupils of the form. Teachers were always on the lookout for this sort of behaviour and did stamp it out at Crewe Grammar.

Mr Worgan had a very good idea of who the culprit was, but couldn't quite put his finger on it! He would spend long periods of time just staring at me and, in the end, it became quite an obsession with him, because he would glare at me even when I was not whistling.

On most days Mr Worgan would stride into the classroom, look at me, open the window, look up and down Ruskin Road, and then turn quickly and look straight at me, as if to say, "Right! I'll have you today!," After 2 or 3 minutes I would test the air with, `Colonel Bogie.' Classmates would start to smile and giggle, and Mr Worgan would glare at them and move to the window constantly watching for any lip movements from anyone. He would peer through the window, and there would always be someone walking up Ruskin Road, for example the window cleaners or the postman. Initially he thought it was one of them whistling, but Mr Worgan was not stupid, and he knew who it was alright! It had no doubt been discussed in the staff room and he was just waiting for me to smile or do something out of place.

In one particular lesson I did smile, but it was nothing to do with the whistling, but that was his cue.

"Goolding, get out here quick!," Mr Worgan shouted.

Out I went and he gave me a smack across the head that made me see stars - banging me against the wall, and I couldn't hear a thing for a few days afterwards. I could never understand whether the smack was for the whistling, or the laughing, but I had a good idea in the end. It certainly taught me a lesson, and the whistling immediately stopped - much to the relief of Mr Worgen who was a very nice person really, so why I picked on him I will never understand. This certainly was another case of where the punishment fitted the crime.

Hedley Barker and Billy Hannah were the other two masters who could hold the discipline in a class. Hedley Barker was the school history master - a bit like Yul Brynner in looks. Rumours had circulated the school one day that one of the sixth formers had hit Hedley across the face in a heated argument, and Hedley had just sat there completely dumbfounded. This sort of behaviour was unheard of in those days, and could quite easily have lead to expulsion for the lad concerned.

Since leaving school I have met up with the sixth former concerned and he assured me that the rumour was in fact true, but that he had only slapped Hedley Barker across the face. By the end of the day the story had been exaggerated and the rumour was that John Noden had actually knocked out Hedley Barker!

The period leading up to Christmas was very nostalgic for me, with the choir singing carols in the school assembly hall, practising for Christmas carol service. The acoustics in the hall were very good; the sound would echo all around the school. I would drift into one of my many dreams as the snow floated passed the window when they sang, `Silent Night.' This carol would immediately take me back to Little Budworth and the memories of the happy Christmases I had spent there.

Having left the fourth year I was going up in the world - literally onto the next floor and into the lecture room. This was the only room on the top floor used for teaching, as all the other rooms were used for storage. It was to be our classroom for the next 12 months - my final year.

The lecture room was tiered like an amphitheatre with an alley up the middle which divided the boys from the girls. It was a good design as all the class could see the blackboard without leaning or standing, and the teacher had a low vantage point in that he could see all the pupils.

It was the year of my GCE exams and therefore `swotting' was the order of the day. Unfortunately I didn't take to the idea too keenly and consequently I did not obtain as many `O' levels as I should have done. I couldn't blame my results on the asthma either, as my theory was play plenty of sport and fight to the death, if necessary, the dreaded wheeze. I did play cricket and football for the school teams on occasions, but missed a lot due to the asthma, and Mr Jones would be very reluctant to pick me. Nerves seemed to play a large part in the attacks, for as soon as I knew I was even in the trials, it seemed to induce an attack.

During the fifth year we had a young biology student teacher. She would, on occasions, come in with the regular teacher, Miss Slee, but on one particular occasion she was thrown in at the deep end, and took us on her own. She was only about 20 years old and was very attractive so was onto a loser as soon as she walked into the room. The lads would give her whistles and cat calls and, although she tried very hard to maintain discipline, it was only the girls, naturally, who would listen.

One particular day that sticks out in my memory, was the day of the `ink throwing', and I suspect all the lads who were in the class remember it well, and still feel guilty about it.

It started playfully enough. I can't recollect who actually started it, but it was definitely not me on this occasion. I was busy writing for a change and then, suddenly, a big blob of ink appeared on my book obliterating everything on the page (except for the date!), and it also splashed my face into the bargain. Well, as you could imagine one thing led to another and when the student's back was turned to the board, a volley of ink was thrown in the general direction from whence the first attack came. She turned around and saw all the lads throwing ink everywhere, stray blobs going over to the girls side, no doubt to try and involve them in the proceedings, but they would not get involved. The student did attempt to intervene by shouting at the top of her frail face, "Will you just stop throwing ink around."

However, her pleas were ignored and she ran out of the room crying. We were all dumbfounded as we waited for the `Beak' to appear, but nothing happened, so we all went quickly to our next lesson as soon as the bell went for the end of the period.

It was some days later when the Headmaster burst through the door. We were all messing about, as usual, first thing in the morning whilst waiting for our form master. There had been a mention in assembly that morning regarding certain classes misbehaving and that he was not going to tolerate it. However, we had dismissed this as being in respect of one of the lower forms. How wrong we were.

The Headmaster was closely followed by `Jasper Powell', the woodwork master. Jasper was a little Welsh wizard whose hair, glistening with brylcreem, was parted down the middle with a parting that looked as though it had been put there with an axe, and he had the sort of face that it looked like the axe had been used on! He was, incidentally, a very good shot with a piece of 4 x 2 wood - I have the scar to prove it.

Mr Dowling still had his gown on and this was a sure sign of impending doom. Jasper also had his gown on but his was very shiny and didn't look nearly as impressive. As I looked at them, their gowns changed into SS uniforms as the interrogation commenced. Mr Dowling spoke first in a soft tone. "I will ask this question once, and only once." "Who was throwing the ink about on Tuesday of last week?" We all looked up at the ceiling, some rubbing their chins, others looking over to the girls' side to try and put some of the blame on them - laughable really!

Then Jasper, as if possessed by the devil, brought himself up to his full height of 5ft 2in and said, "Right," and goosed stepped up the aisle until he stopped in front of me. He then stared straight at me - his eyes penetrating my mind as if they could see into my head, and all the things that had occurred that afternoon and that they would be revealed. I was able to hold his stare for a while but backed off when his arm twitched. I think if he'd have had a gun in his hand, he would have shot me for even daring to try and stare him out.

Eventually the Headmaster realised that Jasper was taking over the proceedings and shouted, "Open your books on the day Miss......... took the lesson." Jasper immediately repeated the statement and added, "Let's see whose books are covered in ink."

Mr Dowling again gave him a long, hard stare, as if to say, "Why don't you shut up?" The class went very quiet as brains ticked over trying to think up a good excuse. There was a rustle of paper behind as a couple of lads tried to remove the offending pages. That was like a homing device to Jasper, and he shot up the steps again and screeched, "Stop!," and with that the lads froze and he quickly followed this up with, "Don't anyone move!."

He had taken over the proceedings once more, and Mr Dowling again had to caution him with, "Alright Mr Powell, I'll take it from here." However, Jasper was unstoppable now and he turned his attention to me again. "Gudling out to the front!" he ordered. He always pronounced my name wrong - perhaps it was the Welsh translation.

"Goolding Sir," I said quite emphatically and, again, I thought I noticed a slight twitch of his arm, but he must have thought better of it with the Headmaster standing alongside him. I ambled out to the front, and he moved again to clip me around the ear as I passed him. However, the Headmaster shook his head slightly and nodded his head over to the girls who were all sitting, not moving, with their mouths agape watching the proceedings. Jasper nodded back to the Headmaster in approval.

The Headmaster then ordered, "Pass Goolding's books to the front." There followed another scuffle as my classmates displayed undue eagerness to oblige. He then opened the book at the offending page and there, looking as if someone had used the page as a blotter, was all the evidence that would condemn me, although it had been done by other members of the form, of course they had the blotches on their books which had been thrown by me. In the meantime, Jasper was watching intently, his eyes firmly locked onto other members of the form. Some books dropped onto the floor but were quickly spotted by Jasper and he again shouted. "O'Keefe, Sherwin, Bolton - to the front!" In the end most of the lads were at the front of the class with their books open at the page in question. Some of the throwers did get away with it, because they had the good sense to shut their books while the ink was flying around on that particular day - hence no blotches. I had to hold up my hand in the end and admit that I had thrown ink and had no excuse whatsoever - many others did the same. Did Dicken get away with it? I will never know.

"All of you go and wait outside my study!," ordered the Headmaster. Those words sent a chill through me as we all made our way down to his study - three flights of steps down to the ground floor. Teachers came to the classroom doors and glared at us as we passed. Some pupils strained to see over the heads of other pupils, standing on chairs and desks in order to get a good look at the criminals. I have never felt so guilty in all my life as I did on that day.

Outside the Headmaster's study, standing in line is if about to be shot, I was half expecting someone to offer us a last cigarette. Mr Dowling eventually arrived at speed, foaming at the mouth and having lost the close attention of Jasper. His face was rigid and pale with anger, as he disappeared into his study without a word.

By this time my stomach was turning over and other lads along the line were the same as they tried to control their fear of impending punishment. "Get in here the lot of you!" he yelled. We looked at one another as if to say, "You first."

The call from behind the door sounded very angry and so, nervously, we all filed into the study. It hadn't changed from the first day I had arrived with my Mother many years ago now. I noticed the quill pen still stuck in the inkwell. Mr Dowling then beckoned to his Secretary to leave the room, and I thought to myself, "Ivor lad, he's going to come down hard with that cane today." As I looked up and down the line, I thought, "Where's the rest?" The Headmaster turned and went over to the cabinet behind his desk and brought out the cane. It was not like the cane that I had imagined, and that other people had described to me (who themselves had never had it, but enjoyed putting fear into us all before we had even entered the study!) The Headmaster gave a few trial lashes of the cane through the still study air. My knees buckled slightly - the noise was frightening. He winced slightly and rubbed his shoulder as if he had a touch of rheumatics. Some of the other lads swayed a little and I thought he was going to call it off when he rubbed his shoulder. However, it transpired that he was just loosening up so as to get the maximum follow through. "Hold out your hands," he whispered. Some went out immediately, others were reluctant, having never known punishment of this sort before. "Get those hands straight out!" he demanded. All hands were straight out and level, quivering as they waited their turn. The Headmaster then juggled his feet like a golfer dressing the ball before his shot, but in our case it was across our hands so as to get central and then WHACK!! I expect the crack could be heard all over the school, as he had discreetly left the study door open in order to get the maximum amount of volume (no doubt to deter other pupils from wandering off the straight and narrow). "Next!" he screamed, as we all moved to go out.

By this time I thought Mr Dowling was tiring - how wrong I was. "Now hold the other hand out!" he bellowed. We all looked at one another as if to say, "We haven't got another hand." In all we had three canes each and it was a struggle for me to hold the tears back. My hands were numb for days afterwards. However, the punishment did fit the crime and I had no recriminations towards Mr Dowling whatsoever - he was absolutely right. I will never forget the expressions of O'Keefe and Sherwin as Mr Dowling came down with that cane and no doubt they will never forget the expressions on my face. I can still see them now and laugh at the very thought. I still feel very guilty about that poor student on that day of the `Ink Throwing.'

Sports Day was a big annual event for the school and the local press reported the day's events. All the teachers participated - either as judges or starters, and I was taking part in the hurdles and the javelin. I couldn't understand how I had been nominated for the javelin - I think it was probably because none of the other members of the form would do it. I was lucky on this particular Summer's day, because there was no sign of my asthma.

It was a warm, shimmering hot day from the start in June 1953 - first test match was underway against Australia and, eventually, England won very easily thanks to the new firebrand of a young fast bowler named Fred Trueman. At 21 years of age he was one of the youngest players in the team, together with Colin Cowdrey. Fiery Fred was built like a brick shed and had the most perfect run up and delivery since the legendary Harold Larwood. He wasn't as fast, but he could move the ball both ways through the air and off the wicket, as well as throw the odd deceptive bouncer down at the unlucky batsman.

I can recall on that Summer's day, standing outside the staff room listening to the wireless and the John Arlott commentary through the open window. This was during our lunch hour as the wireless crackled away. John Arlott's silky voice would then go through all the records of fast bowlers over the years. In the afternoon we heard that Australia were struggling against Trueman's pace, and that he had taken several wickets. My Father always said that John Arlott was from Gloucestershire, but I'm afraid he was a county out - he was, in fact, from Hampshire, although their dialect was very similar. Peter May and Colin Cowdrey knocked the runs off and England had won by a substantial margin.

As the morning of the Sports Day progressed, different classes were detailed to take chairs and tables out onto the sports field, lining them up along the running track from the start to the finishing tape. Excitement was now building up inside me as the time ticked away, knowing that the local press were going to be there. Would I trip and make a fool of myself as I ran up with the javelin? Would I knock the first hurdle over and fall flat on my face? My lack of confidence in my ability would remain with me for my entire life.

2 o'clock loomed nearer and the Crewe Chronicle photographer had arrived with all his equipment. He set about training his camera on individual pupils to get the correct focus and the right setting for his light meter. I thought he was a genius for knowing all the technical data and using all those many different pieces of camera - surely he must have an `O' level in physics!

At last the time arrived for all the classes to go out onto the sports field in an orderly fashion, with the competitors assembling in the gym to change into their sports gear - pumps, vests and shorts, with each pupil wearing their house sash around their person. Purple was the colour of my house, Delves, and it became my favourite colour. The rest of the school wore their school uniforms - boys in their blazers etc and the girls in their green check dresses with black headbands.

On the sports field all the competitors assembled into their respective houses - Delves, Dutton, Foulhurst and Hawkstone - names of well known gentry of the district in years gone by. Purple, Green, Blue and Orange were the houses respective colours.

Prior to the start of all the events, one of the school Governor's gave a speech over the tannoy which had been set up by Mr Walker, the English teacher, and Ben Reay, the Physics master. They had done a very good job with the small amount of equipment available to them - one microphone and two speakers. I was down by the start now, looking very bemused and nervous when the Governor started his speech.

"I...I...I...would...would....like...like....to....to...thank... thank...," stammered the Governor eventually finishing with... ."Enjoy...enjoy...yourselves...yourselves...."

As the sound echoed around Crewe, I felt like adding to the Governor's speech, ..."or else....or else..."

The Governor must have given a good speech, because I could see the people around the start applauding for several minutes or more. Mr Dowling then made a gesture like a Roman Emperor, waving his hand as if to say, "Let the games commence."

I thought to myself, "If we are the Christians, where are the lions?" I was very soon to find out.

I think the master plan was to try and get all the minor events over as quickly as possible, so that they could concentrate on the seniors. Jasper had taken charge of the starter gun, whilst Mr Walker attended to the tannoy system, which had shown signs of cracking up, so to speak. I thought it appropriate for Jasper to be in charge of the start and the gun. He had a few practice shots to make sure it was working and I imagined him pointing it at me - no doubt that would have got a few miles an hour extra out of me up the running track.

Jasper fired a couple of shots into the air, twirled it around his fingers, John Wayne style, and then flicked it back into an imaginary holster. A smile of satisfaction came over his face as he ordered the competitors into line. "On your marks, get set..." Everyone wavered as they waited for the bang. Concentration was lost and the favourites were left at the start as the gun went off unexpectedly, and an outsider won the race, much to the delight of the crowd. I could see the Headmaster wandering around and smiling at parents in an apologetic smile and he then moved rapidly down to the start to see what was happening, and why the blasted gun hadn't gone off properly. Jasper tried to explain that a bit of damp had got into it. I could think for the life of me where damp could have possibly come from on such a hot and shimmering day. However, the Headmaster seemed satisfied with Jasper's explanation and jogged back to the finishing area - a mite faster than some of the competitors, might I add.

The first and second year pupils had finished their events and it was now time for the third and fourth years and my event, the javelin. We were all loosening up and Jasper was shouting his orders out in broken English, "Gudling - over here quick!" Some contestants were touching their toes, while others were lifting their knees up to their chins - what good that would be in the javelin, I could not imagine. However, I thought I had better do something athletic, so I swung my right arm as if throwing an imaginary javelin down the course.

The spectators needed to concentrate very hard while the third and fourth year pupils were throwing the javelin around, because they could literally go anywhere. After the measuring up, I was adjudged to have come third, so I was very happy about that, and I had also gained some points for the Delves. Most importantly though, was that I had not made a fool of myself.

I actually felt sorry for Jasper who, during the course of the afternoon, had endless trouble with the starter gun. Actually, he did come over to me and said, "Well done, Gudling." Apparently I had amused him with one of my wayward throws which had headed for the crowd, scattering them in all directions and landing two feet short of the boundary rope. The javelin was twice as long as me and as I ran up I had great difficulty keeping it off the ground behind me.

All the field events now over, it was time for the runners and I was down for the 80 yards intermediate hurdles. Again, I was a little apprehensive about making a fool of myself. I could never get it into my thick skull that it didn't matter whether I fell or whatever, but may be that was just part of my character, and nothing would every change that.

We were all now lined up at the start and Jasper had the gun held aloft and then "`Crack' - we were off first time! As I approached the first hurdle I had to change my step and more or less do a standing jump, but luckily I cleared the hurdle easily. After that my nerves seemed to ebb away and I picked up speed and a sense of the winning spirit (something Mr Dowling had mentioned many times during the my time at Crewe Grammar), came over me and I cleared the next two hurdles, knocked the next two down, and finally finished third again.

I was really pleased with myself on that day for achieving two third places. At the finish I had fallen flat on my back exhausted to gulp as much air into my asthma racked lungs as possible. One of the masters came over to me and said, "Hand your number into Mr Jones quickly." I didn't have the voice to say, "Yes Sir," but managed to scramble to my feet and stagger over to Mr Jones who said, "Well done Goolding." To me, those words meant more than coming third in the race. If only my Father had praised me for some of the things

I achieved, even if they were only minor ones, then maybe I would have become a winner earlier in life and got rid of my damned asthma much sooner.

My event over, it was now time for the sixth formers and there was talk of records being broken. It all added up to excitement for me on that Summer's day in 1953, Coronation Year. Most people will of course remember this year for the Coronation Year, but I remember it for the school sports day.

I can remember a lad named Higgins holding the lead from start to finish in the 880 yards and winning in record time, closely followed by Micky Love. I could never understand how they kept going for so long - they must have had lungs like whales. Another lad who won a lot of events that day was Robert Holmes, a winner if ever there was one! I wonder what happened to him in life. As well as winning many events, he also won the cup for the best performance of the day, together with a girl named Pat Lewis who was a keen sportswoman and excelled at everything.

At the end of the day everyone gathered around the finishing line and Mr Dowling gave a speech thanking all who had taken part, and all the parents who had bothered to come and shout for their offspring. It was all for the honour of the house and, more importantly, for the school and he really emphasised this point. "Dedication to the spirit of the game" - I will remember his words forever.

The late 40's and the wartime ideas still lingered on and it was always said that competition was the backbone of any country. These were the sentiments expressed in Mr Dowling's speech, and I am proud to have been part of that era. After the speech everyone drifted away and that was the end of another sports day. Hawkstone had won the house cup for the 17th time, which was a record. Although it was not long before the end of term, we were all back in school the next day to talk about the previous day's events - a day in June of the Coronation Year 1953.

CHAPTER THIRTY ONE

The Piano Recital

At Goodall's Corner, we were situated on a busy crossroads as it was the main road from the Potteries to Nantwich, straight across the main road from Crewe to Wybunbury and South Cheshire. It was a three bedroom detached house with a coalhouse attached at the rear. Jock was over the moon because he was back in the country again and would disappear over open fields for hours on end.

A few weeks before we left Crewe, my Father could not find the money that he left in the locked bureau used for paying off my bike on the `Never Never.' I would go religiously every Saturday morning to the bike shop in Mill Street to pay the weekly instalment of three shillings and sixpence which, in those days, was deemed a lot of money.

I became the prime suspect in my Father's eyes and he thrashed me for supposedly stealing the money, not believing my pleas as I cried, "I don't know where the money is." Eventually the money was found under a pile of papers on the top shelf of the bureau which, incidentally, was kept locked! "So how did I get the money, Dad?"

He did realise his mistake and gave me 2/6pence, but it was too late as the damage had already been done, and I never forgave him for that thrashing.

Of course, there were many times when I did deserve a telling off, or maybe a clout around the ears, but instead I always got a `good hiding', as my Father called them. My Mother's attempts to stop him were useless and she was often brushed aside like a piece of flotsam - he was a very strong man. Maybe this was a reflection of his own upbringing, and he knew nothing else, because I know his own Father was very strict with him.

During our last few months at school, there would be numerous recitals given by pupils in the school, who had had the patience to learn to play musical instruments, and they were given the opportunity to try their talents out on the school. We all had to sit in the Assembly Hall for approximately two hours, listening to violins, pianos, cellos and flutes. The instruments were very well played, but to me - boring! However, I can recall a sixth former named Woods playing the violin so well that even I stopped fidgeting to listen.

On another occasion a top pianist had travelled all the way from London to give a recital, and this was to last for about 3 hours. Half way through, many of us were in the first throes of hypnotic sleep with eyes fully open, locked onto the back of the pianist's head, not hearing a single note. Some heads were nodding closer and closer to the floor, only to be saved the misfortune of actually hitting the floor by Mr Richardson, the music teacher, who would lightly tap the back of the end seat and subsequently the nodding heads would automatically come back to the erect position.

The pianist's head was now revolving round and round as he trilled some high notes with one hand and then, tossing his head back like a horse, mane flowing in the air, he then flicked his hair back from over his face with his hand and carried on playing. This appeared to get some of the girls very excited, because they started to nudge one another along the rows. However, Mr Richardson would not tolerate this and he gave another light tap with has baton on the end seat. The girls immediately stopped smiling and again tried to concentrate on the music.

Mr Dowling was really enjoying himself because he kept turning to the very pretty French teacher and smiling.

Jasper was standing at the back with his usual straight face, eyes fixed rigidly on the school clock. Mr Richardson was now completely overcome by the occasion and was swinging his baton in time to the music - his eyes flickering. Jasper's lips moved as he saw Mr Richardson and his head nodded upwards indicating a gesture of disapproval. The Headmaster gave Jasper a smile as well, as if to say, "It's nice to see you enjoying the music as well, Mr Powell."

By now there were quite a number of pupils with their hands over their eyes and gradually ebbing into a deep sleep - elbows slipping off their knees! Mr Walker, the English teacher, had noticed this and slowly moved towards the window cord and pulled it so as it edge the window open slightly. I don't think the window had been opened for many years, because it began to squeak loudly - much to the horror of Mr Walker. However, it instantly brought some of the lads out of their slumber and the pianist glanced over in his direction, having managed to open one eye, giving Mr Walker a hard stare, usually only reserved for inattentive schoolboys.

I turned to O'Keefe who was sitting next to me and said, "Look - the pianist is half asleep now!" I pointed out that he only had one eye open! This statement didn't sink in at first, because O'Keefe did try to concentrate on whatever he was doing and he had just come out of a deep sleep as well. I was dozing off again, having completing forgotten about the half asleep pianist, when O'Keefe went into what can be described as a combined spluttered laugh, sneeze and hiccough, stifled by the hand over the mouth which, unfortunately, reverberated around the hall.

By this time people were now looking in our direction and were looking down their noses and turning away in disgust. The laughter was infectious to me and the tears were running down by face as I tried to stop my laughter. Hancock, Sherwin and Fernyhough who were sitting to my right, were also in tears. I tried looking down at the floor because the pianist had become a comedian in my eyes, and I tried hard to put the incident out of my mind, but to no avail, and the pianist played on regardless.

Another lad in my row, John Saunders, was also trying to keep his laughter from bursting onto the hall, and in his struggle to do so, his face went from red to deep purple until, eventually, the laughter forced his hand from his mouth and that, too, went all around the hall as he dashed out into the corridor, closely followed by Jasper who, by all accounts, was looking an excuse to go outside. As the poor lad arrived in the corridor it was obvious that he was relieved, because his laughter now echoed all around the school.

As Jasper disappeared from the hall, the pianist paused for a full minute and there was spasmodic laughter after that, as Jasper tried to calm him down - with a cricket bat no doubt!

After what seemed like an eternity, Jasper returned, nodded his head as if to say, "He's dead." The Headmaster returned the nod, smiled, looked at the very pretty French Mistress again, and then settled back to listen to the rest of the recital. The pianist was now building up the crescendo, hands flying every-where - around the back of his held aloft head swivelling at the same time, nodding up and down and his eyes flickering ten to the dozen. I thought Mr Richardson was going to pass out as his eyes were also flickering in cohesion with the music. Jasper caught my glance, squinted his eyes and held them on me for a good few seconds. I thought to myself, "Ivor lad, I think you're going to get another 4 x 2 thrown in your direction at the next woodwork class!." I think at that very moment, as he watched Mr Richardson's performance, if there had been a shotgun handy, he would have got one barrel, and the pianist the other.

I thought Jasper's glare was starting to have an effect on the pianist, because he lifted his hands high as if being held up at the bank, as if it was all over. I was the first to clap, followed by a few other lads, but I'm afraid it was not to be, and he went on to play a few more bars. He eventually banged the last notes and stood up, taking a bow as only a concert pianist can bow - forelocks hanging down and nearly touching the floor. (I will have to write this sentence again one day!)

Mr Richardson was up the aisle clapping and smiling as he was in love with the pianist; I think Jasper thought he was. His applause was for such brilliant playing, which, no doubt, it was. However, our applause was because he had finished! But then, to my horror, some daft bastard in the front row shout-ed : "Encore, Encore, Encore!." Jasper made a mental note of this. Mr Dowling had already moved to go onto the stage to congratulate him, when to our horror, he went into an encore. Fortunately it didn't last long, after which he took several bows and then stood back for the Headmaster to make his speech, and thank him for the wonderful recital, and for travelling all the way up from London to honour the school.

Some of the pupils were now edging towards the door to try and get out for some fresh air, and see how the lad who had had the laughing fit was recovering, when the Headmaster announced that there would be many more recitals coming up after which there was spasmodic clapping. He went on to say that it was all for the good of the pupils to prevent them from becoming bored up to the end of term.

To most of the musical fraternity of the school, the concert had been a huge success and well appreciated, and no doubt many tips had been picked up by the budding musicians, for the piano, when played well, is good on the ears. For me though, music appreciation would come later in life, and then it was in the form of Rock 'n' Rollers like Little Richard and Jerry Lee Lewis who could both bang out a mean tune on the piano, and more or less made it talk.

CHAPTER THIRTY TWO

Fishing, Affrays and Interviews

On occasions I would go fishing with a friend from Crewe Grammar School - Geoff Chesters. He also kindly lent me a fishing rod and we would set off early on a Saturday morning for the Shropshire Union Canal on the other side of Nantwich.

After making our pitch and anchoring our rods onto the rest, we would sit all morning watching the float and hope that it would bob up and down. When the float did move, there would usually have been a fish either nibbling the bait or hooked, but when my float bobbed up and down it was almost guaranteed that there would be a hook with no worm on the end. When I pulled the line in, the fish would be just below the surface of the water chewing a worm and smiling. The fish around Crewe and Nantwich were very clever! They had had the practice over the years at nibbling the bait and not being hooked.

The area was renowned for its top anglers and it was the number one sport in the district. Some of the gear that these men carried around with them was unbelievable - baskets full of floats, lead weights, lines, sou'westers, bait, and spinners - you name it, they had it, and most of them carried two rods. Some of the real professionals would have their mouths full of maggots as this was supposed to make them shiny and when they hit the water, they would wriggle and attract the fish more readily.

After sitting there all morning without so much as a nibble, I decided that fishing was not the sport for me. Geoff had caught a couple of fish, but sportingly threw them back, as they were only small sticklebacks.

It had now started to rain quite heavily and one of the older fishermen came over and gave us some advice, saying, "If you go under the bridge you will catch more fish as they go under there to shelter from the rain." Naively, we went, but didn't catch anything there either. They must have had a good laugh at our expense - all part of the sport of fishing I suppose.

Canal barges were a hazard as well. Although they were the ones who were legally allowed on the canal, the fishermen would shout and shake their fists as they went passed. The barge would create a bow wave as they chugged along, pulling the floats and the weights along with them - to the delight of some of the bargees. It would take quite a long time to retrieve the lines and floats from out of the reeds.

Patience was definitely a virtue where fishing was concerned- something I would never ever be high up on.

Although Crewe Station was the top station for all types of trains, I could never bring myself to just sit around the station all day long, collecting train names and numbers. I suppose it would be called `therapy' now. I did try it with a couple of friends but, alas, boredom overcame me once again, and I opted out after an hour. All that running from platform to platform over the footbridges, bumping into station masters and intended passengers, more often than not seeing the train disappearing into the distance, was not for me I'm afraid. Most of the people collecting numbers had the specially printed LMS Book, whereas I had my little note book which became very dog eared and black due to the constant arrival and departure of the trains belching out their thick, black smoke. As we dashed back and forth we inhaled quite a few lungs full of the acrid smoke, and it did my asthmatic lungs no good at all, and I soon started to wheeze. I would arrive home looking like a chimney sweep.

I had now started Sunday School at a church just off Edleston Road called St John's Church of England. I attended there until we moved again and was eventually confirmed there. Confirmation class would be held at night, so I was very happy to go and get away from my Father's watchful eye for a few hours.

After our instruction in preparation for the big day, we would go into the Church Hall either to debate or play games, such as table tennis - a game I came to enjoy. I did go into the debating class a few times but found that I was a listener, rather than a talker - having had no chance at all to talk when at home because my Father was not a good listener, and the conversation was nil between me and him. He was still under the impression that children were only to be seen and not heard, even though I was coming up to 14 years of age.

The Confirmation Class Club (there's a mouthful) was very good for up and coming congregational lists of my age group and the church did a lot for the youth of the Country in the 50's.

With our constant moving around, my Father said it was not worth buying carpeting and furniture for the front room, so it was up with the lace curtains as soon as we moved into a new house. I made good use of the empty room in that I would smack a table tennis ball against the wall for hours on wet days. This quickened my reactions and also kept me out of my Mother's way. The terraced houses of Stamford Avenue were long and slim, with three bedrooms. They all had Victorian picture rails around the walls.

An outside toilet was attached to the building and some necessary time would be spent out there on many a freezing morning. It would be a challenge first thing in the morning in the Winter, trudging through a foot of snow and prising the iced up door open. As soon as one sat down on the bare wooden seat, it would take your breath away. My Mother cut up newspapers into six inch squares and clipped them onto a two inch nail that had been banged into the toilet wall by my Father. These pieces of paper had become quite damp and soggy over the days of the snowfalls and they never ever seemed adequate for the purpose they were intended. I spent a lot of time there trying to read the football scores of the previous Saturday, with my head at an angle of 45 degrees, until the shout came from my Father, "How much longer are you going to be in there?" It certainly wasn't a place to hang around in!

My Father would head out next and I would watch through the bedroom window, and give a loud bang on the window as he reached the slippy part of the yard. He would turn his head in my direction, scowl and then gradually slip down the wall onto the ice. He would pick himself up, mutter, and then disappeared into the toilet, puffing on a very wet cigarette.

The two dogs had also joined me in the bedroom as they had sensed that my Father would not be in a very good mood when he re-emerged from the toilet. I heard the toilet door slam shut, which meant he was on his way back into the house.

On entering the back kitchen he would say to my Mother, "What did you want to go and bang on the window for?"

"You must have been hearing things again?" replied my Mother. She was always ready with one of the quick explanations! My Father would go to shout back, but then thought better of it and sat down for his breakfast.

In the meantime, I had finished dressing and was now bouncing down the stairs full of the joys of Winter, ready for my Scott's porridge oats. I was whistling `White Christmas' as I entered the room. "You're in a jovial mood this morning aren't you?" snapped my Father. I felt like saying, "Wouldn't you be if you had been out delivering papers since 6 o'clock this morning and now had maths for the first lesson?" However, I wisely decided to keep my mouth shut.

My Mother would be smiling to herself in the kitchen as she tendered the bacon and eggs, turning the fried bread over..... ah, I can still smell them now. She would then bring them into the dining room and come out with another classic saying, "It looks as though it's going to snow again."

I think, unknowingly, my Mother would contribute to my Father's periodic moods, with the comments she made. I suspect she was a lot more intelligent than she made out, and would sometimes have my Father going red in the face with anger and completely lost for words. He would often storm out of the room and punch the wall in the hall. Mother was forever patching the wall up in the hall.

My Father would then go on duty and it was now time for everyone to wind down and have a laugh. My Mother would still be in the kitchen washing the dishes and saying, "You shouldn't laugh really." After the fun and laughter had died down a bit, although the two dogs wanted to play all day, I would say, "Here's your Dad," and Jock would be scrambling on the mat getting nowhere as he strove to get out of the way of my Father. Jock knew that when I said, "Dad," that was my Father and it struck fear into him. At last he would get to the door and hot foot it up the garden. I'd follow behind him and eventually find him cowering behind a dustbin in the alley. "Come on you silly thing, I was only playing," I'd say to him. Jock was not convinced but came back to the house with me eventually. He would be on edge for a while afterwards - his ears up and down at the slightest sound. He just did not realise that he had not done anything wrong, but that phrase, "Here's your Dad," made him think that he had - if you know what I mean! Lassie would try to convince him that my Father would not be back for hours, sniffing around him and nipping his soulful face playfully.

As the time drew even closer to leaving school, many games would be played on the school playing fields and in the school playground. I can recall a very good game we played - `Hand Tennis'. The school yard was divided into hundreds of square sections of serrated red flags. Two of these areas of approximately 8 feet square, were used as a court, and there would be many games in progress around the school yard where many heated arguments would develop.   This was a game in which the players had to be quick around the court, as the tennis ball never bounced more than a foot from the ground and was hit with the bare hand.

The scoring system of `Hand Tennis' was exactly the same as for the big game, and played on a knock out basis, best of three, and the winner stays on the court.

Some of the lads were very good at this game. I enjoyed playing, and just about held my own. The winners, if good, could stay on all through the lunch break and sometimes did.

On this particular day I had won a couple of games and my next opponent was a lad named Clive Roffey. He was a tall lad and quite nippy around the court. We were into the third game and it could have gone either way. "Line ball," Clive shouted, but some of the lads watching shook their heads so I immediately realised that there was some doubt amongst the crows, confirming my view that it was inside the line, and therefore my point. Clive wouldn't give way either, because it was a game point to both of us, and I would never give way if I thought I was in the right.

Rather than doing the sensible thing and calling it a `let point', things got a little heated and eventually Clive and I squared up to one another. Someone shouted, "Sort it out after school." (There would always be a promoter shouting from the back of the crowd and then they would craftily disappear when anyone asked, "Who said that?"

I didn't want it to come to anything like that, but it was never in my nature to back down. Why, I will never know - maybe it was because my Father had instilled it into me, saying, "Don't let anyone bully you around lad!"

I don't think Clive wanted to carry it any further either, but unfortunately things had progressed and the people were arranging the time and place, so it was back to the classroom to sweat it out all afternoon.

Clive was head and shoulders above me and I was thinking, "I'm going to get a right good hiding here if I don't back down." But there was NO way out.

The school bell rang at the end of the afternoon and to me this was like the sound of the bell for the first round. By this time the whole school had heard what was going on on the grapevine, and come 4 o'clock there was quite a crowd tagging along as we headed for the arranged venue. It was at the rear of Ruskin Road at a gap in the terraced houses. It was a patch of land with some grass on it next to the allotments.

The referee was Robert Holmes. I was pleased about that because I thought he wouldn't let it go on for too long if either of us were hurt, but then I thought, "I don't know so much after seeing him and Johnny O'Hara going at it hammer and tongs in the gym."

"Ding Ding" chimed the referee and away we went. Unfortunately for Clive, as I was the shorter one of us, his nose was right at the end of my swing, and my punches kept hitting him right on target - or thereabouts. He did hit me a few times, and my nose started to bleed, but we both kept going for what seemed like hours. "A bit more action please," said Robert Holmes, as if he were a professional referee. I was hoping he would raise both our arms and call it a draw. Luckily for me, Clive didn't use his height to the best of its ability, and in the end I hit him with a lucky punch, at which time he backed away - thank God!

Once it was all over and the crowds had made their way home, I burst out crying because I had been so tensed up all afternoon, and I was now so relieved it was all over.

"Why are you crying? You won didn't you?" But I didn't feel any sense of victory at all; in fact, I felt ashamed.

The next day brought with it some hero worship, but it was all soon forgotten. However, it will remain in my memory forever, and it's probably the only thing that I will be remembered for - "Do you remember those two out of the fourth year in 1953? Oh, what were their names? The ones that had a fight over hand tennis?"

Of course, I would prefer to have been remembered as the Head Boy or Captain of the School cricket or football teams. I dreamt of those things many a night in bed.

School presentation day was for those pupils who were bright and had won prizes, and I was always an admirer of them - never begrudging them their glory because I knew that anything like that was beyond my capability. I would loved to have heard Mr Dowling say at such events, "And now the winner of the English prize for 1953, Coronation Year - Ivor Goolding." Dreams....only dreams!

The school gym was controlled by the P.T. Master Mr Jones, a very fit man for his age. I enjoyed P.T. very much, and although climbing the ropes was an effort, I managed most of the tasks, such as the vaulting horse and the wall bars. Mr Jones enjoyed pairing us all off in size and allowing us to box - not a welcome activity for most of the lads.

Robert Holmes, a winner if ever there was one, would always pick the biggest lad in the class to spar with - Johnny O'Hara....whether he liked it or not! The pair of them would go at it hammer and tongs until Mr Jones stepped in and reluctantly stopped it.

Robert Holmes had enough bottle for the whole school and I had to admire him from a distance - everything he did was so positive; surely he must have got on in life. We did become friends outside of school, mainly because we were both in the same Confirmation Class at St John's Church.

One day we were talking about things in general and I knew he wanted to play for the Crewe Schoolboys Football team. "I'll give my little finger if they would only pick me for the schoolboys team," he said. I thought at the time, what an amazing thing to say, "I'd give my little toe if I could get rid of this damned asthma," I bravely thought.

Robert didn't have to give his little finger because he was picked on merit - he was a good player.

On the days of the P.T. lessons my Mother would sometimes give me a note to hand to Mr Jones to excuse me from showers, thinking that the shower was making my asthma worse. I often forgot about the note and readily went into the showers. Why, I will never know, because they were absolutely freezing and the shock of the first spray would take what little breath I had left in my lungs, and leave me gasping for air and diving out for the towel.

I did play the odd games for the school cricket and football teams, but I think Mr Jones was reluctant to choose me because of my recurring asthma attacks. Well, that's my excuse and I'm sticking to it!

In the June of 1952 we had moved again to a small village outside Crewe called Shavington. We lived at Goodall's Corner on the main Nantwich to Stoke road, and I had to cycle the 10 miles there and back every day to Crewe Grammar School in Ruskin Road.

Near the end of term the school photographs would be taken and this was an achievement for the photographer in charge. He would have to organise approximately 500 pupils into an orderly fashion, and keep them still for the duration of time it took for the camera to move across the whole school. During the morning most of the school had been involved in carrying chairs out to the school playground and, under the supervision of the photographer, had arranged all the seats and benches. The pupils at the back would have to stand precariously balancing on one leg. The camera would take about 5 minutes to go across; after it had passed me I was tempted to nip down to the other end and be taken again, but in those days, things that entered ones head would not usually be carried out - due to fear of the consequences of one's actions!

It took about an hour to get everyone into position - teachers and prefects on the front seats in order of seniority form the centre outwards, with Mr Dowling and Miss Slee in the middle and so on along the line to Benson, the Head Boy at the time, along to all the prefects and then upwards in rows of forms in numerical order - forms 1,2,3,4 etc etc.

CHAPTER THIRTY THREE

Those Lazy, Hazy Days of Summer

The last few months at school were spent revising by most, or just aimlessly walking around the school sports ground. From the school to the sports ground there would be the tennis courts, used mainly by the older pupils and prefects and prefectesses. I can recall watching Benson and Pace playing for hours. There were courts on both the girls and boys sides (separate playgrounds but mixed classes - strange!), and when some of the more mature girls were playing they seemed to attract a much larger crowd - mainly boys.

Moving through the small wire netted gate leading onto the sports field, there would still be air raid shelters relics from World War II; some still used by the groundsman for storing his seeds and gardening implements. They were also frequented by some pupils for a quick drag on the old weed and sometimes for rehearsing the school play, where they could have a bit of peace and quiet!! Whenever I hear Nat King Cole singing, "Those Lazy, Hazy Days of Summer," my mind drifts back to those far off days spent either in the cricket nets or making a vain effort to Putt the Shot, throw the javelin or, for some of the more energetic members of the school, to attempt the four minute mile which, until then, had not been achieved. It would be a couple of months later when Roger Bannister collapsed into the arms of an official, gasping for breath, having just got under four minutes by tenths of a second.

Teachers were also trying to take it easy as the end of term approached and they would organise some games inside. Chess was the game Mr Worgan liked and he taught most of the lads in our class to play. One of the good players in 5T was a lad named Milligan, and I never ever beat him. He was a bespectacled lad who had the annoying habit of sniffing quite loudly whenever he had made his move and put one into check, and as I racked my small brain he would continue to do it over and over again, until in the end I hurriedly made my move. I always meant to ask him if it was tactics or whether he did it unconsciously. Whatever it was, it always worked!

My Father, in the meantime, had taken it upon himself to cheer our household up a little and went out and ordered a radiogram, together with records by Winifred Attwell and Mario Lanza. My Mother always maintained that my Father had a good voice, although I thought that was debatable after hearing him trying to get the right notes while he accompanied the great Mario. It was a painful experience as my Sister and I glanced at one another whilst trying our best not to burst out laughing. However, it was good to see my Father so happy and, of course, we enjoyed it for as long as it lasted.

Lassie, the Spaniel, usually lay peacefully on the mat in front of the fire, her ears going up and down as my Father threw a bit of broken Italian into the song.

Jock would look up at my Father as if to say, "What a really good singer you are," and seemed to be on the verge of one of his loud howls, usually only reserved for the bagpipe music.

It certainly did cheer us all up in those dreary early 50s - not just the music, but the sight of my Father singing and smiling.

As the Mario Lanza records ground to a finish, Winnie was then put on and this record, in my opinion, was the forerunner to the Rock 'n' Roll era - Black and White rag. Why he bought this one I'll never know, because his whistling was not much better than his singing. I realise now why my Mother thought my Father had a good voice; it was because the pints and the whiskey chasers lubricated his tonsils and put a smooth edge on his voice, as he sang his favourite song, "Danny Boy." I could never understand why, because as far as I know, there was no Irish connection in our family.

Needless to say, my Sister and I would put the records on when my Father was out and have a good sing-song along, with my Mother and the two dogs. I think eventually Jock knew all the words to - "Because You're Mine," because when my Father sang, Jock's lips would move as his eyes followed my Father around the room, watching him as he made all the gestures the same as Mario had done in the film - "The Great Caruso."

On occasions my Father would move his arms extra quick and Jock would dive under the table and my Father would pause for a little laugh, knowing that he had frightened poor old Jock. "Drink, Drink, Laugh and be Merry," would be his last song and a hint of a tear would come to his eyes as he ended the song.

CHAPTER THIRTY FOUR

"The Robins" - my Heroes

In the 50's, Crewe Alexandra Football Club were a good side, but never quite made it into Division II. I had become an ardent supported and I would go to Gresty Road to watch almost every home game - come rain or shine, and on occasions, when I had some money, I would also go to the local away games such as Port Vale, Chester and Wrexham. Initially my Father took me and we would stand in the same spot in the paddock at every game.

At this particular game it was a Cup Game against the old rivals, Port Vale, and nearly 20,000 people had squeezed into the ground, spilling over onto the pitch all round the touch line.

The game still went ahead, and it proved to be a record attendance at Gresty Road. Names like Frank Blunstone, Johnny King, Frank Mitcheson, Peter Elson and Jack Meaney were some of the stars in the team. Frank Blunstone went on to Chelsea and England fame, Johnny King to Stoke City.

Mighty Bob Young was the right back and nobody hardly ever got passed him - he had legs like ham shanks and once tackled by Bob, there was no comeback. Many a winger and the ball were taken over the line and into the crowd by Bob during the course of the season. Mind you, his tackles were always fair.

Peter Elson, the goalie, was brilliant on occasions and attracted scouts from many top clubs like Arsenal, although he never actually left Crewe, staying on to coach youngsters after his playing days were over, and he was there when I left school.

We would train with the first team players on the hallowed Gresty Road turf and Peter would be there giving advice.

Crewe Alex had their share of ups and downs, but never finished bottom of the league.

My Father had also been a keen Liverpool supporter and he would often go to Anfield whenever he was off duty. His supporting Liverpool rubbed off onto me, because I also started to support them in those early 1950's.

Saving football programmes was a hobby that many lads got into, myself included, and I think I had just about every programme of all the teams, except Arbroath. I should have kept them, as they would have been of some value now.

Stamp collecting was another craze but I wasn't very interested in this, because to get good stamps one had to spend money. Some of the keener collectors would send for approvals and get free stamps, and would then sell them to other lads who would buy them gladly. I would never get drawn into that sort of thing, because to me approval was `On the never never' - something very much disapproved of by my Father.

CHAPTER THIRTY FIVE

Weeding and Waiting

While settling in at Goodall's Corner at Shavington, it was 1953, Coronation Year and all the arrangements were in full swing - not only in London but in all the towns and villages throughout the Country.

My Father, together with many of his drinking partners on the force, had been `selected', as he called it, to go to London the previous year, 1952 (the year King George VI had died), to line the route as the King was carried to his resting place, and now the same team had been selected to attend the Coronation.

I had become a member of the Shavington Church Guild, and spent most of my Tuesday evenings there learning the art of table tennis.

My Sister was still at school and was doing very well at swimming, in that she had been picked to represent Cheshire at the Olympic Pool in Blackpool. I can recall the excitement in our house as my Mother prepared everything ready to get on the coach from Crewe with all the other swimmers.

My Sister was a natural swimmer and with a little coaching would have made the top flight. The event was also treated as an England trial, because all the Counties were represented. My Sister finished second to Linda Ludgrove who went on to swim for England - beaten by a touch (fingernail) but that's the difference between success and failure. However, she took it all in good heart, not realising how close she had come to glory and being selected for England. My Mother blames the chips they had eaten for their tea prior to the race, `chips!' - my goodness, no wonder she came second!

After a few months at Goodall's Corner, my Father again fixed me up with a job at Joe Case's Nursery in The Hough, about a mile from our house.

The nursery was jointly owned by two Brothers - Joe and Bert, and was about 4 acres in area providing a living for the two families. They enjoyed the work and no doubt were up very early in the mornings getting all the produce ready for the market. I had my own opinion, because I was constantly on my knees moving along rows and rows of young lettuce plants, removing weeds and nettles - a chore that could only be done by hand. My fingers and hands would be red raw and full of nettle stings from the wet nettles.

It seemed to be constantly raining during the time I spent at the nursery - usually on my school holidays and every Saturday morning; my Mother blamed the Atomic bombs - maybe she was right and it was them that blew the hole in the ozone layer. Who knows?

On some of the warmer sunnier days I was allowed to pick raspberries, filling hundreds of punnets in a day. All the produce would be loaded onto the back of Joe's little trailer and taken to Crewe Market for selling. Some, of course, would not get sold, and Joe would more or less give it away and on many occasions would bring a lot back, and I would take it home for my Mother.

Joe was the careful one and worked out all the bills, while Bert would like a pint and a bet in the "Buck" (The White Hart pub), across the road from the nursery. Joe let us convert the loft into a table tennis room, and there we would spend hours in the dust filled old loft, smacking a table tennis ball back and to on a table we had made ourselves out of some old plywood.

On some nights there would be as many as 10 lads milling around eating the odd apple or pear that was stored up there for the Winter.

Christmas was also a busy time for Joe and Bert. They would disappear with their car and trailer down to Wybunbury Moss where they would collect bales and bales of moss for packing into wire rings to make wreaths for the festive season. I was never permitted to do this, as it was an art - fitting flowers and sprigs of holly all around the wire frame and, when finished, they were very effective. The whole set up was a one-off only reserved for the early 50's - a much slower pace and people enjoyed themselves although they made most of their own fun.

1953 was also the year that all my practice knocking the table tennis ball around under the dark lights came to good, in that I managed to win the Crewe Junior Championship with a lad named Ray Platt. Ray actually went on to become a much better player than me, playing for the Crewe Town team for years.

Table tennis was not a sport widely publicised during that era, but taking part was my idea of beating the dreaded asthma and to win something was an added bonus, as it meant that I would forget about the asthma and therefore I was able to concentrate on whatever activity I was taking part in.

For all its rows and rows of smoky terraced houses and swirling fog, Crewe turned out to be a general building of my character. Although still much to be desired, I was very much under my Father's brand of discipline and, in a way, this kept me in my shell. I was frightened to express myself and make my own decisions. All in all, I just could not communicate with people.

My Mother attempted in her own little way by creating a few laughs and generally bring good cheer to the household, but what was really needed were books to read - something that we could not afford. My parents were not to know, because undoubtedly they had a strict upbringing and knew no different. After all, no one is taught how to bring children up - it is something which is picked up from ones own parents.

Finally the great day arrived for leaving school. However, it turned out to be somewhat of an anti climax really. We all just went out different ways - some had jobs, others stayed on into the sixth form to try and obtain more `O' levels.

I went to work at the nursery whilst waiting for interviews at various companies in the area. I spent most of the Summer of 1954 on Joe Cases nursery until one day my Father came home and said, "You've got an interview at Radway Green."

I immediately thought that Radway Green was another nursery, with a name like that. However, it transpired that it was in fact an Ammunition Factory (Royal Ordnance Factory). I travelled to the interview on my bike, eventually finding the place in the middle of nowhere. It was an interview for an apprenticeship and I failed miserably.

In those days there were no Careers Officers and most of us had no idea what an interview entailed.

A couple of weeks later I had an interview at Rolls Royce in Crewe and I fared much better. In fact, the following week I received a letter saying that I had been accepted for an apprenticeship. I didn't know whether I was excited or not, because working in industry was the furthest thing away from my mind. However, once I had settled in, and realising that there were a few of the lads from my class at school also there, I actually began to enjoy my work.

Chapter Thirty Six

Bolts, Bodies and Benches

My first year was to be spent in The Millwrights Shop - a place where I would learn many different forms of crafts; a sort of multi-skilled training. I commenced my apprenticeship on the first Monday in September and I cycled the 6 miles from Shavington to Rolls Royce - a mile more than I was used to from the previous 2 years of cycling to Crewe Grammar School. Most people had bikes then and the factory gate would be blocked solid at night time as the men raced to get home after a 9 hour shift.

On many occasions it would be throwing it down with rain and inevitably I would arrive at either work or home saturated to the skin - something accepted as part of the everyday drudgery of those far off days of the 50's.

By this time my Father had begun to lay the law down a bit heavier, and his discipline was now making my life a misery. He would not think twice about giving me a clout around the ears for minor offences; such as riding on the footpath and, more often than not, riding without lights to save my batteries. He always seemed to know - it must have been something inbuilt into his Copper Brain.

Today it is acceptable for children to ride on the footpath, although it is still against the law, it is safer for the children.

The Millwrights Shop was a dull and smoky place with shafts of light streaming through the holes in the roof, as if pulling the smoke and dust spiralling up to the roof forming patterns as it went. The extractor fans would very often be broken and the smoke would hang just under the roof with nowhere to go.

A Maintenance Fitter named Roy Whittaker was given the job of showing me around and teaching me the many skills involved in the repairs of pumps and the marking off of materials for different projects.

Roy had been assigned the work on the experimental side of the Millwrights insomuch as he had to make a body turnover truck for the world famous Rolls Royce car body. I found this work very interesting and my interest never waned the whole time I was with Roy.

The Engineer was a man named Crutchley `The Baron' who hardly ever came out of his office. Men were frightened of him and this fear was instilled into me - even though I had not done anything wrong. Whenever he went past me, I would start to sweat nervously. He was probably the nicest man you could ever wish to meet, and he knew he could rely upon his foreman and the leading hands to run the job. He was a very tall erect man built like a Guards CSM.

After several weeks and many alterations, the `Body Turnover Truck' would be ready to go over to the paint booth. It had four wheels around its bulk and we had to push it round. It must have weighed a ton, and consequently it would veer off into its own direction.

Although the designs were created in the Drawing Office, Roy would add his own modifications which would improve it in many ways. However, he received no recognition for these bright ideas, because Roy's ideas would be swallowed up by the Drawing Office and used on the finished model. Roy was the type of fella who didn't mind them using his ideas, so long as it made life easier for him. But Roy, you were not getting any extra money for your ideas!!

We would arrive at the paint spraying booths after bouncing off several walls swearing and short of breath. The completed model consisted of a length of 4 inch pipe right up the middle and off centre - this being about 20 feet long with two 6 foot diameter wheels at either end: like the wheel of a ship, and the whole thing would swivel around in a 360 degree turn.

The first designs brought out were even heavier, but we somehow managed to get them to the paint shop; sometimes having to travel around the factory as they were very reluctant to go around corners. It became quite an event: like the launching of a ship, because as we arrived with the latest model, a loud cheer would come up from the paint shop and the paint sprayers would come out with some choice wisecracks like, "Here's another Titanic!"

One of the men had suggested that we all go on Charles Atlas courses to build a bit of strength up so that we could turn the contraption over. Roy would sometimes look hurt and I felt sorry for him as he tried to show them how easy it was to turn them over ably assisted by me. I would be at the other end and as we both turned the wheel, the whole mass of pipe and steelwork would rotate, and on a given signal from Roy, I would have to plunge the pin into a hole to stop the thing from turning back on its force of gravity and falling to the bottom of its rotation.

On many occasions I would miss the hole and the machine would spin freely out of control on its axis with Roy hanging on for all he was worth at the other end, and screaming at the top of his voice red around the gills, "You dozy bastard....get the pin in!" and many other shop floor phrases reserved for a wet behind the ears apprentice!

What with Roy shouting and screaming, and the paint sprayers on the sideline not knowing whether to laugh, cry or assist in the general melee, I was really trying my hardest to locate that hole with the pin. However, in the end, I had to burst out laughing uncontrollably, much to the annoyance of Roy, who was still hanging onto the wheel - feet gradually being lifted into the air as the weight of the machine started to move slowly to its base.

The main concern for Roy was the thought of a month's work crashing all around and being destroyed in one minute. Luckily, I found the hole and it stopped with a jerk and nearly took it off its feet.

"Put some hair around it," the paint sprayers were shouting.

"Put a ton of lead weights in it," I thought to myself, as that would balance it.

We would then need a crane to take it round to the spraying booths.

I had been warned about practical jokes, but did not know what to expect and in what form they would be.

"Go up to the stores and ask for a long stand, will you, there's a good lad," instructed Roy. On arrival at the stores I asked the craggy little storeman, Wacker Wakefield, "Could I have a long stand, please?"

"Wait there a minute and I'll get you one," he replied.

About half an hour had elapsed. The storemen were always in with the tradesmen on practical jokes, but unfortunately this one had backfired on Roy, as he was struggling to lift a pump. Eventually Roy appeared looking annoyed.

"Have you got it?" he asked.

Wacker then reappeared and said, "You've had it," and laughed.

"No I haven't," I innocently replied.

"How long have you been standing there?" asked Wacker.

"About half an hour," I replied indignantly - and then the penny dropped!

The foreman had now appeared worrying about the pump that Roy had left, then realising what was going on and gave ROY a mild telling off!

Of course, there would be many other occasions when practical jokes would be played, but by this time I had sussed them all out. For example: glass hammers, bubbles for spirit levels and, the classic, a rubber hammer to keep the job quiet!

On many occasions I would be in the welding shop, but this particular day was my first and I was holding pieces of metal to be welded onto the main channel. I was doing this for a couple of hours and had not been forewarned about the electric arc and the rays it gave off.

When I returned to the Millwrights Shop apparently my face was as red as a Crewe Alex scarf. Again, I got a telling off - through no fault of my own really, although I expect I had been told by the apprentice supervisor, but had forgotten.

"Always cover your face whilst in the welding bay," I was instructed by the Union Man. An arc burn on the face and especially in the eye can be very painful when the ball of the eye is scarred and it would be very sore for days afterwards.

The Union would advise and fight for better conditions and were doing a very good job; they were certainly needed on the shop floor. I had joined the Union because it was my choice to do so, realising that they were genuinely concerned for the welfare of the working man. They did manage to get things altered through negotiating and not by striking - something that was to commence in the 60's, and was always politically motivated. It was like joining a club of one's choice, not being forced to join as in the closed shop, a something resented by many tradesmen.

My asthma was still hanging around, but I tended to shrug it off, as I had many more things to occupy my mind, while learning all the crafts of the trade. What I will say to all asthma sufferers is: never give up. Eventually the problem will go. That was my motto. Although I still had a few years to go before it cleared up, I was always thinking positively.

All of the machinery in the Millwright's Shop looked twice as large as anywhere else - mainly because most of the work was heavy maintenance.

The power hammer would be going from dawn until dusk; the full nine hours of the shift on some days, and we were still working a 48 hour week which incorporated working on a Saturday morning.

Bill, the man who operated the power hammer, had been a blacksmith in the old tradition and had developed very muscular arms over the years, as a result of banging away on the anvil. Bill always maintained that the power hammer took all the toil out of the blacksmiths days, and he was quite happy with the modern day workhorse.

The small anvil would not be adequate for the large pieces of metal he had to hammer into shape.

With all the dust, the constant hammering and the giant guillotine bouncing up and down, it was like a day on the Somme at the height of the battle. The noise was literally deafening.

Sheet metal workers would throw their individual notes in while they knocked a piece of 8 x 4 sheet metal into some elaborate shape; mechanical saw blades wearing their way through big chunks of 6" diameter solid round bar; the radial arm drill with all its many devices for locking and feeds sometimes being accidentally knocked and bringing the drill in at the wrong place; Welding Bays with the splatter off the end of the electrodes sending out their fiery sparks like erupting volcanoes and invariably landing on unprotected skin and burning holes to be there forever; the screams of the windy gun as pilot holes were drilled into the sheet metal as the Tin Bashers tried to line up off cuts into a perfect conical shape, and sighing sighs of relief as they fitted perfectly.

All of these noises would be tolerated in a day's work, as men strove to contribute to produce the best car in the world.

Roy would often give me jobs to do on my own now, some successful, some big failures - but I was learning.

The Millwrights Shop was well laid out - the plumbers had their working benches alongside the tin bashers in one half of the bay, and the fitters and the turners were on the other side. I was to move around all the different trades during my 5 years, including a spell in the Drawing Office.

Now and then, if Roy was waiting for another job, he would take me on a tour of the factory, in order that I could get an idea of the main production line, and how it functioned. I was able to see all the little bits and pieces that went into making the great Rolls Royce.

There would be rows and rows of multi spindled drilling machines, centre and turret lathes on the assembly line, spitting out thousands of nuts and screws. People would be standing there like zombies pressing buttons and lifting levers as machine tools came down on to the engine block drilling out the holes. The engine block would then move along slowly on rollers to the next stage, tapping of holes etc and so on until it went through the very stringent inspection at the end of the line.

Roy's Wife worked on the line and he would often stop for a chat. I could also move around and talk to some of my friends of that time in the various departments spread around the factory.

Everything at Rolls Royce never ceased to amaze me, mainly because I was new into the trade.

One day we went into the Engine Testing Department to change a filter. The man in charge of the department told me that this particular Rolls Royce engine had been running non-stop since before the War, with only the oil being changed.

In the early 50's Rolls Royce completed about 30 cars a week. Automation was just starting to come into the car industry but Rolls Royce prided themselves on the hand finished car for a long time afterwards.

To just sit in one of these marvels of machinery, knowing that one could never, ever possibly own one, was an experience never to be forgotten. The smell of the leather upholstery, the wood finish on the dashboards, all done by a special type of craftsman.

Eight coats of paint would be put on each of the bodies to give it that immaculate finish. Unfortunately this craft was to be speeded up by the `Body Turnover Trucks', as they were appropriately called.

As far as I was concerned, anything alongside a Rolls Royce would be seen as just a truck, in comparison.

The Shah of Persia visited the factory one day to see how his car was being modernised. It already had smoked glass all around so he was probably having air conditioning installed. This would be 1955. I could only look around in disbelief at all these famous people, because, up until then, I had only read about them in the newspapers, or maybe a brief comment had been made about them in school.

Cars would be sent back from all over the world if they had been involved in accidents; they would be completely stripped down in order to see if there were any flaws in the chassis or the metal. At this particular time a sports model had been returned - namely the Bentley Continental, which had been involved in a crash in Italy at a speed unheard of in this Country of 120mph. The car was hardly recognisable but on close examination it was found that the paint, in which the paint sprayers prided themselves, was not cracked but had peeled back like a piece of bark off a tree. The engine in the Continental was as long as the Mini Minor and had remained intact after the impact, whilst the body had concertinaed. The engine was that finely balanced, it was said that you could blow on the fan blade and the engine would rotate for an hour.

To think that this marvellous engine would now have to go for scrap and maybe used in another Rolls Royce.

It was an experience in the Finishing Shop where the final completed cars would go through many inspections before being allowed out of the factory for testing.

The price of a Rolls Royce then was in the region of £10,000, with eight white horses under the bonnet, the world would undoubtedly be your oyster. It was a King's ransom to pay, but then again, only Kings and Shahs could afford them.

M. O'KEEFE

F. FERNYHOUGH

J. SAUNDERS

R. BOLTON

M. JOHNSON

K. SHERWIN

CLASS 5T 1953

CREWE GRAMMAR

D. PRESTON

A. HANCOCK

A. MILLIGAN

I. GOOLDING

C. DICKIN

P. BAILEY

BRYLCREEM your hair

Keeps hair in top form

DENIS COMPTON
1949

For handsome, tidy hair that keeps its good looks all through the day, use Brylcreem, the perfect hair dressing. Whether it's a day out in the open or in the office, you can rely on Brylcreem to keep you right on top. For Brylcreem not only gives the hair life and lustre; the pure emulsified oils it contains tone up the scalp and prevent Dry Hair. Brylcreem your hair and make smartness your goal. Brylcreem is supplied in jars and tubes.

BRYLCREEM — THE PERFECT HAIR DRESSING

DENIS COMPTON, MIDDLESEX AND ENGLAND

FATHER WITH "MOGGY MINOR" 1954 SHAVINGTON NR NANTWICH

CHAPTER THIRTY SEVEN

"The Haircut"

'Haircuts', were my Father's favourite subject - why, I could never quite understand, because he was completely bald! From the age of 11, I seemed to be permanently in the Barber's Shop. "That hair's getting too long....go and get it cut on Saturday," were the words I dreaded.

My Father insisted that I use a Barber's Shop that was situated at the top of Edleston Road in Crewe - probably because he had given the Barber strict instructions for it to be "Cut down to the wood," as he jokingly put it.

I arrived early on the Saturday morning but there was a queue as usual, although I can't think why, because he was no Vidal Sassoon. As soon as the Barber opened the door, the older men nudged me out of the way so that they could get off to their fishing or take their pigeons for a walk(!), release them and hope they would fly back to the loft. This was their way of training the pigeons up for the big races.

My Granddad was a hard trainer. If the pigeons didn't land on the loft board immediately, instead of strutting up and down the house roof, `billing and cooing', then my Granddad would be very annoyed - to say the least! On many occasions a pigeon would arrive back long before any of the other birds in the district had reached the outer limits of the Wirral. I think he was telepathic where pigeons were concerned, because about half an hour before they were due to arrive, he would take a chair out into the backyard and sit there looking into the sky, jumping up at every bird that appeared on the horizon, only to realise that it was an old crow, before sitting down again muttering.

My Gran would be watching from behind the lace curtains trying to control her laughter, but overdoing it sometimes and my Granddad would glare in her direction.

His next move was to bring out a tin of dried peas and start rattling it as one of his pigeons had landed on the roof, and was strutting up and down. Granddad would start off very politely, "Come on my old beauty," he would whisper, whilst at the same time giving the tin several rattles and throwing odd peas onto the loft landing board in an attempt to entice the pigeon down. After repeating this three or four times with no effect, he would start to get very annoyed and the language would start to get a little heavy and even the parentage of the pigeon was now in jeopardy.

At this point my Gran would be holding her sides with laughter, and tears would be streaming down her face. If only they had gone straight into the loft and let him take the ring off their legs to put into the clock, then life would have been much easier for him and he would have won many more prizes, and money. However, that's another story!

The point was that after being first in the queue outside the Barber's Shop, I had now been demoted to 8th inside the shop and some of the men in the queue looked as though they had had their hair cut the previous day!

I picked up a copy of a tatty Picture Post with a picture of a girl in a bathing suit on the front cover, but several men looked at me and frowned, so I quickly opened it up only to be confronted by more scantily clad girls in bathing suits!

"It'll make you go blind looking at them!," one stubby faced man said, as he leaned over to get a better look.

At last, a page with good old Winston on it, and I could feel all the eyes on me now, so I moved my head from side to side as if reading the magazine, much to their annoyance. When I put the magazine down there was a mad scramble to look at it.

In the meantime, the two Barbers were cutting and clipping chunks of hair with clumps falling to the floor all around the swivel chair. One of the Barber's was still using hand shears and as he cut I noticed the tendons and the muscles that had developed on his arms due to the constant opening and shutting of the shears. He did use them extremely skilfully, although I thought if he only used the electric ones I would have been on my way home by now!

It was a cold snowy morning in January and I was wearing my school uniform, with my cap perched on the back of my head. I kept the cap on until it was my turn to get my hair cut - after I had been in the Barbers Shop for about an hour. The smell of Brylcreem was overwhelming but some of the customers had the audacity to request Silvikrin! This was obviously more expensive, as the Barber gave quite a frown when it was requested.

I had now counted the number of bottles on the shelves about 10 times, and thought to myself, "Dennis Compton looks very smart with all that Brylcreem plastered on his hair, but I wonder who washes his pillow slips or does he, perhaps, wash his own hair every night before retiring to bed?" Whatever he did, he was one of the best cricketers of all time. Maybe the sun reflected onto the Brylcreem and dazzled the bowler as he ran up to bowl.

All of these silly thoughts were drifting through my mind as I waited my turn, and the next thing I knew, the Barber was making gestures at me through the mirror, waving his hands up and down. I hadn't realised that I was unconsciously picking my nose and he was waving his hands at me to stop!

I thought that at last it was my turn - but it was not to be. A giant of a man stood up lifting the chair with him as his buttocks were too wide for it! I certainly wasn't going to jump in front of this man!

Every now and then, a young boy would come through the curtains, sweep all the many coloured locks of hair into a pan with a brush, and then, without so much as raising himself, he drifted back out again, only to return to watch the Barber very attentively; he was an apprentice. Was he learning, or was he brain dead? I could never really tell. Maybe he became the greatest hairdresser the world had ever known, who knows?

It was now just after 10 o'clock and my calculations told me that it was my turn next - that is counting those who had arrived after we had first come in.

"Anything else Sir?," asked the Barber as he brushed the remnants of the bits of hair from around a customer's shoulders and neck.

The customer stood up and the Barber gave him a hand towel with which to clean the rest of the hair from around his person. He then gave the Barber his money and, in return, the Barber gave him what I thought was a shampoo sachet.

It would be a few years before I realised what, "Will there be anything else Sir?" was the code phrase for.

There was another boy along the row from me and he made a move to get into the chair, but I thought, "Oh no, I've been here too long!," and I dived into the chair.

The Barber had been putting the money into the till and on turning around he automatically shouted, "Next!," but he found me already sitting in the chair. I tried my best to make myself comfortable, although I always felt uneasy in the Barber's chair. I wondered if it was wired up.

The Barber pumped up the chair to the level he required, gave it a few swivels, before asking, "How would you like it Sir?," with a wry smile. It was as if he knew something that I didn't.

I would like to have said, "Could you cut it all around my cap and take chunks out of the back of my head?," and, assuming his reply would have been,

"We don't cut hair like that here Sir," I would have replied with,

"Well - you did last time!"

As the Barber swivelled the chair back and forth to get it to the correct position for a small school boy, I noticed a black shape appear at the window, peer in and then stroll on past. The Barber turned back with a grin on his face.

"That was my Father pounding the beat and who just happened to be passing to make sure I was in that Barbers Shop," I thought. What a considerate Father he was!!

Clippers and scissors were now going in unison as hair fell all around me off my shoulders onto the floor. As he cut the sides down to the wood, my fat face became even fatter, and I tried to contort it into a thin, lean face in the mirror. The Fred Astaire look maybe.

I was beginning to regret annoying the Barber by saying, "Do you want me to take my cap off?," because he had given me one of those, "You'll be sorry!" looks.

He had now worked around to the front of my head and what bit I had saved from last time was under threat. I had managed to comb it up into a bit of a wave (with a little help from the sugar and water), and I was quite proud of it because it stood up a good inch from my head and made my face look a lot leaner! Off it came I'm afraid, and it was left about a quarter of an inch long. Cutting the hair on the back of my head was the most painful part, as the hand shears did not always open as the Barber lost his concentration as he chatted away to the customers about the previous Saturday's football game at Gresty Road.

As he cut and sheared, my head would gradually move down in my effort to relieve some of the pain, and eventually my head would be on my knees! Why did they put those pictures of Dennis Compton in the window if they had no intention of cutting hair like them????

With chunks out from around my ears and the back of my head, it felt as though I had done 15 rounds with Rocky Marciano, instead of having my hair cut like Dennis Compton.

Really, there should have been no ooo's or ouch's in a Barbers Shop - it should have been a place of art and style. Finally the Barber had completed the cut.

"Would you like anything on, Sir?"

"Yes," I replied, "Plasters!"

This annoyed the Barber once again, as the shop was still full of potential customers who had grimaced through every shear, cut and piece of hair that had been prised off my head. One or two of them looked as though they were having second thoughts, but the Barber caught their glances through the mirror, and they stayed put! .....Ah - that's what the mirror was for!!

It certainly wasn't any good for the customer, as the Barber was already programmed to cut the way HE wanted to, and not how the customer wanted it.

Why didn't the Barber ask me, "Would there be anything else Sir?"

After brushing me down, he took a mirror off the shelf and held it behind my head, whereupon I saw a perfect haircut. I was sure it was a photograph of a perfect haircut used only for us schoolboys to make us think it was OK. It didn't show the scars and the places where pieces had been ripped out of my head as the shears failed to open.

Anyway, the Barber considered that I was now finished and lowered me down with a bang. As I hit the floor I shot out of the seat landing on my feet facing the till. I struggled to find my shilling and the Barber moved towards the door. However, fortunately I found the shilling stuck to my chewing gum. The

Barber took my payment and threw it into the till, turned and shouted, "Next!" to commence work on the next patient (as I now called them), only to be confronted by me with my hand held out for my change.

"What do you want?" he bellowed.

"Change," I replied with a smile.

He strode over to the till muttering and returned with my three pence change. It was all I had in the world, and my Father had said that I could keep the change - THREE OLD PENCE!! - this would buy some sweets. The Barber slammed the change into my hand and said, "Good Morning." To which I almost replied: "It was until I came here," but thought better of it because he was obviously a conversational friend of my Father's. How was I to know he wanted a tip?

As I made my way to the door, I waved to the other customers who were patiently waiting their turn, but there was no response as they were also fed up with having to wait so long.

The doorbell rang as I went into the street; I glanced back through the window and gave the Barber a smile. He gave me a long, hard stare as he automatically continued cutting away on another poor customer.

The cold wintry air hit the back of my head like a jug of cold water. This was one occasion that I was grateful of my cap to hide the scars and my bald scalp and, of course, to keep my head warm - although that was debatable!

As I proceeded to walk down Edleston Road, I glanced into numerous shop windows to see if my bald scalp was obvious and also to make sure that my cap was covering it - if not, I would adjust it. Several shopkeepers ran out of their shops and shooed me away.

Back home my Father was eagerly waiting to inspect and, as always, he would say,

"Bah....that's a good haircut lad; although you could have had a bit more off the sides."

"Anymore, and my ears would have dropped off!" I thought.

My Father wasn't at all concerned whether the haircut suited me or not. I did mention the scars on the back of my neck, but all I got from him was "You shouldn't have moved then, should you?."

Bless him. I couldn't win.

CHAPTER THIRTY EIGHT

Lassie - Gone Forever

Marilyn Monroe was quite big in films now and, together with Jane Russell, they made a tidy pair.

Poor old Marilyn was worried about men not appreciating her acting. I don't think many of the lads of my age were worried whether she could act or not, so long as she sang, "We're having a Heat Wave."

Tony Curtis was also flashing back and forth across the screen in many of his swashbuckling films, either on a chandelier or a Trapeze. His hair was always held immaculately in place and copied by most of my generation, with the quaff coming down almost over the eyes - a style also sported by all the Teddy Boys.

The "Teds" as they were called for short, were, on the whole, very smartly dressed and I cannot recollect many incidents in Crewe where there was any fighting with bike chains and knuckle dusters, as reported by the Press in London.

This was 1954-55 and the Teds were at their height of fashion, and gradually falling out of favour as new styles were now appearing almost every year as people had more and more money to spend. I have to admit that the Teds did certainly bring a bit of colour to the dreary early 50's.

The television had been around for a few years now. However, we could not afford one in our house, although we were invited into Mrs Hall's house, our next door neighbour at Goodall's Corner, whenever there were any special events on, for example, Show Jumping from London on a Saturday night, or even a Cup Final. We would watch anything then; even the Potters Wheel at the interval would be interesting to me.

My Mother would sit there completely bewildered by the television and amazed at the pictures coming through from

London, and the following day she just would not stop talking about the previous `television show', as she called it.

"How do the pictures travel through the air and into the television screen over hundreds of miles?," as a typical question relating to the television, and these same questions were asked about the wireless some years before.

It was still only the early 50's and it was the age of Captain Llewellyn and Pat Smythe who were to go on and win many events on the Show Jumping circuit. This was still a sport for only the well to do.

One of my Father's other bright ideas to attempt to bring some extra cash into the house, was to volunteer my labour to the pig farm in Sydney, just outside Crewe owned by a Mr Dawson.

I would go up to the pig farm during my school holidays, and I have to admit that out of all the work I have done, even up to the present day, that was by far the most strenuous! Fortunately it was only once a fortnight!

I would jump onto my bike at about 6am and cycle the 5 miles to Sydney. There would be no fear of never finding the place, because as I got within 2 miles of the farm, there would be this smell of pig muck wafting over the surrounding countryside.

Whether I was suffering from asthma or not, I still went to the farm, arriving at about 6.30am and, without more ado, the boss would instruct me to start cleaning the pigsties out before feeding. Well, the weight of that s... stuff - if I had worked there for a few months, I would have had arms on me like Popeye.

Pigs are extremely intelligent animals and, despite the myth, are quite clean. (It is only human beings that keep them locked up in sties in limited space), and once they get to know you, they greet you with a friendly grunt. The boars can be very bad tempered though, especially at breeding time and if I opened the gate they would try to knock me over to get at the sows in the next sty and, once I shut the gate, they would go for me. - biting my Wellingtons and other vulnerable parts of my body, until I had to jump out of the sty for fear of being badly injury.

A full grown boar was nearly as high as my shoulder in those days, as I was still quite small. I suppose the main reason for my lack of height was the constant attacks of asthma.

My next bout of hard labour was on a farm at Weston. I still had to get up early, but found this work more to my liking.

I was given the job of measuring the amount of milk produced every day for the Milk Marketing Board. Mr Proudlove owned the farm; quite a large farm as I recall, and there must have been over 100 cattle to milk every morning. The hard work started once the cows had been turned out of the shippons and out into the fields, and I had to clean all the sludge and slurry left during the night.

The farm was slowly becoming mechanised in that they had a mechanical shovel at the end of the shippon to lift all the stuff onto a wagon and eventually take it out to the midden to be thrown back onto the fields to enrich the soil. The farm was an organic farm, as were most farms in those days.

My Father thought that plenty of fresh air and hard work was the right formula for clearing my asthma - maybe he did have the right idea, but it did not clear mine at the time.

One night I arrived home from work to find my Mother and my Sister sitting down at the tea table. They were both crying, and my Father was also close to tears. I immediately thought that there had been a bereavement in the family, and I wasn't too far from the truth.

The bin men had arrived as usual on the Friday morning and they had to go around to the back of the house to collect the bin. My Sister, who was on holiday from school, was playing with Lassie on the lawn in the back garden, when the bin man appeared and startled the two of them. My Sister had now stood up and Lassie was barking playfully. The bin man then more or less put his arm on my Sister to put something between him and Lassie, as he edged around the wall to collect the bin. He picked the bin up and started to move rapidly away to the front garden. Lassie then ran at him and nipped his leg.

Apparently this particular bin man made quite a commotion about the whole episode and reported the incident to the Clerk of Works who was given no option but to report the matter to the police.

My Father was on duty at the time that the incident was reported, but was told as soon as he came back in to report off duty. After finishing his shift at 2pm he had arrived home and immediately asked my Mother what had happened. Of course, my Mother denied everything saying that the bin man had shaken my Sister and that was why the dog had gone for him.

Without further ado, my Father put Lassie on her lead - she thought he was taking her for a walk and was wagging her tail in excitement. They only walked across the road to the nursery, as my Father was aware that the owner of the nursery had a 12-bore shotgun. The man at the nursery pleaded with my Father, but to no avail, and poor Lassie was put to rest.

I could see that my Father was very upset and I had to go up to by bedroom to have a cry, because I knew that Lassie was innocent. It was reminiscent to one of the old movies in which the audience knows that the victim is innocent, but cannot do anything about it. However, in movies there is always a happy ending because justice prevails when a witness to the crime comes forward at the last moment.

The following day my Father said that he could not have people talking about our dog, a policeman's dog, biting people! If a case of a dog biting someone on my Father's beat had arisen he said, "What could I have done if they had known that our dog had been let off?"

If only that bin man had not made such a commotion. He came again the following week and must have been completely unaware that my Father had had Lassie destroyed, because he said to my Mother, "Where's the dog then?"

My Mother immediately burst into tears and then gave him a good dressing down and had to be restrained from doing anything silly by my Sister.

There was nothing wrong with that bin man at all. I can now see his point of view in reporting the incident, because he did have to call at our house every week. I knew for a fact that there were many more dogs in the neighbourhood and they were a lot more vicious than Lassie, and that same bin man would have to call at those houses as well.

After my Mother's telling off, that bin man never came up our path again - or maybe my Father had had a quiet word with him.

Chapter Thirty Nine

Marilyn, Movies and Milburn Magic

During the 50's in Crewe there were about 7 cinemas within a hundred yards radius, including the Lyceum Theatre which had its entry facing the market. The Empire, The Kino, The Plaza, The Palace, The Gaumont, The Odeon and The Strand. These picture houses would be packed on the two sessions in the evenings. I remember such films as: `Brigadoon', Johnny Ray in `There's No Business Like Show Business', with Marilyn Monroe and many other stars of the halcyon days of Hollywood.

Burtons Snooker Hall was another place to go and pass a couple of hours before going to the cinema at night. Here, the cigarette smoke would be a murky blue due to the fact there was no ventilation, unless someone opened a door. I can still picture those huge long curtains of heavy velvet hanging to the floor in desperate need of a good cleaning, the windows thick with a yellow film of years of cigarette smoke drifting onto them.

The 1955 Cup Final was the Milburn final. My Father and a few of his drinking partners had obtained tickets for this final and one of them had to stand down as he'd been called to duty on that day, so my Father said that I could join them.

It was at the end of April and they had hired at Austin Sheerline for the day. Of course, there were no motorways so the journey to Wembley took about 6 hours, weaving through the A roads.

I can recall there was Frank Salisbury, Jack Gallagher and Harry Fitton - all members of the police football team at Crewe, and my Father kept saying, "Watch your language lads!"

There would be the usual banter between them all, but the main conversation would be between my Father and Frank

Salisbury who had the same hairstyles (bald!). My Father would start by saying that "Hair doesn't grow on busy streets," and Frank's response would be that it grew wild around his arse! At this point the four of them would roar with laughter.

Arriving at Wembley I was completely bewildered by the mass of colours moving along the Wembley Way - the black and whites of Newcastle and the blue and white of Manchester City and scarves and rattles were waved around. As the television was in black and white, it was very difficult to distinguish between the two teams on the hazy screen.

Manchester City had introduced the `Deep Centre Forward' in that Ron Revie would have the freedom of the middle of Park, the forerunner of the `Mid Field Players'. The `Revie Plan' was well tackled by the Newcastle team in that they moved their defence forward en-bloc as Revie sent pass after pass through, only for the Manchester City forwards to be caught `offside' time and time again.

We had a position right at the back behind the goal and luckily my Father would lift me up every now and again so that I could get a better view of the whole stadium. Eventually the man in front was persuaded to move over and let a smaller chap stand in front of me, and I could then see most of the ground. It looked so big seeing it for the first time and the atmosphere was electrifying especially just prior to Kick-Off when the Military Band struck up with `Abide with Me', and grown men were moved to tears.

Once the Duke of Edinburgh had met the two teams there was a roar as the teams broke rank to go to their ends to kick in, until the referee blew for the two Captains to `Toss Up' for which end they were going to be allocated in the first half. Newcastle won the toss and Jimmy Scoular decided to remain as they were. It didn't really matter at Wembley which way you kicked, because the pitch was perfectly flat like a snooker table.

Within a minute of the kick-off, Len White took a corner from the right and `Wor Jackie' met it with his head on the edge of the penalty area, and it went like a bullet straight into the top right hand corner. Bert Trautman could only stand and watch because he was completely off balance, as he had anticipated the ball going into the other corner of the net.

1-0 to Newcastle and they went on to win the game 3-1 and so crown a hat trick of appearances in the early 50's at Wembley winning a further two matches.

After the game and the presentation of the cup to Newcastle, the crowd surged for the exits and I was literally lifted off my feet and carried out of the ground with my Father screaming, "Hang onto me or Frank!." This I did, and arrived outside the ground rather shaken to be led back to the Limousine.

As we drove away from Wembley I can recall Harry Fitton waving to the crowds as if he were Royalty, because this car was very similar to that which had brought the members of the Royal Family to Wembley. The crowds were waving back and my Father and the other two were laughing that much that tears were streaming down their faces; it was good to see.

We pulled into a grotty old café on the road into London and had something to eat. Afterwards we headed into the middle of London, Piccadilly Circus, where we went to a pub. I cannot recall the name of the pub, but it was the old traditional type, and probably a singing house as well. The windows were of frosted glass with patterns, and various types of stouts imprinted into the glass in sepia colours.

It was about 7pm by this time and as we pulled up in the limousine quite a large crowd had gathered, anticipating that someone very important was going to emerge from such a high class car on Cup Final Day. Harry Fitton got out of the car first, as he was a very distinguished looking man at the best of times; he always stood erect and looked extremely smart. Harry really laid it on as he walked up to the pub waving and gesturing in a very royal way.

"It's Harold MacMillan!," said someone in the crowd.

Harry was closely followed by Jack Gallagher, my Father and Frank Salisbury who kept the charade going. I was left in the car for the night and was ordered not to venture out - on no account. My Father had left me with his new watch to look after. Needless to say, I became very bored and decided to go for a walk around. "I might as well see the sights of London," I though to myself.

I had only ever read about London in the newspapers or been told about it by others, so I was going to take advantage of being here. I was not too far from Piccadilly, so I walked around with my head held high, mouth agape watching all the neon lights flashing around `Piccadilly Circus', flickering their advertisements across the murky circus with Eros balancing on one leg firing an arrow. Coca-Cola and Player Cigarettes were the main neons.

As I moved away from the Circus, a coach with two horses pulling it came into view and there. sitting at the front, was Kay Kendal - beautifully made up in feathers and a large Victorian hat. Apparently they were advertising Agatha Christie's `Mousetrap' in only its second year.

After seeing Kay Kendal, a lady I had only seen in films, go passed on that coach and feeling the draught as it passed just a couple of yards away, I felt as though I had been in a film with them myself.

Glancing around on several occasions I had noticed the same man following me; I panicked as I thought he was after my Father's watch, and I was determined to hold onto that watch, come what may! After reading books about London and how it was full of pick-pockets and thieves and remembering Oliver Twist and all that, my little heart started to increase a few beats and began to pound faster and faster, as I started to run for the Underground. The man following me also increased his pace and I knew for definite that he was after the watch, because as he came alongside me he fiddled with my wrist, trying to undo the strap.

Although there were hundreds of people milling around, there was nothing I could do because if I had shouted out, I would not have been heard. I therefore decided to run again and proceeded down another tunnel and up and back into the same street where smartly dressed women were leaning against the walls of buildings; their faces were made up like film stars. "Fancy a good time love?" they asked.

I eventually found my way back to Piccadilly and by this time I had taken my Father's watch off and put it into my trouser pocket, just in case the pick-pocket caught up with me again.

There was an on-duty policeman strolling by, but I'm afraid I couldn't say a word to him either, because by the expression on my face, I must have looked suspiciously guilty of something - like a modern day Oliver Twist perhaps.

The thief was still lurking in the background and I knew I had to guard this watch with my life, because I had left the car and wandered around against my Father's orders, and was now on the point of losing his watch.

The man came in close contact once more and I lashed out at him, more in desperation than in temper. I thought it was a good right hander, only to discover that the blow hit in the mid-rift somewhere. Luckily it did the trick because people in the vicinity were starting to notice and he ran off not wanting to be caught. I ran for the car as fast as my little legs would carry me and, once inside the car, I locked all the doors, lay on the back seat and fell asleep. I have no idea what time my Father came out of the pub, because when I woke up we were well on our way home.

CHAPTER FORTY

Learning the Hard Way

I had commenced Crewe Technical College in Hightown which went hand in glove with starting an apprenticeship, and several of the lads from my form at school were also in the class studying for an ONC: Peter Bailey, Roger Bolton, Mike Johnson and Dave Preston, all from 5T.

Hightown was in the old part of Crewe and many buildings were built with the old red clay brick, similar to those used in the Manchester area and famed on the Lowry paintings. The college itself was like a wedge about to be driven down Victoria Street - a three cornered junction. One road led down towards the swimming baths and the Hop Pole Pub, made famous by my Father, and the other road to Rolls Royce along West Street.

I found the maths just as difficult here as I had done at school, but I really tried to concentrate. Unfortunately I could not sustain the effort and had a tendency to doze off a little in the afternoons (after my chips and a pint which I devoured at the Market Square), only to be stirred by the lecturer shouting, "What do you think Goolding?."

"Oh I thought it was a good goal," I once replied, obviously not realising what I had said, because I had been staring at the window which I had marked out in my mind into a Wembley pitch, and imaginary players were running around the panels.

At lunchtimes we would often wander into Crewe town centre and buy a bag of chips and take them into the open air market behind the Crewe Theatre, and study the billboard advertising of the forthcoming attractions.

One particular week the board announced that `Jane' of Daily Mirror fame was going to make an appearance at the theatre, something unheard of in Crewe and there was some commotion from the local press and the 'Keep your clothes on' Society. "We'll have to have a look at that," said one of the lads, after seeing the board showing Jane in a very provocative position.

"It'll be a laugh," said another.

"Not at our age," I thought to myself.

Anyway, after licking our greasy fingers and neatly rolling our newspaper wrappings into a ball and doing a few juggling tricks with our feet, ending with a final shot for goal and into the wastepaper bin, it was back to college.

I usually purchased the Daily Mirror - a good working man's paper, mainly for the sports and Garth and, sometimes, I might just happen to glance at the Jane strip, because it was next to Garth!! I often wondered why they never got married, appearing so close to one another every day for so many years in the newspaper.

As it happened, I did not go to see Jane, but I often wondered if any of the other lads did.

Back in college we were having a very uninteresting lecture on moments of force and how to calculate them. "There has got to be a better system than this," I thought to myself, because I was an out and out practical lad. Why I never verbally relayed my thoughts I do not know, but instead I just kept them to myself. The gift of the gab was a marvellous gift to possess, but sadly it was never to be given to me.

At the end of the day it was a short walk down to the Bus Station at Crewe town centre and home to Shavington. Travelling on the bus was a luxury paid for by the company while attending the college; otherwise it was on the old bike everywhere. I had some narrow escapes on my bike, especially on one particular occasion when trying to make it home on a punctured back tyre. The back would go in all directions, rather than forward, and as a result I spent most of my time in the ditches lining the route from Crewe to Shavington. I had to walk up the hills otherwise I would get a crippling cramp in my calf muscles, but I would freewheel down them - a very dangerous practice as the hill at Gresty corner was very steep and swept around into a right angled bend.

As I reached the bottom on the flat tyre, the inner tube was wrapped around the spokes, ripped to pieces and irreparable;

whilst the tyre, which was already threadbare, had holes in it where the inner tube had bulged through.

Halfway down the hill the bike was now completely out of control and cars were overtaking and peeping their horns as they went passed me. The bike was hitting the kerb and bouncing back into the middle of the road. By this time the wheel had sustained a slight buckle and the whole bike was jolting up and down like a rodeo horse. It was impossible to jump off, because the bike had picked up quite a bit of speed and all I could do was hope there would be a soft landing at the bottom! But I'm afraid this was not to be. The bike veered off across the road into someone's front path before coming to an abrupt halt just in front of the garage doors. I hit the garage doors with a loud thud. The owner came out of the house thinking that I had been hit by a car, and ran out into the road to see if she could catch the culprit's car registration number, but returned to me shaking her head.

"Would you like me to ring for an ambulance, or would you prefer a cup of tea?" she asked, before making her way to her house to telephone for an ambulance.

"No!" I shrieked. By this time I had scrambled to my feet after untangling my arms and legs from the bike. I gathered most of the parts of the bike and limped home to spend the next couple of days trying to repair it.

That bike and I went through hell over the years I had it - dynamo hanging off that wouldn't work in the wet, brake rubbers worn down to the metal that would only stop the bike when the metal parts jammed into the spokes, with the inevitability of me being launched through the air and parting company with the bike for a while, the seat (or rather, what was left of the seat) rather hard and prone to jolting back without warning, resulting in me disappearing onto the mudguard.

The racing handle bars were my pride and joy, but eventually I had no rubber grips left to hold onto, and in the wet the bare metal would become very slippery and both hands would pull off the handle bars without warning and with bruising consequences.

As the bike got older and became more rickety and out of shape, the chain would come off every time I put a bit of pressure on the pedal. Luckily the chain was bone dry - otherwise

I would have been in an even bigger mess than I already was! (This was probably the reason for all the problems - no oil on the chain!).

My Father was never concerned about the condition of my bike, as long as the lights were working at night. It didn't matter if I got killed, as long as my lights were still on when the ambulance arrived to pick the bits up!

Repairing punctures was my Mother's speciality, because the patches would never stick properly for me. I would spend about two hours stripping the tyre and the inner tube from the wheel. I would use a couple of my Mother's favourite spoons as leverage to remove the tyre from the wheel (and very threadbare tyres), and if I used extra leverage, for example a screw driver, I would always end up putting another in the inner tube. There were so many bulges from the inner tube bursting through the tyre as I pedalled along, that I could almost tell the time by the number of bumps that hit the brake rubbers.

After repairing the puncture, now came the really exciting part of reassembling tyre and inner tube with bits of old tyre neatly placed over the holes in the tyre to hold the inner tube in place.

I would begin the painstaking the task at the back of the house, holding the spoons and trying to lever the tyre over the rim while holding the screw driver in my teeth to try to get the final bit of the tyre onto and over the rim. With one foot on the wheel to stop it rolling around on the wheel hub and chain cog, I would now be down the side of the house. My knee in the spokes seemed to steady the whole wheel for a while, at least giving me enough time to remove one spoon and put it into a different position on the periphery of the wheel rim, and at last I would get down to the final bit.

Prayers would come thick and fast now as I asked for just a couple of seconds for the tyre to hold on and for me to lever the last piece over. By this time the wheel would have dragged me onto the footpath on the Nantwich Road, but I was determined to get that last bit on - even if I ended up in Crewe with it! I would get some strange looks from people passing by on their way to the shops, and drivers would peep their horns and smile sympathetically, and old women would cross over to the other side of their innocent smiles met my scowls.

Finally it would go onto the wheel and I'd give out a shriek of delight. "I hope I haven't pinched the inner tube! Please God - no!" I thought to myself

As I lifted myself up off the footpath and picked the wheel up at the same time, my Mother would come around the corner of the house. "Have you done it yet? I want you to go to the shops for me?" she asked.

My Mother always had a way of stating the obvious. There I would be, standing with a wheel in my hand and she would ask if I'd done it yet! No wonder my Father was so bad tempered. "Does it look as if I've done it," I would say sweetly.

"There's no need to take that tone of voice," would come the reply.

"Balls," I'd whisper.

"What did you say?" my Mother demanded to know.

"I think I've lost the *balls* out of the bearing," with the emphasis on the balls, I shouted back.

"Oh," was my Mother's response.

Back at the main part of the bike and about to fit the wheel back into the frame, my Mother would follow me and offer her advice as if she was an expert on bikes. "Why don't you pump it up and see if it stays up first?" she would suggest.

"No, it will be alright," I'd say, having every confidence in the way I had stock the patch onto the inner tube, carefully cleaning the holed area and allowing the correct time for the solution to go tacky - it couldn't possibly fail.

After spending a further half hour putting the wheel in position on the forks and tightening the nuts up, giving the wheel a few trial spins checking that it was running true to the forks, and not catching the brake blocks, I was about to pump the tyre up again when, to my horror, I realised that I hadn't put the chain on. "Bastard chain!" I shouted, not caring whether the whole village heard me or not, and off it would come again.

Chain on, pump up the tyre and then off I would go into the house for a rest.

"Don't get any oil on my chairs," my Mother would shout.

After about 10 minutes had elapsed, I went out to see if everything had gone to plan, only to be met with a loud hissing noise. I had had just about enough now, and picked the bike up by the two wheels and, after summoning a colossal amount of strength from somewhere, I threw the bike right down to the bottom of the garden. As the bike hit the ground there was an even louder hissing noise, so I would throw the screw driver at it as well, and then wander out of the garden and along the footpath for a while, to bring my temper back to normal.

By the time I returned to Goodall's Corner, my Mother would have the bike stripped down again and have the puncture repaired perfectly. I had no idea how she managed it, but they always stayed up afterwards. What's a Mum for anyway?

That bike and I remained together for many years and if it could have talked, it would have had quite a few tales to tell!

All in all, Crewe was the beginning of my grown up life - adolescence if you like, and I had already learnt many things about the ups and downs of a working man's life.

Working at Rolls Royce provided me with more independence. The tradesmen at Rolls Royce were very good at teaching young lads the engineering techniques that were to be their future and their bread and butter. Although they all had a sense of humour, it was restricted to the lunch hour and break times, as they maintained that they should lead by example and practical joking was non-existent then because of the dangers that were around every corner. There would be lathe chippings shooting off in their own burning orbit, acid baths for the chrome work, fumes from the case hardening shop, guillotines jumping up and down cutting through sheet metal, waste cuttings flying around and attaching themselves to your boots etc.

It was now early 1956 and, on arriving home from work one day in January, my Mother announced that we were going to move in a couple of months. "I'm not going this time Mum - not halfway through my apprenticeship," I said to my Mother.

I had promised Mr Dyson, the Apprentice Supervisor, that I would not be moving again, and I did not want to break this promise. However, my Father had other ideas.

"You're coming with us, and no ifs or buts about it," said my Father in his usual understanding and considerate way.

I should have argued my case, but in those days my Father's word was the law in our house. I have often wondered how life would have evolved if I had remained in Crewe.

Years after we had departed Crewe, my Mother told me that

a Police Sergeant by the name of Mr Cartlidge had offered to take me in until I had completed my apprenticeship at Rolls Royce.

Having moved around a lot, I left Crewe after having a farewell booze-up at The White Lion at Weston with my friends. I had also made many friends at Rolls Royce. I had trusted anyone up until I reached the age of 18, and at this time as my life progressed, I discovered that some people are not as trustworthy as first thought.

My Father, after he had succeeded in getting me through Grammar School (no mean feat, let me tell you), forcing me to stay in most evenings to study maths, he then more or less let me get on with it and if I asked any questions he would simply answer, "Grammar School is out of my range." Little did he know that if he had only channelled his energies into learning, instead of muscle, he would no doubt have progressed a lot further in life.

Looking back, I think a lot of people's lives are a case of - "*If only...*" - this was certainly the case for me.

CHAPTER FORTY ONE

Out in the Big Wide World

In the September of 1955, Rolls Royce apprentices were sent on an all expenses paid trip to the Motor Show at Earls Court. It was here that I saw how the other half lived; there were people who could afford to buy any car they wanted and they would not even notice the money go out of their bank account. A bank account - what was that?? It must be something that only the people of London had.

The Rolls Royce stand was proudly exhibiting its new automatic gearbox and the brain box had been cut in half to enable people to get a general idea of how it worked. It was too complex for me I'm afraid, although many of the other apprentices understood it, because many of them had been working on it in the Experimental Department at Crewe.

The automatic gearbox was a good seller for Rolls Royce after the Motor Show of 1955. It was a very memorable day for me in the short time that I had been working for a living.

My wage at this time was £2.10s per week which was not a bad wage back then, and I was given 10 shillings pocket money, which would last me all week - well, NEARLY!

I was also approaching the Saturday night and Sunday morning stage of my life, or should I say Saturday night, and broke for the rest of the week.

My baptism into the world of alcohol took place at The White Lion at Weston where I would have three Black Velvets and think the world was my oyster, until I hit the fresh Weston air on my way over to the Village Hall for the Saturday night hop. I'm not sure whether it was the Guinness or the cider in the deadly concoction that gave me the courage to ask girls to dance - something I would not normally do.

The Village Hall had a live band (I did actually see the drummer move on one occasion), and they played everything from Irish jigs to quick steps, with the odd jive thrown in. For our 1/- entrance fee there would also be a buffet thrown in, because once it opened the whole lot would be devoured in 10 seconds flat!

After the dance we would all stagger home singing and laughing. As the ale worked itself around our brains, we would air our tonsils. I would do my impression of Johnny Ray's `Such a Night' with apologies to the great man. The noise would echo all around Weston. The singing would die down (so to speak!) as we passed the cemetery and as the moon shone over the gravestones, our pace would quicken up until we reached the railway bridge on the way down to The Hough.

We were all about the same age and in the same boat financially, although we were in different vocations; Phil Elson was training to be a watch maker in a jewellers in Crewe town centre, Alan Yoxall went onto the railways and became a train driver (how many of us wanted to be one of those as kids?), Mike Jackson joined the Police Force, and Des Jackson and Barry Houghton joined me at Rolls Royce.

Everything at that age was new and our minds were all geared to the same things - looking for girls (preservation of the human race), drinking, singing and football, but not necessarily in that order.

It was a good three mile walk to Goodall's corner and as we approached it our singing would die down, because that was where Constable Goolding lived. Some of the lads had another mile to go because they lived near Wybunbury.

First love is something that many young adolescents had to endure, and I would be no exception. It is a sort of pull imprinted in the brain that the male of the species must look for a mate - no matter what the consequences might be. I suppose an urge to produce the next generation.

However, first love does not always work both ways because, at the age of 17 I thought that when a girl showed as much interest in me as this particular girl did, it was forever - not so! I fell for this girl hook, line and *sinker*, to coin a phrase, with the emphasis on the sinker in my case.

This girl was quite a bit older than me, and had had a lot more experience of life, shall we say.

Sylvia treated me very well, knowing that I did not have much money at the best of times and could only just about pay to go to the cinema once a week, she paid for cigarettes; yes, she would bring a tin of Dumaurier and keep offering me one until I accepted - not a good idea with my asthma!

I can recall that Sylvia lived in a terraced house in Gatefield Street. She always had money to spend because she worked at a hairdressers in the town centre. She was very bouncy and sure of herself - a requirement if one wanted to succeed in this world. Her photograph had been in all of the local newspapers posing in a swimsuit having won a beauty contest at Butlins. She was a natural blonde and had very smooth skin like porcelain - any boy would have fallen for her, and she knew it. Sylvia was a bit of a rebel for the early 50's - she wore tight jeans etc on Sunday nights.

Prior to meeting Sylvia, a night out with the lads consisted of noting who was going with whom, sitting through a movie and then diving out of the cinema before `God Save the Queen!', to get the last two pints at Kettells on Mill Street. However, an evening at the cinema with Sylvia was very difficult. It was like escorting a film star - well, in my opinion anyway. I would feel so proud as we walked passed my friends who would be waiting to go into the `cheap seats' - a place that I had often been in myself!

Sylvia would insist on paying for the balcony seats - no doubt a good vantage point for her to see many of her ex-boyfriends - yes, I was a rebounder! I could just imagine everyone muttering as we strode passed the queues outside the cinema, "Who's that square with Sylvia?"

At this time in my life I was still very much under the close scrutiny of my Father, and I had to wear what he approved - 22 inch grey flannels and a blazer. In my own mind I would loved to have tried a Teddy Boy suit on, gone home and let my Father see, but I knew I would have been thrown out of the house with nowhere to go - after all, he was a copper.

One weekend Sylvia informed me that she was going away with her parents, so, off I went with my friends to the Odeon. We were standing in the queue in the pouring rain on one particular Sunday night waiting for the doors to open, when suddenly my friends started acting peculiar. They were trying to block my view and generally diverting my attention from something. As the cinema doors opened my friends literally pushed me forward. However, I'm afraid their efforts to prevent me from seeing Sylvia and her new boyfriend strolling passed as large as life, were not very successful. I could not believe what I was seeing! I was destroyed to say the least.

However, in a way, it was a lesson learnt early in life and it did prevent me from having a steady girlfriend for a few years after that incident - although eventually the right girl did come along.

I believe that Sylvia thought that by using me, she would get her ex-boyfriend back, but I'm afraid her little plan did not quite work out how she intended. She would often take me to her house when her parents were out and play many of her records (putting my miserable `collection' of three to shame - Heart Break Hotel, Around the Clock and Rock Island line). I don't know why I didn't realise what was going on at the time, as she kept on playing the same records over and over - Doris Day's `Secret Love' and Frankie Laine's `Answer Me,ah'. Oh well, such is life for a 17 year old, and an innocent one at that.

"It's good to be alive in 1955," was Spike Milligan's pet saying, although I wasn't convinced. It did affect my concentration on my main hobby - sport. I did manage to put the whole thing behind me eventually, and I soon realised that I was not the only person on the planet who would have to go through the pangs of first love or, maybe, second love and so on. My Mother didn't help much either once she discovered that my little fling had ended. She would go around the house singing, "Who is Sylvia, what is she," smiling to herself as she went about her housework. I think my Father was also relieved because he must have been tired of clouting me around the ears for riding my Sister's bike without lights on my many rides home from Crewe. Another ending to the perennial Rebounder.

It was now back to the Olde White Lion at Weston and the three pints of Black Velvet.

By this time spots were my main concern - there's always something isn't there? I would wake up in the morning and see yet another spot in a very noticeable position, usually on the end of my nose. Some of the spots would turn into painful boils after I had tried to get rid of them. The Doctor said it was my age and the environment I was working in - cutting oil and dust. He would give me a box of plasters and some cream - the plasters had holes in the middle and once put in position, on the end of my nose, gave the impression that I was trying to balance an object on the end of it! I persevered with them and left them on at night and hoped that the spot would disappear by the morning - but it was not to be. Some mornings the spot would resemble Mt Etna, throbbing and glowing.

Bits of bum-fluff were now appearing around my chin so I decided to try my Father's razor and shave the offending bits of hair off - many times cutting myself and ending up putting little pieces of toilet paper on in order to stop the bleeding. On many a night it would look as if I had just walked into a snow storm with pieces of paper all over my face. My Father blamed my Mother for getting cheap blades; he couldn't understand why they were not lasting as long as the others.

Guess what I got for Christmas that year? Yes - an electric razor! This was the in-thing for parents to buy their Sons at that age.

In 1955 I was 18 years of age and had been working for just over 12 months. My Mother was still buying my clothes, because there was no way that I could have possibly saved any of the pocket money that I was receiving. My Father would make sure that my Mother bought the very conservative type clothes - blazers etc.

The year of 1955 was a very eventful one for me as I was playing football and cricket for the Rolls Royce teams. I was also training with the Crewe Alexander Juniors on the hallowed Gresty Road Pitch - something I had dreamed of when I was much younger as I stood in the paddock, frozen stiff, waving my red and white scarf. I would go along to training with another lad from the village, Tony Hope. Many of the first teamers would also be there and this was an added bonus for me, because I could listen very intently to the instructions thrown out to the professionals, realising that they did swear just like ordinary men.

Swearing was something used in ordinary conversation at work and went unnoticed once I had been at work for a few months. My Father would swear and would be a frightening sight as he walked around the house, cursing this and that. It was "bloody this," "bugger that," or "sodden hell," and when he really got going his voice would reach a very high pitch and he would more or less screech at everyone within distance. "Shut up will you or you'll waken the dead!" my Mother would finally demand. That statement rather startled him and he would then shut up.

CHAPTER FORTY TWO

The Dancing Years

The next step, excuse the pun, was to learn to dance and preferably to jive. To me this would be a kick against society or a bit of devilment against my Father, because now he was starting to get more and more of a disciplinarian as I reached adolescence and he was saying things like, "Don't you ever bring any trouble here, because if you do, I'll swing for you!"

To me, that meant that I was going to die as well, so I never took any trouble home - much to the relief of my Mother. Anyway, what was the trouble I was going to take home? Getting some girl pregnant? There was NO chance of that - we were lucky to see a girl's ankles in those days. In those innocent days some girls actually thought that they could get pregnant if they stared at a boy for too long; therefore, passing glances were VERY brief. They say that eyes talk and most of the girls I looked at during my spotty adolescence had it clearly stamped on their eyes - "Get Lost!" - well, most of them anyway.

Dancing years meant the 7.30pm bus from Goodall's corner with my friends to Crewe and alighting at Mill Street right outside Rattigan's Dancing Studio. We were all 17 years of age and everything was new as we felt out way into the big wide adult world - Phil Elson, Mike Jackson, Alan Yoxall and myself, all with shoes gleaming - a condition of entry into the studio.

The admission fee for the studio was 2/- which paid for the instructions and the music was played on an old gramophone. After paying our fee it was up a staircase and the music of Victor Sylvester wafted around the corridor like one of the old Humphrey Bogart films. It was then into the main dance hall with its highly polished wooden floor and the revolving crystal glass in the middle, to give it even more atmosphere. Just inside the door on the wall was a chart showing feet in the various steps of many different dances. "I'll never learn all those steps," I thought to myself.

I did eventually learn to do the waltz and I more or less did the same step to every dance that was played. I could never ever get the hang of the Tango, although some of my friends were quite natural dancers. The Tango, when danced by a good dance team, is very nice to watch and I can understand why all the women would swoon over Rudolph Valentino in the 1920's - he was the master of the Tango and no doubt a lot of women too.

At the beginning of the lessons Mrs Rattigan would have the girls on one side of the room and the boys opposite, and then she would give a demonstration with Mr Rattigan - her back arched like a Spanish bullfighter. Mr Rattigan's head would be held aloof, his moustache bristling in time to the music. Oh, those turns - they made them look so simple as they whirled up to the far end of the studio. They would finish and take a bow as if to say, "Follow that."

After the demonstration we formed two circles - one inside the other, with the girls forming the inside circle. The two circles would then rotate in opposite direction to the tune of a Paul Jones record and when the music stopped, the person opposite you was your partner for the following dance. This was an extremely good method of getting everyone to know each other for the night, although there would be a lot of shuffling around as lads moved up and down to try and get opposite the pretty girls, and Mr Rattigan would get quite annoyed if the scrambling and shuffling went on for too long, and he would swiftly call a halt.

"Now, if we're all quite ready, we'll start the music - a Waltz to start with. Thank you Henri," he would call to the gramophone operator.

Henri was a bit of a character; he had an eye for the women, in between changing the records he would be watching the girls and occasionally winking at the pretty ones. He had a little brush which he cleaned each record with before putting it on the turntable and for a bit of fun he would touch some of the girls on the shoulder as they passed by - giggling and smiling like they do. The girls took in all in good fun but Mrs Rattigan was not amused and even seemed to be jealous when Henri looked at the girls.

During the course of the evening Henri would have a dance with Mrs Rattigan and I noticed he stood much closer to her than to Mr Rattigan, who had now gone downstairs to collect the evening's takings from the doorman.

I thought that my dancing was now progressing quite well - it was just the turns I couldn't get the hang of. When I came to the end of the room, I would tend to turn my partner straight around, instead of going into the Victor Sylvester glide around. I must have looked like one of those clockwork soldiers as I shuffled around the floor. There were mirrors placed around the hall to help individuals to improve their posture and style, and on looking in one of these mirrors as I flashed by I looked just like "Question Mark" holding onto a capital "X."

Mr and Mrs Rattigan would mingle amongst the eager pupils and cut in now and then to show individuals the finer art of the dance movements. Mr Rattigan was a tall, slim man in a charcoal suit with Dickie Bow to match, ideally built for dancing, especially the Waltz in which he excelled. In his enthusiasm to show us how good he was, he would literally lift Mrs Rattigan off her feet in the turns, she would give a wry smile. There would also be a smirk on his face as he made a little extra speed along the straight, and she would have to change step several times in order to keep up as they glided over the highly polished floor. Henri (this had to be a nickname - surely!), who also had his charcoal suit and bow tie on for the occasion, and resembled a waiter in one of the top French hotels, would have the extra chore of sprinkling granules onto the floor to make it more slippy - as if it wasn't slippy enough. It was a struggle to stay on one's feet even in the slow Waltz. Jiving was strictly out. "We will have none of that modern day muck in my studio!" Mr Rattigan would say.

By now I thought I was an expert at dancing, although I did the Waltz to every tune and I couldn't understand why my partners never came back to the Tango. I had to learn to Jive somehow!

Our next move was the Mecca of dancing - Crewe Town Hall, where all the top bands of the day would play on a Saturday night: Ken Mackintosh, Ted Heath and Chris Barber, to name but a few.

Inside the hall, which overawed me because it was so big (absolutely nothing like Rattigan's studio), I almost turned around and went back to the pub. There would be an area laid out for jiving with a row of chairs separating the jivers from the steady waltz and quick step brigade.

Later in the evening as the Yanks (who, incidentally, were still based at Middlewich and Burtonwood, not far from Crewe 10 years after World War II), staggered in, together with the `Drapes and Drainpipes'. They all headed for the `Jive Area' to put on their own brand of dance and the floor would bounce. The way those Yanks moved it would put the Teds to shame. It was small wonder most of the girls made a bee-line for them, although they also had plenty of money. I sat there for most of the evening like a wallflower, not really interested in dancing, just a spectator, staring in wonderment.

My friends had been tripping the light fantastic and showing off their own Rattigan type of dancing - slow, slow, quick, quick, slow. It was fortunate I had downed a couple of pints in Kettells before I made my entrance into the big time, because I plucked up enough courage to ask a girl to dance. She immediately pulled me over to the jive area; I was like a young boy pleading with his Mother not to take him into the jive area. "But I can't jive," I said in a panic.

"Neither can I," she smiled.

Well, the looks from the `drapes and drainpipes' as I attempted to put on the style, or rather, more like the agony! The girl with whom I was dancing was not in the least bit embarrassed - maybe she had consumed a few drinks herself. However, she did tell me a little white lie, because she could actually jive quite well. Perhaps she had noticed me with my mouth agape watching the Yanks doing their own brand of jive and felt sorry for me. Whatever, I did pick up the jive movement and from then on I never looked back. I had the last Waltz with her and then along with my friends we moved to the door, carefully treading over Yanks and Teds in their weekly brawl, trying our best to avoid any hard stares, just in case we got drawn into the fights and, of course, remembering my Father's immortal words, "Don't you ever bring any trouble here lad, because I'll swing for you if you do!" I bet he would have been in the middle of it all if he had been there!

After that we turned our attention to the Nantwich Civic Hall - a building which had only recently been built.

Jiving was not permitted at the Civic Hall *under any circumstances* and was stopped by the M.C. as soon as anyone tried to have a go. It was to be a few years before jiving would be allowed in the dance halls around the Crewe area, although by this time Rock 'n' Roll was starting to get into its stride with the arrival of Bill Haley and his Comets. Like many other people of that time, my first records were `Rock Around the Clock' and `Heartbreak Hotel', and I played them over and over again, until the needle on our old gramophone player wore out!

CHAPTER FORTY THREE

Gorgonzola Cheese
and Gypsies

It was now approaching Christmas 1955, and I was determined to make it an enjoyable one, because, as an asthmatic I tended to worry about things that were totally out of my control. For instance, I would worry about Atom Bomb tests in Australia and in the South Pacific with our "Squaddies" being used as Guinea Pigs. My spots had now taken second place in the worry stakes!

I was now buying the Daily Mirror in order to keep up to date with world news and seeing how Garth was coping with the evils of the world. One day, emblazoned across the front page of the newspaper, was a diagram of the H-Bomb blowing up - 100 times more powerful than the Nagasaki Bomb. "Why," I thought, "100 times more powerful?"

They called it a deterrent, and it probably was, but it didn't stop me and, no doubt many other young people of my age, from worrying if the Russians would ever launch an attack on this beautiful little island of ours. "I definitely must enjoy this Christmas, as it could be my last," I promised myself.

My Father had now turned his attention to the local youth population in Shavington. Tired of chasing them from outside the local Chip Shop and clearing them off the footpaths, he had approached a local farmer to see if he had a spare field he could use as a football pitch. The farmer willingly agreed and in next to no time a football team was formed consisting of many local youths of the district.

The team made its debut in the Crewe League and had a big press write-up and, in fact, they actually did quite well in the first season. My Father had even relinquished one of his strict rules and allowed me to go out on a Sunday morning to play football on Coopers field. I was grateful for this, as it meant that I would no longer have to make the excuse of taking Jock for a walk and hiding my boots underneath the back of my pullover every Sunday morning. The problem would arise after the game, but I thought I had solved it because about 50 yards from home I would hang the boots around Jock's neck and he would run straight into the coalhouse and drop them in there.

One night on returning to the living room with a shovel full of coal, my Father also had my boots attached to the front of the shovel. Jock shot out of the room as soon as he saw those boots, and more or less gave the game away. "Oh," I said guiltily "I was cleaning them yesterday."

My Father gave me a long, hard stare and then went out again. I thought I noticed a hint of a smile on his face as he went through the door - perhaps he was remembering his own youth at last. Could this have been a new outlook on life for him? I sincerely hoped so, although he could still change moods in a flash!

Maybe he was going all out for promotion at this late stage of his career (he only had 3 years to serve for his 25 years and a pension). His little Moggy Minor was still circulating around the district and I could detect that engine miles away, as he headed for the Chip Shop in Shavington where, on most nights, we tended to congregate for a natter. The lads got to know that whenever I disappeared, then so should they. My Father thought he had cured the local youth population from hanging around the Chip Shop, but little did he know that my swift movement was their cue to move as well. It didn't matter if all the houses in Shavington were being burgled, as long as there was no one standing outside that Chip Shop.

My Father, being the devout copper that he was, would very rarely accept gifts from the local farmers. The farmers wanted to give these gifts as recognition for the good job my Father did in keeping the law and order around his 7 square miles. One evening my Father relented when a farmer offered him 10 slabs of cheese, because he loved cheese. It was a blue cheese, very similar to Gorgonzola and, whatever it was, it was very ripe. My Father kept the cheese in the kitchen and it stunk to the high heavens until, eventually, my Mother could stand it no longer and told him to get rid of it. My Father would not throw it away and instead he took it up into the attic where it remained for months. My Father loved the stuff and we would watch him on many a night struggling to lift his huge frame through the cockloft door and then reappear with a large slice of cheese for his supper. He would then devour it, together with half a jar of my Mother's home made pickles.

The following morning at the breakfast table, it was down with my porridge as quick as possible before my Father came down reeking of blue cheese and onions. I think if he coughed he would have burnt most of the wallpaper off the wall with his breath! On many a night I would wake up thinking that I could hear the cheese going for a walk around the attic; or perhaps I was the mice thinking it was their birthday and having a celebratory dance.

Chapter Forty Four

Quick Decisions

One night at Goodall's corner, I was awoken by a commotion outside and the banging of the front door. As I pulled the curtains back I could see three men - traditional gypsies drunk, shouting about ancient byelaws etc. I knew there were gypsies parked up on the common at The Hough because while they were there we tended to give it a wide berth, mainly through superstition.

My Father had now opened the door and was listening to the leader who was demanding that my Father run them back up to The Hough in his police Moggy Minor. My Father wouldn't have anyone in that vehicle, not even family members. Initially this statement stopped my Father dead in his tracks and he squinted through the night to see if there were any more gypsies hanging around the side of the house. It was about 2am in early September and there was a mist hanging over Goodall's corner.

"By an ancient byelaw of the Borough of Nantwich, it is your duty to take us home," said the gypsy to my Father. On hearing this statement my Father was stumped for words.

The gypsies were dressed in the usual gypsy attire with the traditional white silk scarf draped around their necks. My Father edged nearer to the leader, unfortunately they had picked on the wrong copper, whose motto was: "Hit first and ask questions after," and who, incidentally, had to get up at 5am that morning to report for duty at Nantwich for 6am. As I squinted into the chill September night, the biggest of the gypsies made a run at my Father and he made a very quick decision; he had to hit him and then the second one. At this point the third one of the gypsies must have thought better of it and ran up the road in the general direction of The Hough.

The other two gypsies then picked themselves up and muttered something at my Father as they moved onto the road. With that, my Father again moved towards. "That's an ancient byelaw of Goodall's Corner - now on your way!," shouted my Father, before turning and glancing up at my window as I quickly dodged back behind the curtains and jumped back into bed.

"Father," I thought, "If you're going all out for promotion, I hope the Superintendent doesn't hear about your `Quick Decisions'."

The following afternoon my Father was pottering around in the front garden when about 6 gypsy caravans approached Goodall's Corner - no doubt heading for fresher pastures. As the third caravan passed the house, there, in the front, were the two gypsies who had confronted my Father the previous night. "See you next year, Ivor!" they shouted, as they drew level to the house.

My Father couldn't help but smile, and I wondered why on earth he didn't smile more often - because it really did suit him.

At this time Frankie Laine was No. 1 in the charts with `Answer Me' (the longest running No. 1 in the charts ever recorded), and Doris Day was airing her tonsils with many numbers, and a young upstart known as Elvis Presley was starting to swivel his hips, and had also moved into the charts. "He won't last long with David Whitfield's `Caramia Mine' moving up the charts," said my Father.

Well, I'm afraid he was wrong, because those `Blue Suede Shoes' walked right into `Heartbreak Hotel', and there began a legend.

I had now moved into the machine shop at Rolls Royce; this being a part of my training. My first stop was on the small Herbert capstan lathe, and my instructor was Derek Johnson. He was to show me the `cuts'. I was setting up and turning out thousands of parts for the stores, mainly brass fittings used in the everyday practice of maintenance. I thoroughly enjoyed this part of my training because, occasionally, I would be asked to go onto a bigger lather - The Turret. This would turn out more precision work for other departments. I suppose the other regular turners who had been working there for years found this quite boring, but not me.

266

Before moving on permanently, I was to train another lad on the Herbert capstan and his name was Mally Worthington - his ambition was to become a Middle Weight Boxing Champion of the World.

Mally had been boxing from a very young age and was now at the age where his career as a boxer would have to take off and he would probably have to turn professional to realise him ambition. He had won the ABA Championships.

When I left Rolls Royce I did try to follow his career and I know he did join the Johnny Campbell stable in Birkenhead, and had a few professional fights. The last I heard was that he had broken his arm which unfortunately more or less brought his boxing career to a halt, and I have never heard of him since.

Mally did persuade me into sparing with him a couple of times at the St Joseph's Gym in Nantwich, mainly because I was the same weight. However, unfortunately I was not quick enough to get out of the way of his very fast punching, and I was pleased that I came out of the ring unscathed; although Mally informed me that he was only `shadow boxing'. Mally and I remained good friends until I left Rolls Royce.

During the Winter, Rolls Royce decided that they would organise coaching sessions for all apprentices who were interested in improving their cricketing ability. They recruited the Nantwich Professional, Ramchand (who had finished playing in Test Cricket for India the previous season), to come along every Saturday morning until the start of the season to put us through our paces.

Ramchand was an extremely good coach; even though the training was indoors and using a tennis ball, it still helped us to perfect the shots that would have taken years in the nets with a leather ball.

Although professionals had been in the Lancashire league for many years, the North Staffordshire League had only just started to play and pay them after World War II.

Together with Ramchand, there was also Mankad playing for India who was also a professional with one of the teams in the league.

I must say that Rolls Royce really did look after their apprentices - both at work and socially. Playing in the North

Staffordshire league, albeit only for the Rolls Royce second team and playing on grounds such as Great Chell, Knypersley and many more, was like playing on County Grounds every Saturday. As far as I was concerned, the wickets were perfect in 1955.

CHAPTER FORTY FIVE

"Keep Away From That Majestic!"

I travelled for interviews to the, then, Boom Town of Ellesmere Port on the Wirral. Interviews at Shell and Metal Containers (Van Leer) came to nothing. I was hoping that my Father would suggest that I remain at Rolls Royce, but unfortunately he did not, and eventually the whole family moved to the area - and I was without a job!

What a fiasco! My life was in total disarray just because my Father wanted to keep his eye on me!

It was 9th March 1955 and, after a few weeks of collecting my dole money, my Father came home and informed me that there was a job for me at Offleys Garage, and that it would do until another job came along. "What was the other job?" I wanted to know.

After a couple of months working at the garage learning how to clean cars and mow the boss's lawn, I attended an interview at a firm called Wakefields (it was latterly changed to Castrol). Here I met a giant of a man named Bill Hampton who gave me a brief interview before informing me that I would start work there the following Monday. I would still be in an apprentice-ship, but it was entirely different work than Rolls Royce; I would mainly be working with pumps and valves, although there was a certain amount of construction work involved - something that Bill prided himself in.

Now a Sergeant, my Father seemed to take on an even more disciplined approach with me, and I could hardly go anywhere unless he vetted it first. Even prior to our move to Ellesmere Port he reeled off a list of places that were strictly out of bounds to me.

One of these `out of bounds' places was The Majestic Dance Hall which was situated at the bottom of the town, together with all the pubs along the `Dock Road' - nicknamed: `The Barbary Coast', as all the pubs were frequented by all the sailors from the ships that docked at the Wharf to offload timber for the Bowaters Paper Mill. Needless to say, I ventured to the banned Majestic Dance Hall the first week I arrived in Ellesmere Port, and found myself totally out of place in my grey flannels and navy blue blazer.

The `Teds' were in full swing at the Majestic and it was also the nearest dance floor for all the `foreigners' (as they were affectionately called) off the ships which had docked at the wharf for a few days. I sat there in wonderment at all the activity in this very dimly lit place, with the crystal ball revolving and reflecting its many colours around the dance hall from its central position.

Each `Ted' had his own style of jiving and it was an education for me just to watch the girls being thrown up in the air, over their shoulders and sliding between their legs along the floor, to be caught on the other side with perfect timing.

"One, Two, Three o'clock Rock..." the band would strike up and dozens of shuffling feet would descend onto the dance floor as if receiving a signal from some unknown force, smiling, laughing and giggling. I just could not understand why my Father banned me from this place of enjoyment and happiness.

By 10.30pm some of the seamen would arrive from the pubs that were scattered around the Dock area, namely: The Bull, The Horse and Jockey, The Dock, The Grosvenor and Canal Tavern. These were all located within 50 yards of one another, and made up the `Barbary Coast'. The seamen would be very drunk and would ask the girls to dance, not realising that some of them had their boyfriends with them.

Before long the inevitable happened and all hell broke loose as the locals got very annoyed and there would be bottles and fists flying everywhere - arms and legs in the air, screaming from the girls as they helped their boyfriends by scratching and biting. The `foreigners' found this all very amusing because some of them were very big men - mainly from Norway and Sweden, and probably ex-lumberjacks not being able to understand a word of English.

The band continued to play on for a while, and even played some waltzes in an attempt to cool the trouble down. I just sat there frozen to my seat and nursing my pint of beer, not daring to move a muscle in case someone decided to pick on me!

By this time many of the girls had sat down next to where I was sitting in order to keep out of the way of the trouble. I must have looked like a wallflower because there were plenty of empty seats around me! Some of the girls got chatting to me and one or two even asked me to dance once the trouble had died down. They must have felt sorry for me as I was sitting there, mouth agape, just taking everything in.

It would be 11pm by now and I was just thinking about making a move for home when, suddenly, without warning, the double doors of the main entrance burst open and there, standing in the doorway was....guess who? Yes, the very one - Sergeant Goolding with Constable Davey Roberts. They had come on duty at 10pm and were looking for a bit of sport no doubt. There were still the odd scuffles dotted around the dance hall, but nothing of significance. However, Father and his colleague headed straight over to the group that were still fighting and started laying into them - the locals and foreigners alike.

The Manager had now switched all the lights on and I looked very conspicuous with a bevy of women around me. My brain had completely disengaged, as I hadn't been prepared for anything like this occurring.

Someone hit my Father on the head with a bottle which had hardly any effect whatsoever and, as he stumbled slightly, his leopard-like eyes settled on me!

Grabbing two men and dragging them to the door, he told Davey to bang the handcuffs on them, and he then did an immediate about turn before heading straight in my direction. The girls surrounding me gaped in amazement as I jumper over rows and rows of seats, as I tried to make my getaway. Some even tried to block his way and the Manager opened the side door and I was out in the street.

I was running around like a chicken with its head off not knowing which way to go. I had only seen these types of situations in the `Movies', and as I tried to get my senses together, Davey came around the corner and pointed to an entry. "Run down there as far as it goes, and then turn left and you're back on the main road through the town," instructed Davey.

Although I didn't know Davey at the time, he must have realised that I was `Young Ivor' and he knew what would happen if my Father had caught me there and then. I will always be indebted to Davey for showing me some compassion because he, also, was a very hard man. My Father and Davey were very alike; they both had quick tempers, and they would often have arguments, sometimes resulting in actually coming to blows - according to policemen who knew them very well.

The tale goes that my Father and Davey would settle their arguments in the cell at Westminster Road Police Station where no harm could come to anyone but themselves, only to be halted by the cry, "Here comes the Inspector!"

My Mother would often spend many hours holding a piece of steak on my Father's black eyes in an attempt to get them back to normal for his court appearance the following day.

After escaping, so to speak, from what would probably have been one of the biggest hidings of my life, I walked along the canal bank, passed the Carbon Black Works and into Wolverham Road and up to No. 31. I stood across the road in the shadows of the flats for about an hour, just in case my Father did come home. I knew deep down that come the morning I would be in for quite a hiding, and when my Mother let me in I went straight to bed lying awake, contemplating whether to leave home or not.

The following day I arrived home from work to face the music. I would always face the consequences and take my punishment - God knows why. I should have kept running when I left the Majestic, but there was always my Mother to consider, or else I would probably have left home a long time ago.

Anyway, as it transpired, I certainly did get quite a hiding and so began the silence between my Father and I, and this was to continue for a very long time.

CHAPTER FORTY SIX

The Lathe

Ellesmere Port, in the oil producing belt of Cheshire, was to become the place where I would spend the next 25 years of my life (apart from a two year spell when I did my part for Queen and Country on the National Service).

Sport was still very much a big part of my life, although it didn't assist me from a career point of view. Some of my supervisors (*God Bless them!*), really did try very hard to get me interested in the art of engineering maintenance. Looking back, I know that I should have listened to them. However, it's easy for me to say these things now....hindsight is a wonderful thing!

Many of the tradesmen attempted to show me the ins and outs of repairing various types of machinery; some were interesting and others were very boring, routine jobs - like packing pump glands, oiling link mechanisms and, if the foreman gave me a telling off for anything, I would be put on the lathe for days on end renovating used flanges, turning, skimming, boring with red hot chippings flying everywhere. Concentration was an absolute essential requirement of the job (something which, unfortunately, I had never had), because as the cut for ripping the weld etc was switched into automatic, sometimes, with the slag being harder in some places, the boring tool would be pulled into the side of the revolving chuck. This would create a terrible crunching and grinding noise, instantly stopping some of the tradesman dead in their tracks. Others would dive for cover under their work benches. I would also dive for the knock-out switch, but very often I was too late as the carriage of the lathe would also drive into the chuck with awesome results, fusing the lathe's electric supply and most of the workshop.

The foreman, Eddie Sheard, and the Engineer, Bill Hepburn, would by this time have plucked up enough courage to come out from behind the office wall and would cautiously walk over to the lathe, gingerly eyeing the smoke rising from the electric inlet. "What the f***ing hell are you playing at?" the foreman would shout, in an angry, quivering voice; his face quite ashen.

I would do one of my Stan Laurel impressions and edge along the wall to try and put some distance between the foreman and I. By this time the foreman was, to say the least, fuming. "What am I going to do with you?" he pleaded, giving the engineer a swift glance to see if he could come up with any bright ideas; but there was not even a flicker from Bill.

I would have been quite happy if he had given me a belt around the ear, as I was used to this type of treatment at home from my Father periodically. The foreman would eventually shrug his shoulders and look towards the electrician's bay. "Jacko! Fix that f***ing fuse before the whole complex goes up in flames!" he demanded.

All the hammering and welding would cease and everyone would be looking in my direction - some would be sniggering behind the foreman's back, pulling faces in an attempt to make me laugh, and giving the "V" sign. Naturally, I was very rarely given weekend overtime shifts.

It was now early 1957 and just over 10 years out of Little Budworth, and in the big wide World. Bill Haley was still giving his all with `Rock Around the Clock' and others were fast coming onto the scene. Buddy Holly was an up and coming legend to be, and David Whitfield and other ballad singers were coming to the end of their era.

CHAPTER FORTY SEVEN

Chemical Plants and Compressors

A s I progressed through my apprenticeship, I did gradually improve my overall ability to repair things. However,
the foreman usually selected the less complicated tasks for me
which included making coupling guards for rotary pumps or
doing some sheet metal work. Strangely enough, I quite enjoyed making things because there was some job satisfaction in
seeing something useful put into position.

Some of my first efforts had to be packed up with washers in
order to clear the rotating shaft, and some had a slight lean-to
starboard on them - but, nonetheless, they did the job.

Eddie, the foreman, (Bill Hampton had now retired), had
begun to acknowledge me as he passed me in the workshop,
so I must have been back in his good books. He would give me
a wry smile, and I can recall that throughout life I would have
many of those!

As the months elapsed, Eddie must have felt that I was ready
to have a go at something a little more complicated, because he
gave me a small compressor to overhaul. I was delighted by this
and told my Mother that Eddie had given me a big job to do. My
Mother gave me an understanding smile - as if she had a degree
in engineering!

I worked extremely hard on that job, being very careful
when removing parts and labelling them, and ensuring that I
gave the sump a very thorough cleaning. The odd pieces of metal that I would find amongst the pieces of white metal from the
damaged bearings would be thrown into the scrap bin. I was on
the overhaul all week, scrapping the white metal bearings to fit
the shaft, carefully bluing etc and making doubly sure that they
bedded in correctly, reassembling the whole compressor and

then, carefully, transporting it to the compressor house and lining it up with a very accurate dial test indicator. Everything was perfectly level and in line and I gave it a quick turn by hand. It turned freely on its own, the pulley wheel turned for a couple of minutes with perfect balance. Finally, all of my Rolls Royce experience was coming together, I thought.

"The whole chemical plant relies on this compressor," Eddie informed me during the week, as he passed my workbench. I was proud of my effort, but Eddie would not allow me to work the weekend shift. Or maybe I had refused; the latter was probably the most likely explanation.

On the Monday morning cycling into work, I was full of the joys of Spring as a result of having had a good weekend playing cricket on Saturday and Sunday.

My happy outlook was soon to change. As I walked through the workshop door, there was Eddie leaning on what can only be described as the charred mess of a shell of a Compressor Unit. With one hand on the compressor top and both eyes transfixed on me, Eddie beckoned me over, and here commenced the biggest bollocking of my life! "What's this?" he asked sarcastically.

A burnt out compressor," I replied cheekily.

Eddie's face started to colour up slightly and by this time the engineer, Bill Hepburn, was on the scene to throw his two pennyworth in,though he was normally a very mild tempered man, there was more than a hint of anger in both his voice and his facial expression.

"What have you done?" he asked.

"I don't understand it. I did everything right - put all the parts back as they came out, and I really spent a lot of time cleaning and lining the damned thing up," I said.

"We know that," Eddie chipped in, very quickly.

All of the other fitters were at the other end of the workshop trying to look busy and smiling sympathetically as the bollocking continued. Eddie had now picked up what looked like a piece of scrap metal which was about an inch in length, with a hole at one end and a taper at the other end. "I found this in the scrap bin," he informed me. "Do you know what it is?"

My eyes rolled to the back of my head. "It is part of a plumb bob?" I stammered.

Eddie's face was now beginning to contort and his knuckles were gradually turning white as he clenched his fists even tighter. "It's an oil thrower!" he screamed, after putting the hammer shaft down, having almost squeezed it into a pulp.

At this point all of the other maintenance men who were watching attentively disappeared to their various hideouts. "An oil thrower?" I queried innocently.

With that Eddie attempted to explain friction to me, and tried his best to omit swear words in his explanation. Bill was still stood there.

"Don't move," he said, as he started to undo the cover of the compressor.

Once it was removed there was an awful smell of burnt oil and metal, and Eddie gave me one of his tight lipped, hard stares - eyeball to eyeball.

By this time several of the many maintenance men had wandered back into the workshop and were trying to catch my eye once more; one or two of them succeeded and forced me to smile as they pulled faces and nodded their heads as Eddie extracted the burnt-up shaft with globules of white metal attached to it.

As a final year apprentice, I should have known better.

"You find it funny do you?" Eddie snarled.

"You could get the sack for this," he continued, obviously trying to frighten me, because Eddie was not the sacking type. In actual fact, he was one of the best.

Although Eddie was a very good foreman and knew the job thoroughly, over the years to come I was to infuriate many more foremen, and still live to tell the tale - JUST!

Eddie had now got most of the bits out of the sump of the compressor.

"I suppose you realise that all the production came to a halt in the Chemical Plant over the weekend do you?" he turned to me and asked.

"Er, no," I stuttered, "Is that serious?"

Eddie was left speechless and all he could do was bite his bottom lip.

"As you can see, there is a sight glass on the side - can you see it?" he asked.

"Yes," I replied.

"There is a mark for the correct oil level," he pointed out.

"I did all of that - oil to the correct level and everything," I said.

"Good," said Eddie, rather sarcastically. "Well you see this little bit of metal in my hand? That picks the oil up from that level and throws it over the white metal bearings. Missing wasn't it?" he asked.

"Was it - amazing!" I said, searching for something to say that would satisfy Eddie. However, unable to think of anything, I had to keep repeating - "Was it," "Is it?" "Will it?" - much to the annoyance of Eddie who, undoubtedly had taken a lot of stick from higher up.

"You will now clean up all this mess and start to reassemble, and you will call me out of the office every time to put a piece on or throw ANYTHING away, and I mean ANYTHING, so that I can make sure that everything is OK," he said, before turning on his heels.

After a couple of days the compressor was reassembled and Eddie helped me to fit it and line it up to the coupling, and the time came to start it up. I thought I would show some initiative.

"Is the oil in?" I asked. Well, if looks could kill! I thought Eddie was going to pass out.

Jacko, the electrician, had appeared trying to keep a straight face.

"Put the fuses in Jacko, will you?" instructed Eddie.

On his return Eddie pushed the button but nothing happened, so Jacko went back and really put the fuses in this time. Eddie pushed the button and the machine started to move and a look of relief came to Eddie's face.

There followed the usual bangs on the walls by the tradesmen to give the impression that something was knocking inside the compressor. Eddie turned to me and smiled for the first time in a week. "I'm going for a smoke," Eddie said, once the machine had been going for about 10 minutes. I moved to go with him, but Eddie had other ideas.

"Don't you dare move out of here for at least an hour!" he screamed at me.

I'm afraid that Eddie was extremely disappointed with me and forever after, and was very reluctant to give me a big task. I never really got the chance to conquer Eddie's fear of giving me important jobs, as I was about to disappear into the Army on National Service for two years. This probably came as a relief to a lot of people at the Castrol Oil Production Factory at Stanlow. They were good times for me though.

CHAPTER FORTY EIGHT

Unsung Heroes of the Trade

During the course of my apprenticeship, I met many great characters in the engineering trade. At Castrol I spent quite a while with Bill Halligan, an ex-seafarer who could tell many a tale about his days at sea. He was born and bred in Liverpool, and went to sea at 15, just as the sailing ships were coming to the end of their life, with the conversion to steam power.

On one occasion Bill and I were working on a rotary pump on the second floor of the Chemical Plant and in those days fire precautions were not all that stringent. Other engineers were fitting a new elevator from the ground floor up to the top floor to carry chemicals in bags to blend into an agitating pot.

As the morning progressed and Bill had lit a few "Woodies," and we had spent most of our time attempting to dodge the spatter being given off by the welding arc above as we strove to lift the shaft out of the rotary pump, unbeknown to us, an inflammable liquid mixed with sawdust had been used to clean the floor.

A lot of this liquid had been left around on the platform and as the slag and spatter continued to tumble down in cascades, eventually the inevitable happened - it ignited, isolating Bill and I at the end of the platform with a twenty foot drop. I panicked but there was nowhere to go.

The flames were gradually lapping towards us and the vessels, full of chemicals, the majority of which had tightened down lids. If those flames had reached the vessels, I suspect that Bill and I would have been launched into orbit.

People down below were shouting for us to jump, but Bill was now almost 65 years of age, and he knew that if he jumped he would not land very well on the concrete floor - come to think of it, neither would I.

Whilst I was still trying to make up my mind, Bill ran through the flames, without any thought for his safety, and through the heat haze I could see him running around, as if he were searching for something. I was about to run through myself, when I heard a loud hissing noise from the other side of the flames.

Bill had managed to get two fire extinguishers from somewhere and was firing one at the fire and holding the other underneath his arm. Bill put the fire out on his own, much to my relief.

Bill certainly saved my life that day, because I would only have run through those flames as a last resort. He also saved the Chemical Plant from going up in flames and, as a result, saved the Company a lot of money. However, he didn't even receive so much as a "Thank You" from the firm.

Bill was a very quiet and modest man - the likes of whom are usually only seen in films until then, but they were only actors; Bill was genuine.

This was the first of two occasions in which I almost died as a result of insufficient safety measures on those days. As a young apprentice, one never thinks about danger, because you think it will never happen to you. This episode did make me more aware of the dangers, but the dangers of chemicals are often hidden and appear only as vapours. Such an experience occurred shortly after this incident.

It was a cold December morning in 1958 and I had gone into the Chemical Plant on Gland tightening patrol on all the steam pumps. I must have done something to upset Eddie again, but this job was a king of "Jankers" for doing something wrong. However, as least it was a warm job, so I didn't particularly mind.

Later on that morning I was given a task on the Chemical Vessels renewing studs on the inspection hatches as they had corroded away where the chemicals had seeped through. I spent most of the morning painstakingly trying to remove the studs which were screwed into the vessel and at last the last one came out. I began to lift the sight glass and jointing - and that is all I can remember.

Apparently the vapours had knocked me out immediately and, luckily, I had fallen from the stand and hit the handrails around the second floor and remained there out to the world.

One of the other fitters, Timmy Ireland, had pulled me out of the building and carried me to the ground floor and had propped me up against the wall outside the Chemical Plant. The next thing I knew, the works Nurse was wafting smelling salts under my nose.

I came round completely no worse for my experience thanks to Timmy.

They say you learn from experience but this is not always the case, because I had two experiences where, if it were not for the quick thinking of colleagues, I would have died. Mind you, I was certainly a lot more careful following those episodes in my life. I also noticed that people tended to steer clear of me for a while, thinking that perhaps I was a jinx!

IRENE NEWQUAY **1959**

WITH BRIDES MAIDS, FRIEND DOT AND AUTHORS SISTER SUSAN

WEDDING DAY, 27TH MAY 1961

**AUNT ETHEL, MOTHER & FATHER 1960
IN THEIR EARLY FIFTIES**

ORT NEWS & ADVERTISER, THURSDAY, DECEMBER 11, 1958

Liverpool F.C. trial for local boy

A LOCAL police officer's son who has been playing with local amateur league side Wakefields for the past two seasons, will be on the first rung of the ladder to football recognition if a satisfactory report follows his trial with Liverpool F.C. on Tuesday.

He is Ivor Goulding, who by his consistent displays of clever football has been helping Wakefields to maintain a satisfactory league position. They are at present holding the fifth position. Ivor's favourite position is at outside-left, and it is in this position he displayed his talents before Liverpool's top coaches.

Ivor is the son of Police Sergeant Goulding, of the local force.

"A DREAM COME TRUE"

INSIDE-RIGHT for Wakefields, Ivor Goolding, aged 21, has been invited to take part in a trial match by Liverpool F.C. Ivor is the son of Police Sergeant Goolding and before coming to Ellesmere Port he played football for the Rolls Royce team at Crewe.

Soccer Personality No. 7

I. GOOLDING

Signed during the close season, Ivor Goolding, former Castrol player, is one of Great Sutton's outstanding players operating at outside-left.

An all-round sportsman, Ivor plays cricket for Castrol in the summer, and is also a sound table tennis player.

(PHOTO: E. HUXLEY).

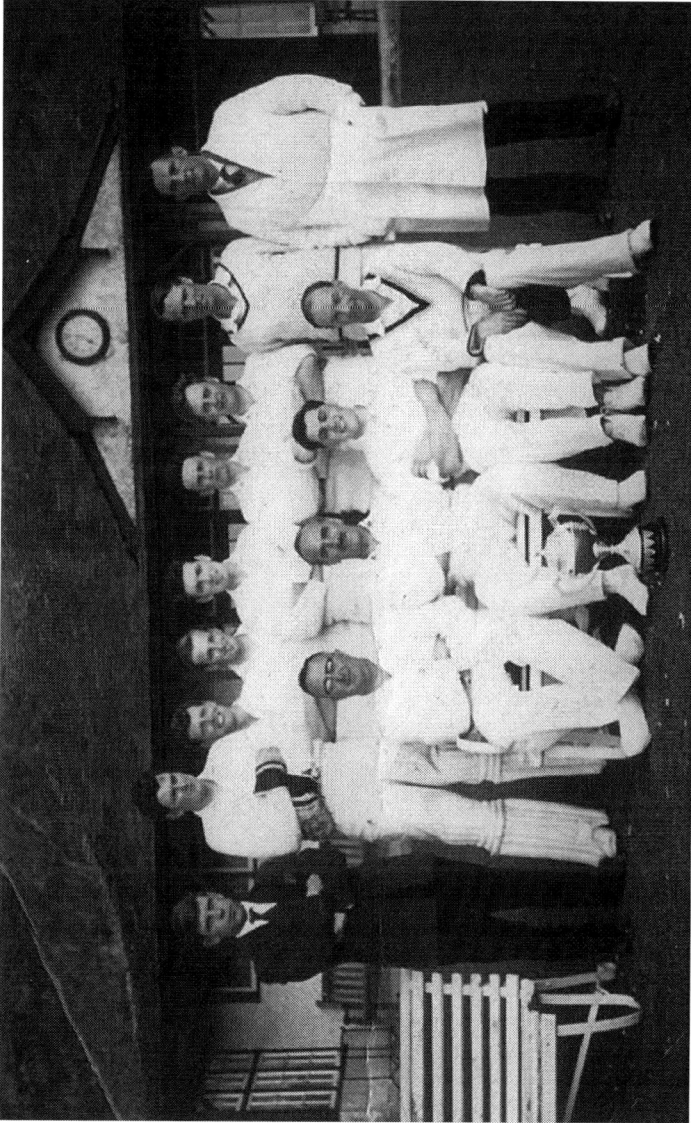

AFTER WINNING 3RD DIVISION CHAMPIONSHIP AT TIDWORTH 1961
AUTHOR NEXT TO WICKETKEEPER J. SHONE

**FIGSBURY CAMP GUARD WITH FRED CARTER 1961
PICK HELUES & WIRELESS IN CASE OF ATTACK!**

**"A" AND "B" PLATOONS, ROYAL WELCH FUSILIGRS CRICKHOWELL
END OF TRAINING 1959. AUTHOR 2ND LEFT BACK ROW**

MAJOR COWLEY & CSM WILLIS CENTRE
HQ 51ST INFANTRY BRIGADE

MONEYVRES ON SALISBURY PLAIN WITH SIDBROWN RIGHT

AUTHOR, LENNY WILLIAMS & JOHN SHONE
WINTERBOURNE GUNNER NR SALISBURY 1961

THE AUTHOR LEFT AND LENNY, FIGSBURY CAMP, 1961
ABOUT TO GO ON ADMIN. PARADE

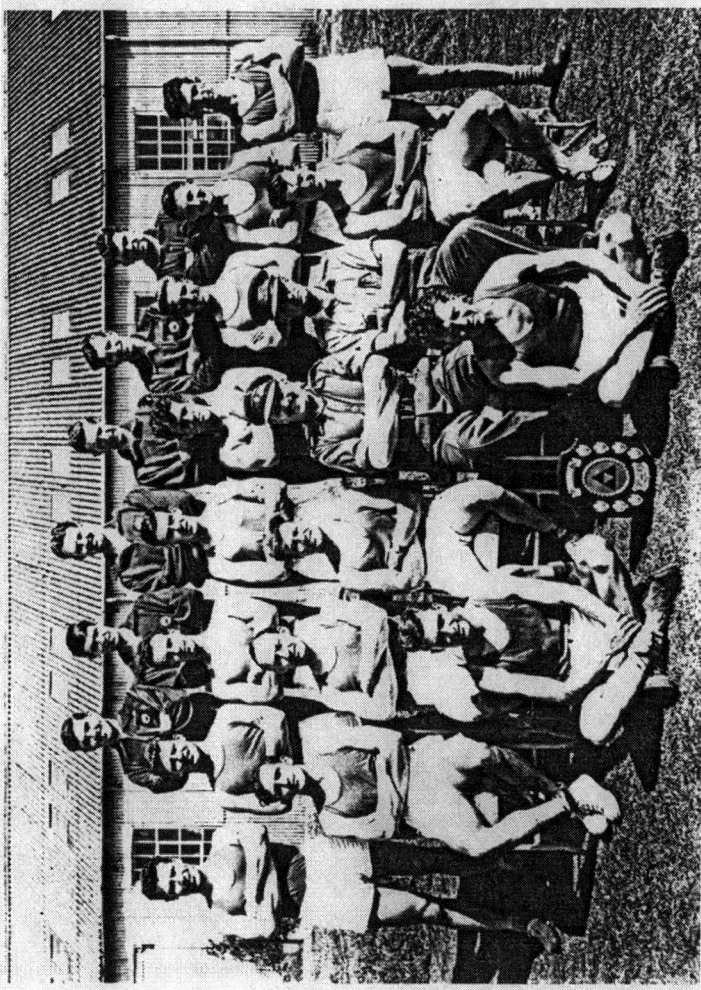

WINNERS OF 3RD DIV ATHELETICS 1961 BRIGADE HQ FIGSBURY CAMP
AUTHOR 2ND FROM LEFT MIDDLE ROW

CHAPTER FORTY NINE

Trials and Errors

By this time in my life I had met a very pretty girl, Irene, whom I was to marry and here we are some 30 odd years later. Irene gave me a different outlook on life and I started to settle down. I never thought I would meet another woman that I would fall in love with, because I had become very reluctant to stay with a girl or even trust them since my first experience with them.

Irene and I became engaged in March 1959 and it would be the first time I had ever been away for a holiday in my life - a week in Newquay, Cornwall in June of the same year. Every minute of that holiday still remains very clearly in my memory. Buddy Holly and Newquay go together:-

> *"The sun is out, the sky is blue,*
> *There's not a cloud, to spoil the view,*
> *But it's raining, raining in my heart."*

It was so hot in Newquay, and I had never been in such heat before. We spent most of our time sunbathing on the Tolcarne Beach which was just a stone's throw from our hotel - The Cavendish.

Our Labrador, Jock, who had been with us through thick and thin for most of my life, had died 12 months earlier; he was just unable to cope in the `concrete jungle' and old age had taken its toll.

My asthma had fortunately eased off by now, and eventually I was having no attacks at all. It would appear, therefore, that it was having a dog in the house which was causing the asthma attacks, and not, as I had originally thought, a nervous condition as a result of my Father's strong discipline that had been administered by him all my life.

When my asthma ceased, it was almost like receiving another lung - I was able to run without getting short of breath after 10 yards!

Just prior to my 21st Birthday I was playing in the local amateur football league for Castrol as a right winger, in the Matthews mould, attempting to emulate the great master with swerves (but usually only fooling myself and not the fullback!).

On this particular Saturday I must have had a good game, because at the end of the game one of the lads in the team said there was a bloke wanting to speak to me over by the club pavilion.

Covered in mud, which was a rare occurrence for me, I went over to the man in question. To my joy and amazement, he was a scout for Liverpool Football Club - the club I had supported all my life, mainly because my Father was a keen supporter and had often gone to Anfield on his days off. "How would you like a trial with us?" asked the scout.

"Well I would love to, but I'm due to go into the Army any time after I have completed my apprenticeship," I replied, although, why I said that, I do not know!

"Well, if you get picked we will try to arrange a posting nearer to home," he said.

In those days I often ignored advice and, after giving him my name and address, I went back and had a shower with the rest of the team. They all wanted to know who I was talking to.

I was over the moon for weeks afterwards and when the letter arrived inviting me over to the Melwood training ground; I couldn't wait for the day to come. It was December 1958 and I had had my 21st Birthday the previous month. My Father and I were speaking for the first time for years and he and my Mother had bought me a gold ring as a Birthday present. This was certainly a somewhat weepy evening for my Mother.

I was to go over for my trial with Liverpool on the Thursday, so I knocked-off work at about 3pm in order to get the bus to Liverpool. I actually had to catch 3 different buses and finally arrived at Melwood at about 6pm, where I was met by Ray Lambert, one of the Liverpool players of the past who was now in charge of the scouting. After we trained and had a game, I left the club and went home.

The trip to Melwood was repeated several weeks running, and I would play a few games. However, I found that it was too much trouble getting to the ground, especially having to travel by bus. I did get a card to play some games on the Wirral but, after biking to Hoylake, I returned to the works team because it was obvious that I was not going to make the grade as a professional footballer.

It was now the middle of January 1959. It was nice to be able to play as an amateur for years after this because I knew in my own mind that if my asthma had remained with me, I would never have been able to play at all. It was the proudest period of my life, so I say to all asthmatics - "Never give up hope."

The music in these days was, of course, `Rock 'n' Roll' with Elvis still in full swing. When the film `Rock Around the Clock' was shown at the local cinema, there was dancing on the stage and in the aisles, and many seats were being damaged during the course of the week.

The night that my friends and I were there, the place was bouncing and suddenly the lights went on and the film stopped halfway through. The row of seats that I had been sitting in had been pushed back, and I was flat on my back still singing. As I glanced back towards the doors I could see three policemen standing at the back of the cinema, and I immediately recognised my Father as one - even looking upside down!

I made a swift exit stage left on hands and knees into the toilet and through the window and away as fast as my legs would carry me. I believe there were a lot of lads thrown into the cells at the Police Station that evening. My Father told my Mother the following day that they had thrown some lads into the cells, but they had only kept them for an hour and then let them go.

I thought to myself how close to death I must have been if my Father or one of his Constables had caught me. "Just you keep away from that Hippodrome while that idiot Bill Haley is on," he said to me as we were sitting at the table. I nodded in agreement, but when my Mother looked at me, she knew I had been there because of the look on my face.

As I left the house singing `One, Two, Three o'clock Rock," my Father gave me a very hard look as if something was ticking over in his head, and he was wondering whether I was there or not.

As I had some of my own cash I decided to go and get measured for my first suit at Jackson the Tailors - the "in" tailor of Ellesmere Port.

I arrived at the tailors early on the Saturday morning and was greeted by the boss himself. "Yes Sir?" he asked as I walked in, and I had to glance behind me to make sure that Royalty hadn't walked in after me, before I realised that he was, in fact, speaking to me!!

I was shown all the various patterns and colours. I thought that a loud colour would brighten up my drab world, so I chose a light blue. "A popular choice," Mr Jackson assured me.

The measuring up for the suit was all new to me - chest, arms and inside leg.

"Relax" he firmly commanded, as I tried to throw out my chest. Mr Jackson took my inside leg measurement about 3 times because I kept on moving when the tape was pressed under my private parts - a little too heavy for my liking; but it brought a smile to Mr Jackson's face.

"Would you like a full length drape jacket and 16" bottoms, Sir and maybe a velvet collar?" asked Mr Jackson, because, being the mid-fifties, this was the era of the `Teds'.

He produced some photographs of lads in the full regalia - one in an orange suit, the other in lime green. I thought to myself that I would be called all the "Puffters" under the sun if I dared to walk through Ellesmere Port in one of those!

"17 inch bottoms," I said daringly, "But no drape, and just the normal length jacket, please."

About 2 or 3 weeks later I called into the tailors to see if my suit was ready and, sure enough, it was. "Erm, just one small point, Sir," Mr Jackson said somewhat nervously. "A Sergeant Goolding has been in and changed the trouser bottoms to 20 inches."

Well, what could I say? The suit was complete.

"Well, make me another pair of trousers of the same colour with 17 inch bottoms and I will call for them in two weeks time," I instructed.

The tailor duly carried out my request and my Father never found out, because I would keep them at my friend's house, change and then go out on the town.

After a few weeks, the light blue started to lose its colour somewhat, and it picked up the dirt very easily, so I had the bright idea of getting it dyed Royal Blue. Oh my God, when it came back, `bright' was not the word for it! It really stood out amongst the charcoal greys and the blacks like a sore thumb, and once I put it on I realised it had shrunk and the inside leg was now about 28." They had become very tight under the crutch, making me walk even more quickly. I complained at the launderette but they reassured me that it would hang to its original level eventually. Liars! I hesitated to try to understand what they meant by "hang to its original level! So, now I had a pair of 20" sky blue trousers and a Royal Blue jacket.

For weeks afterwards my Father would watch me like a hawk, as I went out of the house at night in my sky blue trousers, with my coat on my arm turned inside out not daring to wear it because of the clash of colours.

My Father started to get even more disciplinarian towards me as his time for retirement grew nearer. I suppose he thought that if I got into any trouble now he would be immediately sacked, and 25 years of plodding the beats of Cheshire could have been wasted, and he and my Mother would have been out on the streets.

My Mother was also under the same impression, although why, I do not know. I just can't imagine what sort of trouble I would get into. "You bring any trouble here lad, and I'll swing for you!" he was forever saying. That was good enough for me Dad.

One Saturday night I had been out until about 2am, having walked back from Chester as I had missed the last bus, and having thought that my Father was on nights. How I miscalculated I will never know, because usually my Mother would tell me his shift times. Anyway, I arrived home and noticed the wrapper still around the knocker on the door. This was an invention of my Mother's to stop hawkers or postmen knocking while my Father was in bed - off at 6am after 8 hour nights.

I gave the door a slight knock and waited for my Mother to answer, but there was no movement inside at all. I therefore proceeded around the back of the house and lobbed a hand full of small stones at my Sister's bedroom window, hoping she would hear me. No sign of life again I'm afraid, so I went back to the front of the house and was relieved to see someone coming down the stairs through the frosted glass in the front door.

The door opened and I walked through with a smile, when suddenly I was on the receiving end of the biggest thrashing of my short life. "Where have you been until this time?" screeched my Father, in that very high pitched voice reserved only for when he was very angry.

Apparently my Father had swapped shifts in order that he could play his bowling handicap in the afternoon.

On this particular occasion, he laid into me a little heavier than normal, and my ribs were quite sore the following day, and I vowed after that I would never be home later than midnight while I was still living at home - much to the relief of my Mother, who must have been fed up with making excuses for me.

It is only now looking back to those days, that I realise my Father really believed in what he was doing, and the way he was bringing me and my Sister up, although to us, he was always a figure of fear. I have to admire him for what he was - a copper through and through, but at the time, the hidings seemed to be much too harsh for the `crime'; if they could be called a crime, for a skinny teenager growing up in the early 50s.

No doubt other people with very strict Fathers who they hardly ever saw also only remember the worst times of their upbringing.

My Sister, Susan, had to be in for 10pm every night until she was 21 years old, and she would not dare be as much as a minute late. Fear had been instilled into us both over the years. When I did eventually settle down with a steady girlfriend, my Father seemed to lay off, as if he thought his job was finished and I was no longer likely to stray onto the wrong path.

"You will go in the Army - no `ifs' or `buts' about it!" my Father said, a few months prior to undergoing my medical for National Service.

In a way, it was a catch 22 situation for me, because I did want to get away from home and see what the big wide World was like. However, I was now engaged and wanted to stay with my fiancée, who was very pretty and would no doubt have plenty of lads asking her to go out with them whilst I was away. Unfortunately for me, I had inherited my Father's very jealous nature so it was twice as difficult for me and consequently there would be many arguments when I was home on leave. The cure for my jealousy would only come with age.

My Mother would often tell me when I was young of how my Father would go into a blinding rage if anyone so much as looked at her when they were out or in a dance hall. These things were told to me even before I became interested in the opposite sex, and I thought no more about it until I started to meet girls in my teens. Some girls can be extremely devious so I suppose this triggered my own jealous streak. It must be a fantastic gift not to be jealous, but I suppose love has many ways of revealing itself. Luckily I did manage to come out of it - it was all in my mind and unfortunately very difficult to understand.

During my three years stay at Castrol prior to joining the Army, I learnt a lot about engineering taught by some very good craftsmen, mainly ex-seafarers. Eddie was originally a trades-man and I served a number of years with him, together with Bill Halligan and the one and only `Robbo' (Bob Roberts).

CHAPTER FIFTY

Elvis Eat Your Heart Out

At Christmastime the Company would arrange a free dinner in the canteen and staff from the factory would get up and sing after the foreman had waited on the workers, serving the Christmas Dinners to all - a kindly gesture by them.

I was now approaching 19 years of age and, like a lot of lads of that age, I thought I could do a good impersonation of Elvis. The first time I got up and sang a couple of easy numbers which we had rehearsed for weeks before during our lunch hour - `Rock Around The Clock' and `Heartbreak Hotel', and I managed to keep in tune with the pianist.

The following year I was much more nervous. The first singer had been on and sang, like a Nightingale, one of Ruby Murray's hits - I think it was `Softly Softly'. The songs I had chosen were `Rock with the Caveman' - one of Tommy Steele's hits, and `Be My Girl' by Jim Dale. They are two songs that have never been heard of since.

The tradesmen had been making fun of me, which only resulted in me being all the more nervous.

I ate my Christmas dinner and had a cigarette or two to tune up my throat and give it that husky sound. Bruce Barrett had finished his rendition of the Johnny Mathis hit, `A Certain Smile,' and received tumultuous applause. Bruce actually went on to form his own group, `The Magpies', and he was the lead singer with them for many years. By this time I was ready to run out of the canteen and head for the nearest pub!

"You're next!" my friends were now shouting and clapping at the same time, giving me one of the biggest build-ups ever known in the Castrol Canteen Christmas Concert. Of course, this was all to make me even more nervous!

A few of the lads had even saved their bread rolls and were tossing them in the air like cricket balls about to be launched at speed at some unsuspecting batsman.

The MC, Mr Johnny Reynolds, then announced me and, might I add, did a very good job considering I was only going to sing two numbers. Johnny Harris was tapping the drums like some sort of `Build Up'. "Here he is ladies and gentleman - the lad who gave us Elvis and Bill Haley last year, Ivor Goolding!"

No turning back now, and up I went, trembling and holding the microphone in an attempt to stop the shaking (so that's what they are for is it?). The two Johnnies were waiting for me to start and they would follow, so to speak. As some people may know, `Rock with the Caveman' starts with a sort of howling lead in with no music at all. I gave it my all and shut my eyes, so that I couldn't see the audience cringing and wincing with every note. The overall consensus at the Castrol Canteen Christmas Concert, that it was the nearest they had heard to `A dog chewing holly!'.

Eventually the drummer caught up with me and there was a sigh of relief from behind as I finished. I got a clap here and there from the audience, mainly out of sympathy and then I went straight into my next number - `Be My Girl', and completely lost the drummer again, because I was that nervous. I rushed through the song to get off that stage and disappear into the nearest manhole.

I still maintain that I was 30 years ahead of my time!! Even now, if I ever see a singer on stage struggling a bit, I feel nervous just watching him and remembering those far off days in the 50s at `The Castrol Canteen Christmas Concert.' I realised that I was only up there to give the lads a laugh.

In spite of my asthma, I had always tried to set myself goals and this wasn't always easy - especially for someone brought up with sport all around him, as a result of having a sporting Father. During my childhood, if I came third in any competitions at school, as far as I was concerned, that was an achievement, and I had to tell anyone who would listen, mainly my Mother as a rule. This was not a case of blowing my own trumpet, but rather to let people know that I was really trying to overcome the dreaded wheeze that occurred every so often.

I very rarely had a day off work and I did eventually get rid of the asthma and was able to lead a normal life. From then on my lungs got bigger and bigger and I was able to enjoy sport to the full.

CHAPTER FIFTY ONE

National Service, Army 1959 - 1961
Royal Welch Fusiliers

I knew that I would eventually have to go into the Army for my National Service, and it was now getting close, because I was due to complete my apprenticeship in September 1959, after five years. Irene's brother John Williams (Wigsy) was already in Malaysia with the Cheshires serving his national service.

Finally the buff coloured envelope with OHMS stamped on it dropped onto the hall mat and I handed it to my Mother for her to open. "Yes," she said, "It's from the Army; you have to report to Brecon, South Wales on the 3rd of September."

"Brecon - where is that?" I asked.

I had had my medical the previous year and passed A1, like most of the lads, so they were on the ball with my papers considering I didn't come out of my time until 31st of August. I was also considering going to college for a further year so, in effect, I would not have had to do my National Service at all.

Looking back, I am glad that I didn't go to college because the Army was an experience I am grateful for, as it helped me to appreciate a great many things in life. Of course, my Father had laid down the law a few months earlier. "You will go in the Army and no `ifs' or `buts' about it!" he had said.

Apparently, he didn't want the MPs around arresting me or, even worse, having to arrest me himself because he was now in his final year of 25 years of plodding the beats for the Cheshire Constabulary. He certainly didn't want anything upsetting his exemplary conduct record, and also the reward of a pension (what a joke that was!).

I would never have even dreamt of not joining the Army; as far I was concerned, this was something that young men accepted as the right thing to do for Queen and Country then.

However, even then there were a few Conscientious Objectors and they would serve three months in Gaol rather serve their time in the Army.

"You'll love the Army," my friends all said - even those who weren't going in.

When completing my application form, I had deliberately put down REME, RE's and RASC, and what did I get as a Tradesman? "Royal Welch Fusiliers! Maybe it was because my Christian name was Ivor.

At work that day I shouted the news to another friend, Bobby Attwood, was going out to the North East delivering oil with his wagon, and would not be back for a few days. When I told him he laughed loudly. "What mob?" he asked.

"The Royal Welch," I replied.

But every dog has its day, because on Bobby's return he discovered he had received his papers to join "The Cheshires." This meant that he would only have to travel up the road to Chester for his training. We were both in the "Footsloggers" - me the 23rd afoot and Bobby the 22nd afoot.

Eventually the big day arrived, if one can call it that, and both Bobby and I were going in on the same day - the 3rd September 1959. I was going quite willingly, although I would be away from home for the first time and would also be leaving my fiancée behind, since I was by this time engaged.

On my day of departure, breakfast was a very quiet affair. My Mother and Sister did not say much that morning, and my Sister even let me have the square side of the toast without argument. I seem to recall that my Father was on duty, and therefore there were no "goodbyes" from him. My Mother had provided me with enough "butties" to last the whole two years that I would be away. "Don't forget to write," she said, whilst giving me a little kiss on the cheek.

Off I went to catch the bus to Chester Station - my Mother waving until I was out of sight.

My Cowboy and Indian escapades, together with my time in the Church Lads Brigade and Boys Brigade, were all going to come together now, and turn me into a good soldier. What a shock I was in for!

Settling down in the train carriage at Chester there was someone I knew by sight, but had never spoken to. He recognised me too, as we were both from Ellesmere Port so that helped a lot. He informed me that his name was Denis Fairbrother and he was going to Brecon to join the same regiment, and he was also engaged.

As the train left the station amidst a flurry of steam and smoke passing under the Hoole Bridge, I could not help but to cast my mind back 10 years when, as a boy of 11, I had sat on that bridge watching all the trains going in and out to various destinations in Wales. At that time I would have been on my way home from school, with nothing to worry about, except extra homework and the odd asthma attack. I thought to myself, if only I could turn back time, and I could be whisked up onto that bridge before heading for home.

The train continued to chug on across the Roodee Bridge and on into Wales, until we arrived at Wrexham where some more recruits joined us who were also on their way to Brecon. They, too, had long faces!

Once out of Wrexham the train began to pick up a bit of speed as we went down into a valley, only to strain as we started to climb steeper hills and, eventually, quite high mountains and greenery, which was extremely picturesque, as we went deeper and deeper into Wales. As an Autumn scene it was a wonderful sight - all the light browns and the ochres that are associated with the fall of the leaves.

As the train puffed its way through valley after valley, my mind again started to wander and it suddenly struck me that I was on my own for the first time in my life, and going to make my own decisions - whatever they might be.

Finally, after several hours, the train arrived at Brecon Station and my everlasting memory of that station was of all the cattle pens - no doubt to keep the sheep in as they awaited transportation to various meat markets around the British Isles.

It was now 4pm and, having left home at 9am, we had been travelling for an awful long time. Not only that, I had finished my sandwiches which my Mother had made for me hours ago, and I was now absolutely starving!

We disembarked the train with our little suitcases at the ready for storing our civilian clothing. We were all sorts of shapes and sizes, sporting drapes and Tony Curtis haircuts with DA's being combed every few minutes.

We had now been waiting for about 15 minutes and there was still no sign of any military personnel. I thought to myself, maybe we're in the wrong place, and we should be in Brechin in Scotland NOT Wales!

However, shortly after this thought, a tall, slim and very smart Lance Corporal appeared from the bottom end of the station and very politely introduced himself as Lance Corporal Jones. (Well, what other name was there in the hills of Mid-Wales?)

Most of us were about 21 years old and the Lance Corporal appeared to be about the same age. We learnt that he had joined the National Service when he was 18 years old and was due to complete his service in three months, about the same time we would be completing our training.

Lance Corporal Jones swiftly formed us into two straight files and then marched us down the main street of Brecon to the barracks. The barracks were quite an awesome sight; it must have been a keep or maybe a prison in bygone days, because it had 20 foot walls all around and battlements on either side of the entrance, which consisted of two 10 foot high oaken gates of about 3 inches thick with a small personal gate built into one side. No escape from here I thought to myself.

Inside we were setting foot on the drilling square which, unbeknown to us, was sacred ground - a place of perfection and strict discipline to the Training Sergeants. The barracks were the South Wales Borderers Head Quarters and had been for 100's of years - a Regiment like the Royal Welch was steeped in history and bravery on all the battlefields around the world.

Unfortunately for our draft (incidentally, one of the last drafts to do National Service; the last drafts having gone in at the end of 1960), a few months before the RWF depot at Wrexham had closed for training, and so the Army in its infinite wisdom had thought it a good idea to send us into Borderer country to do our training. The regulars of the SWB's were very proud of their nickname - "The Swabs" (S.W.A.B.S) and there was some friction between the Borderers and the Fusiliers. This had nothing to do with us at all, as we were from the Wirral, Cheshire or South Lancashire, but we were Royal Welch Fusiliers from North Wales, and as a result we were not really liked down there. Granted, there were a few lads from North Wales and they, like us, were unconcerned about the Regimental rivalry.

Lance Corporal Jones then showed us to our billet on the second floor of the block which, no doubt, would have been filled with hardened Squaddies during World War II, as they trained to do battle against Hitler. The billet was a rectangular room with a door at one end leading out onto winding stairs - which we would run up and down thousands of times during our three months of training in and around The Brecon.

Lance Corporal gave us Chapter and Verse about the Army and that there would be two training platoons - "A" and "B." I was to be in the "A" platoon with Sergeant Smith, whom, as yet, we had not met. We were shown the cookhouse and the NAAFI, and then left to sort out our kit for the following day.

A reveille by the regimental bugler woke us up at 6am. "Come to the cookhouse door boys!" he instructed. Some of the lads were very reluctant to get out of bed at that unearthly hour, but were soon aroused by the orderly Corporal banging his drill stick on the edge of the steel framed beds and creating a racket in order to attempt to move the laziest soul.

We got up and put our Army issue kit on; this was a novelty to us and we had quite a laugh looking at one another's attempts to look smart.

I had brought with me a writing pad on which I recorded the number of days I had to do inside - 730! It appeared that everyone else had also done this. I had also brought a photograph of my fiancée and I walking hand in hand through the main street in Newquay only three months earlier. Most of the other lads were also courting or engaged, but some had children and were married, even at that tender age, and it was these lads who were hit the hardest. I thought I had been hard done to, having to leave my fiancée behind, and I hoped and prayed that she would find it in her heart to wait for me.

We had only been at Brecon for a couple of weeks when the "Dear John" letters started to arrive. Who would be next?

We were all ordered to the Briefing Room to meet our Platoon Officer and Sergeant for the duration of our training. We were divided into two platoons of 26 Platoon. On arrival at the room we were again greeted by Lance Corporal Jones' friendly face and told to sit. "Here are your Sergeants for training," said Lance Corporal Jones.

It was reminiscent of acts coming out at the London Palladium! First Sergeant Brown "B" Platoon, followed by Sergeant Smith. My first reaction to him was one of fear, because he was built like a weightlifter with a back as straight as a ramrod and a barrel chest that looked as though it had been carved out of a piece of solid oak. He had a South Wales voice of velvet but could spit orders out to frighten even the most hardened Soldier or Officer. He could also come out with jokes mocking unfortunate "Sproggs" who couldn't cope with the drill at first, and dare anyone else laugh.

We were informed that we would be earning 39/6 per week.

"Yes," said Sergeant Smith with a wry smile, "we pay you for your holiday."

He also said that he would not bore us with details about his parents.

"Sergeant Bastard Smith will be quite appropriate, but whisper it very quietly. You will find me a very fair Sergeant or else."

The adjutant then gave us the information we required as far as food and issues of extra clothing were concerned. A real live Captain! I had never been this close to a Captain before; the only ones I had ever seen were in those never ending World War II films and, more often than not, they were played by the excellent actor - David Niven. He had always been my idea of an Officer, and a lot were like him, but times were changing.

We were then handed over to Sergeant Smith again who told us we would have to have our boots "bulled" up for the next day - our first muster. We were also informed that we were not allowed out of the barracks for one month until we were `acclimatized', as he put it.

The following day we were all lined up for muster at 8am precisely. What a shambles! Sergeant Smith looked as though he had had a bad night and he started to scream orders to Lance Corporal Jones, who was up and down the files poking some of the lads who looked as though they were dozing off again! I was extremely frightened, and whether any of the other lads were, I don't know, but, none of us dared reveal the fear.

We resembled a field of mushrooms with our oversized berets perched on our heads and it was very difficult not to laugh at some of the bemused faces up and down the files. Sergeant Brown who had "B" Platoon managed a smile for his lads, but Sergeant Smith was not as friendly. "Look at that dozy lot!" he shouted, pointing to the "B" Platoon.

And so the pattern was set and we were in competition with one another, and this competition lasted right through our training and was intentionally created by the Army, undoubtedly producing results. After a while the platoon were escorted out.

In the Army height was a crucial factor; the tallest were at either side of the Squad and tapered down to the smallest in the middle.

Army numbers had been issued - "23640068 Fusilier Goolding, Sir," and woe betide anyone who forgot that number after a few days.

We were introduced to the Regimental Sergeant Major of the Depot. He was a small man compared to other Officers we had seen - RSM Martell. I thought to myself that that would make a very good Officer's name; popular in the Officer's Mess when a round of drinks were ordered no doubt - "A small brandy."

After several weeks of running up and down those stairs, changing for this and that, staying awake until the early hours of the morning, burning leather off boots with a spoon heated by a candle, cleaning brasses and pressing uniforms night after night, we had adjusted to Army life and got to know one another very well.

The Corporal had developed a loud shriek as he gave orders for us to stand to attention or quick march. All of his sentences would end in `hun'. For example `right - hun," `left - hun' or `open order - hun' (March). It would be the last syllable that we moved on, so it was his way of getting everyone to move at the same time. However, it didn't always work, because some of the lads would be dangling their foot forward in anticipation of the order, and as a result they would receive a bollocking from Sergeant Smith, who would sit back sometimes like an artist and admire his work. On the whole it wasn't good enough, and he strove for perfection because he was getting close to the end of his 22 years service in the Army.

Sergeant Smith's voice, when angry, could he heard 20 miles away in Merthyr! It was a rough, loud voice now - not like the voice we had first heard when he introduced himself not so long ago, and once he had given an order, you do not misinterpret it or you would suffer the consequences.

Slowly we began to trust the people who were training us and we gradually started to get things together - although one or two would never be able to get it, so these would be hidden in the middle of the ranks.

The NAFFI was a welcome retreat in the evenings, but more often not we were too tired to go down there for a pint. There was a juke box though, so I usually went down with a couple of the lads I had got to know from the Wirral - Lenny Williams, Kenny Bratley and Eric Thomas (otherwise known as Thommo). We had many laughs during the two years of our National Service.

I put a few records on - Peter Gunn was good for a bit of noise after slogging it out around the "square" all day, played on the twangy guitar of Duane Eddy. Bobby Darin's two hits were also played regularly - Dream Lover and Mack the Knife. My own favourite was Buddy Holly singing `It doesn't matter any more."

We had downed a few pints and were having a sing-song after about an hour, when suddenly we heard what could only be described as someone breaking up stones in a gravel pit. We looked around and there, to our utter amazement, was one of our draft biting the rim off his pint glass and chewing the pieces in his mouth! It was hard to believe but this lad did this kind of thing for bets.

It was extremely unfortunate that whilst he had been on shore leave from the Merchant Navy, the Army had grabbed him for National Service. His name was Lee and he was from Liverpool - where else?

The cracking and chinking could be heard all over the NAFFI and eventually the Duty Corporal went over to him and told him to pack it in, and called him a "Scouse Crackpot" - which I thought was quite appropriate for the incident.

CHAPTER FIFTY TWO

Over The Wall

Four weeks into our training there was to be a Barrack Room competition, and the winners would be given a weekend pass. This was another method used by the Army of getting the Barrack Rooms redecorated and spotlessly cleaned. We worked extremely hard on our billet, well into the early hours of the morning, leading up to the adjudication day - which was on the Friday. We even utilised the professional talent of one of the lads who was a sign writer by trade in Civvy Street - Dave Price, also from Ellesmere Port.

We had to come up with a name to hang over the fireplace to impress the judges. Several names were mentioned but Chez-Nous was finally agreed upon. We thought we couldn't lose. We came second!

We had a hurried meeting of The Wirral Committee and took the decision that we were going on leave anyway - pass or no pass. Saturday came, and no one was allowed outside that Barracks unless they had a pass, even into Brecon itself, and the RSM had given orders to watch any movement by the present intake during the weekend.

Being unaware of what the punishment would entail, we started to move out when all was quiet just after midday, through the side door on the far side of the square - one every 10 minutes in full Battle Dress. I went last and an Officer was walking across the square with rugby kit on. He glanced over to me, gave me a puzzled look and, fortunately, proceeded on his way down to the Sports Field.

We thumbed it home and spent that Saturday night with our families. In those days, getting a lift was quite easy, especially if wearing full Army Uniform. I prayed that we would not be missed back at Brecon, because I knew there was often a spot roll call on the occasional Saturday evenings in the barracks.

On the Sunday, after saying goodbye to my fiancée, I made my way up to the Chester Road in Little Sutton to be picked up by Lenny in his Morris Minor at about 11pm. Not many people of our age could even imagine owning a car, but Lenny, who had worked in a garage before he came in the Army, had done this car up himself. Five large lads in a Moggy Minor, some full of ale, some full of food - you can imagine the stench that was emitted on that long and tedious journey back to Brecon. Incidentally, this was a journey that would be made many times during the course of our little "holiday" in the Army.

We would arrive back into barracks at about 3am. It would be pitch black, except for the very dim Toc `H' type lamps which threw faint light across the road - it was like a ghost town.

Without thinking, we foolishly made our way to the little side door at the main entrance but, luckily, it was locked, or we would have been caught there and then, forgetting about the "Guard." That meant that we had to climb the 20 foot wall! Fortunately the wall was covered in ivy in parts and we were able to climb up easily enough and perch precariously on the top and look down the other side, which was a sheer sandstone wall with a drop onto the white gravel below on the drill square. Thommo went first, as he was the most agile, and we heard him land on the other side and then there was silence. We all eventually landed safely on the other side and took our shoes off and, one by one, went stealthily across the square and into the billet.

No one was any the wiser for us going missing that weekend. We did the same thing on other occasions during the ten weeks, Lenny leaving his car parked in the town for a few weeks.

Snippets of information were now beginning to filter through from HQ and the latest posting after training was to be Cyprus.

This was now our 6th week in training and our boots had been burnt down and the pimples flattened, ready for more spit and polish. The boots were quite highly polished, and to get them looking like that had taken about a month, night after night, of putting polish on a duster and doing little circles all over the boot, whilst adding a little bit of spit to the polish. Apparently this gave the binding and the build up for the very highly polished surface of the boot, but once on the parade ground, and after a few "Attentions," it would gradually crack and so the process would have to be repeated night after night.

I eventually got my beret down to size by constantly boiling and cooling it and finally got it to the shape of my head, with the badge perfectly lined up with my left eye.

Pressing my clothing was also a new experience, as up until now it had only been done by my Mother. Using brown paper and wetting the trousers gave the perfect crease, so they said, but there were a few wavy creases on parade on some mornings.

One morning, completely out of the blue, we were introduced to what Sergeant Smith said would be "Our Best Friend" during the course of the two years - a rifle, the latest Belgian FN SLR twenty rounds. As I drew my rifle out of the armoury I was a little frightened of it, since I, like many others, had never ever seen a gun before, let alone hold one. We were shown how to load, clean and strip down blindfold, and then would come the great day when we marched down to the Rifle Range. Until now we had only used the rifles on the drill field as Sergeant Smith screamed his orders - "Shoulder, Arms, Port Arms. 1-2-3, 1-2-3, 1-2-3, and eventually "Port Arms For Inspection." Fix bayonets was the one that was the hardest and there would be a lot of ironwork falling onto the parade ground as "Sproggs" struggled to fix their bayonets as they looked straight to the front. I could just imagine the married lads having sex when on leave to numbers "In 1-2-3, Out 1-2-3."

CHAPTER FIFTY THREE

Clear As A Mountain Stream

"**Y**ou are now ready to fend for yourselves in the Brecon Beacons!" announced Sergeant Smith, eight weeks into our training.

This announcement made us very proud. However, once again, this was just another method of installing courage into the raw recruit.

We were issued with our rifles (but no ammunition), and a three day supply of food; although a three tonner would come out every so often to replenish the stock of food.

Although it had been an "Indian Summer" during the period of our training, it was now November and was starting to get quite chilly and frosty in the mornings. "Brass Monkey" weather. There was some snow on the Brecon Beacons which was very picturesque from a distance.

Sergeant Smith was a very hardened soldier having been through many campaigns and as we rested a while, he appeared to be musing over something with the Corporal.

The stream was flowing quite quickly as the overnight snowfall melted into it and the water sparkled in the frosty sunlight but it was quite shallow. Sergeant Smith informed us that he was going to show us how to crawl along with the rifle held across our arms, as if holding a baby. He gave us a very good demonstration alongside the stream, ably assisted by Lance Corporal Jones who seemed to have a smirk on his face the entire time. "Right, first one - Thomas, into the stream!" bellowed Sergeant Smith.

We all looked at one another in amazement. In the event, each and every one of us had to crawl for 50 yards into a swift flowing freezing cold stream, and ensure that not a drop of water got onto the rifle. Of course, it didn't matter if the Squaddies got wet - I have never been so numb in my whole life!

We were up in those mountains for two nights. We had to make our own makeshift shelters to protect us from the freezing cold night, and the imaginary enemy. I was so relieved to return to those barracks for once!

It transpired that "B" platoon had it even rougher with Sergeant Brown, and as they marched back through Brecon at about 6pm they broke rank and headed for the nearest pub with the Sergeant and Lance Corporal Leahy screaming at them. In the end they were unable to stop them and raced back to the barracks where they rang for the MP's at Derring Lines - the home of the SAS in those days. They were then rounded up and treble marched back to the barracks, where they were put in the gym for the night with only a ground sheet (the Gaol was not large enough) on the concrete floor.

The following day RSM Martell was marching up and down waiting for both platoons to fall in at the rear of the barracks and out of the sight of any Officers, so that he could give us a good lecture on discipline. He warned "B" platoon that if it happened again, the culprits would be put on orders in front of the Barracks Commander, whoever he was.

After about 7 weeks we were trusted to leave the barracks again. Unfortunately there was trouble in the pubs in Brecon with fighting and such like, and on one such occasion apparently one of the lads, a Fusilier, had chatted to one of the local girls. "You've got the wrong badge on," the girl said to him.

He then told her to go away, after which her boyfriend took offence and the rest, as they say, is history.

RSM again on parade. He was never, ever seen until something happened to make sure that all soldiers in that barracks behaved themselves in and around Brecon, whether they be South Wales Borderers or any other Regiment. He demanded to know who the culprit was but, of course, no one knew. He offered to fight him himself in order to teach whoever it was a lesson, but that was just a show of bravado, as he was only about 5'3" tall and the culprit was 6 foot - and just as wide! He was from Tiger Bay in Cardiff. Confined to barracks for another week. I'm sure that the RSM had shares in the NAFFI - the number of times he confined us to barracks, as the NAFFI was the only place to go.

CHAPTER FIFTY FOUR

Sergeant Smith's Party Piece

Guard Duty was the next phase of our training, and it was the most important part, according to Sergeant Smith, because we were guarding the barracks and, more importantly, the Armoury from the IRA. I thought it was very exciting to be there all night, watching imaginary figures prowling around the barracks - but this excitement would soon wear off as I progressed through my two years of training.

A usual guard routine stag would be two hours on and then two hours rest and, if you were on the first stag, your second stint would be from midnight until 2am, giving over 4 hours in the bunk until Reveille at 6.30am. Naturally, everyone preferred the first stag.

After several cups of NAFFI tea, which had been stewing for most of the night in the urn, my mouth felt like the bottom of a bird cage. My mind drifted back home and the thought of a lovely pint of bitter in the Castrol Club. I wondered how the football team were managing without me (quite well apparently!).

Most of the lads, including myself, would write to their girlfriends or fiancées while they were off stag. I was on the second stag so I would be back on again at 2am for two hours on my own watching for intruders, like the good soldier I was, with a wooden pick helve in my hand. I held it up to the very dim light in the Guard Room.

"This will frighten any potential enemy away or maybe even make them laugh as they fire their automatic weapons!" I thought to myself.

Moving up and down and peering into the very early misty morning air, I leaned against the wall to take the weight off my feet, when I got the biggest fright of my life. A Squaddie dropped down over the wall, obviously a regular Soldier, and put his finger to his lips, indicating for me to be quiet. I went to speak but thought better of it, as he had been AWOL for weeks and was trying to get back into the barracks ready for orders on Monday morning.

Most of the new recruits in our draft had now settled down to Army life, maybe not enjoying it, but accepting it and myself, I was putting everything into it.

Back home I was advised by ex-Squaddies never to volunteer for anything. I took no notice of this advice, and would do the complete opposite!

I held my hand aloft for the boxing; if there had been no volunteers they would have been chosen at random anyway, but there were a few other hands held up, so I was not alone.

I had only previously sparred or, to be more precise, been used as a punch bag, for Mally Worthington as he trained to win the ABA Championships in 1955, before eventually turning professional, when I lived in Crewe.

I now carried a weight of 10 stone 10 pounds and there had to be a middle weight from the "B platoon to be paired off with me. It was a lad from South Wales who was just as scared as I was. The lads built me up into a Rocky Marciano, and told him that I was a professional in Civvy Street, and had so many fights. However, this didn't seem to impress him at all.

On the night there had been quite a lot of blood spilled around the ring, as a lot of the fights were mismatched and some of the lads were just not cut out for the fight game. My fight lasted for the full three rounds, and I was absolutely knackered at the end, as was my opponent. I was adjudged to have won the fight on points and received a medal for my triumph. This was to be one of my proudest possessions because, in a way, after defeating the asthma, I had more or less achieved one of the things in life that my Father had found easy and which came naturally to him - and that was strength.

However, I didn't ever go into a Boxing Ring again, not that I have anything against it, but I just was not cut out for boxing. It's fine if you have the know-how and the speed, but if, like me, you bruise easily, don't bother; there will always be someone who is quicker and harder - and that is a fact of life.

The day following the Boxing Match was Sunday - Remembrance Day, and the whole barracks were on parade. I woke up looking forward to the parade, but when I looked in the mirror as I prepared to shave, I noticed that my eye was black and half shut.

We all lined up on the parade ground and, unfortunately for me, I was the left marker, which meant that I was at the front and marching more or less in the gutter through the very narrow streets of Brecon. Oh boy - did I get some stick from the youngsters as they marched with us!

"Who did your make up mister?" shouted one of the young boys.

"Why didn't you wash your face for the parade?" asked another one.

"Piss off you little horror!" I murmured, without the Sergeant noticing. This was a foolish thing to do as we strode up the steep hill to the cathedral. Yes - a cathedral.

The youngsters were now moving in close and kicking my leg so I had to take evasive action again, and they eventually fell back and pestered the lads at the back of the platoon - thank goodness!

I have to say that the Royal Welch Fusiliers on parade are one of the smartest in the British Army, and in the end I was proud to be part of their history. The white Hackle on the front of the beret was looked after like a baby. It was kept in an empty Brasso tin full of talcum powder to keep its shape and maintain its pure white colour. There was also a black flash fastened onto the back of the collar of the Battle Dress; this was said to stop the crease coming off the plaits that the soldiers had during the American War of Independence. The White Hackle apparently evolved from the same campaign. The soldiers would pin the white briar roses into their hats in order that they would be recognised by their own men as they fought in the woodlands around the East coast of America.

Although we had tried our best on the day, we were no match for the regular soldiers from the depot who looked immaculate in their best Battle Dress or Ceremonial Dress, as they like to call it. It was navy blue with purple stripes down the side of the trousers, purple sashes and the white Hackle, much larger and better groomed than ours, and their marching was a lot sharper than ours. Well, I suppose it had to be really, because they were training us, and obviously they led by example.

As we left the cathedral and lined up again to march around the town, side by side with the South Wales Borderers, all rivalry was forgotten, as the men who had given their lives in two World Wars was remembered.

As the band struck, the sun broke through the lime trees that ran along the path and up to the cathedral. With our backs straightened and our chests pushed out to the full, the medals of the regular Soldiers glistened in the sunlight. There is nothing quite like a military band to get all the marchers into perfect timing.

As we proceeded to march down the hill, the same little brats that had been pestering us as we came up the hill, were now smiling and giving us the thumbs-up; so, finally, it appeared as though the RWF had been accepted in the little town of Brecon.

After another week getting lost on the Brecon Beacons, we were still waiting for orders to go to Cyprus - everything depended on the meeting in London with Archbishop Makarios and the then Prime Minister, Harold Macmillan.

On the last Saturday of training, we were all invited for a night out and Sergeants Brown and Smith enjoyed themselves, laughing and singing a duet - "It wasn't the Yanks that won the war, Parlez Vous etc." Many Army songs were sung and even the barmaids were smiling at some of the lads, despite them being RWF's. Up until this evening I had not seen anyone drink as much ale as Sergeant Smith, although my Father would have given him a run for his money.

As the night rolled on, the songs became dirtier and dirtier, and finally the Landlord had a word with Sergeant Brown as it was also getting close to closing time. Apparently Sergeant Smith did a party piece whenever he was having one of his `booze-ups', and that would signal the end of the night. From what I can recall, it was a rhyme about Alexander's giant penis. Everyone laughed, Sergeant Smith more than anyone else.

We eventually staggered out into the cool night air and returned to the barracks after a nightcap of shorts. I believe that this was another Army tactic - having the end of training celebration right opposite the barracks.

Back at the barracks, and just about to retire to bed, there was a commotion on the Drill Square. Sergeant Smith was shouting orders at imaginary ranks of soldiers. Sergeant Brown, who was laughing to himself, was trying to persuade him to leave the square, but he knew he would just do his own thing, as he was an extremely powerful man.

Names that he had some trouble with during our training were being shouted around. "Williams, you're hopeless!" ....which one, I thought to myself, there were quite a few in our draft. But then it went very quiet. There was then a clatter up the wooden stairs leading up to our billet.

"Please God, don't let it be Sergeant Smith!" we all thought to ourselves. However, the door was kicked open, and our worst fear was confirmed - it was Sergeant Smith. He was swaying and attempting to focus on different members of the platoon. Finally he settled on Lenny (Williams).

"Hello Williams," he drawled "I've come to let you get a bit of your own back on me."

We all moved to try to restrain Sergeant Smith, but to no avail.

"Keep away, or I'll have you all put on a charge; this is between me and Williams!" demanded Sergeant Smith.

He then proceeded to remove his jacket but had great difficulty, and in the end it came off with several buttons and was hurled up the barrack room. One of the lads moved to pick the jacket up.

"Leave it!" barked Sergeant Smith.

"Right Williams, `Out of School', you can have first punch - come on lad," he said, toe to toe with Lenny.

Lenny didn't know what to do.

"No Sarge - go to bed," he said quietly.

But Sergeant Smith was not going to leave without letting Lenny have a go at him. I think it was probably a sign of guilt because he had given Lenny quite a lot of stick on the Parade Ground during the course of training, and it must have been on his drunken conscience. "I'll tell you what," said Sergeant Smith in his South Wales drawl, "you have first smack."

But Lenny still didn't want anything to do with it. This wasn't because he was afraid of the man, as Lenny himself was a powerfully built lad, but he was afraid of being put on a charge and gaoled for striking an NCO. Lenny turned to put his jacket in his locker and as he turned around to face Sergeant Smith again, a full blooded right hander caught him on the jaw and Lenny fell back onto his locker. However, to Sergeant Smith's amazement, he did not knock Lenny out. "OK Sarge...that's enough," we pleaded, but he was still not satisfied.

"No! It's your go Williams - come on lad!" shouted the Sergeant.

Lenny hit him fair and square on the jaw and he shot across the room, hit the door, slid down and went out like a light. He came around 5 minutes later. "What happened?" he asked, before climbing to his feet and leaving.

Five minutes later a rather drunken Lance Corporal Jones arrived shadow boxing around the room, which was quite a funny sight. "Who hit the Sarge? I'll take him now - in fact, I'll take you all on!" he slurred.

He was subsequently bundled through the door without any more ado.

At muster the following day, Sergeant Smith had come to say goodbye to us all. His jaw was bruised and very swollen. He looked straight at Lenny, managed a smile and then looked away, and the whole episode was forgotten. In my opinion, that was the mark of a man to be looked up to - Sergeant Smith, what a character! I wonder what Lenny thought of him?!

CHAPTER FIFTY FIVE

Sugar Loaf Mountain

After a weekend pass we were posted to Cwrt-y-Gollen, just outside the market town of Crickhowell. This was a transit camp and had been built for the American GI's during the second World War. The barracks were like the Ritz compared to what we were used to - it even had central heating that actually worked!

The whole atmosphere was a lot quieter here, and it was as if the Army were letting us wind down before our posting to our Battalion. We were to remain here for approximately two weeks, running around the woods and hills in the immediate vicinity of Cwrt-y-Gollen with the famous "Sugar Loaf" mountain, which could be seen from our barracks, and which was a very picturesque sight, with a fluttering of snow covering its apex.

We even found the time to venture into Crickhowell in the evening to have a good old sing-song in the pub in the market square. We were fortunate, because we had a pianist in our midst - a lad named Holmes, and he could really bang a Rock 'n' Roll tune out on that `Old Joanna'. Jerry Lee eat your heart out!

We were all now wondering if we were going to be posted to Cyprus, and it was all dependent on the Peace talks which were taking place between Makarios and the Prime Minister. All we could do was await the outcome of the talks.

I must have had a dozen haircuts during the 10 weeks of training (I wonder if my Father had a word with Sergeant Smith?). "Fusilier Goolding - get that hair cut!" the Sergeants would instruct. I think they must have said that phrase over and over again in their sleep.

After those 10 weeks in training, I must admit it was the fittest I have ever been in my life.

It was now early December 1959 and orders had come through for us to go to Bulford on Salisbury Plain to join our Battalion. Although the main force had not arrived back from Cyprus, some of the advanced party were there organising the camp for occupation.

Bulford was about 2 miles from Tidworth - the main administration town for the Army in Southern England. The New Zealanders had been in the camp during World War II and during their wait to go to various parts of the globe they had etched out a huge kiwi in the chalk on the hill facing our camp.

CHAPTER FIFTY SIX

A Feeling of Loneliness

Our kitbags were loaded onto three tonners at Cwrt-y-Gollen and each platoon would follow a separate three tonner. We must have travelled for 100 miles as we sat on the wooden planks on either side of the truck. It was extremely uncomfortable and my bottom became numb as we carved our way through the countryside, the rain pouring in as we slowed down through all the towns and villages en-route.

After passing through several villages on the border of Wiltshire, the landscape began to change and trees became scarcer and scarcer, as we drove further and further into chalk country. Tank tracks covered the terrain and they had churned up parts of the road as they turned and manoeuvred for fresh positions. Little did I know that this is where I would spend most of my time for the following 2 years.

As the three tonner came to the top of another small hill, I glanced around the edge of the canvas to see what was ahead, and then, for the first time, I had a feeling of complete and utter loneliness. There was nothing but sky and open land - no hedges, just miles and miles of Plain; obviously an ideal place for the Army to train.

The convoy came to a halt in Tidworth for a while before moving on into Bulford and, although surrounded by members of my platoon, I was alone and I knew that the Army would either make me or break me.

By this time I was 22 years old and had, up until now, given it my all. It seemed the only way to approach the next 2 years of my Army life, but things were starting to liven up as members of the advanced party were returning from Cyprus. The battle-hardened regulars were out to prove how good and hard they were - some of them were bastards, but most were National Service, like us.

The regulars (and by `regular' I mean 22 year men; some of whom had even seen service in the Korean War), would rather be on active service than be based at home in England. Whilst they were in England they were always on edge and would be at the centre of any trouble in the towns around the camp. Consequently they would have to be posted abroad again, because no town could hold them in England. They were so highly trained that they had to be where the action was, in whatever part of the World where trouble erupted. I suppose this was a tribute to the NCOs and the Officers who had contributed to their training and had moulded them into perfect Soldiers. They, like us, could now be flown to any part of the World within 24 hours, and as soon as they hit ground they would be ready for action.

According to my brief I was to be the Company Clerk. We were taken up the lines, as the CSM's called them, which was a block consisting of a central walk-through with 8 rooms branching off - 4 on either side, and were known as `The Spider'. We spent a few months in these rooms and during out settling in time the Main Battalion came back from Cyprus, as the trouble there was now over.

Guards were now the order of the day, as all the weapons had been brought back and chained in the Armoury. I was put down for Christmas Guard unfortunately, and this would be my first Christmas away from home. Fortunately a lad from Mid-Wales named Rhys wanted New Year at home, and so we swapped.

After returning to camp following Christmas at home, I was feeling really down, knowing that I was to be on guard all New Year's Eve. It was, once again, a time of isolation and as I stood in that sentry box for two hours, my mind would often revert back to happier times not so long ago, of sunshine and Newquay. "What the hell am I doing here? It has to be a bad dream!" I thought to myself.

The temperature was well below zero and I had lit a cigarette (not permitted on guard), and had cupped it in my hand behind my back after inhaling to keep the glow away from any prying eyes - it also kept my hand warm. Tea was brought down from the cookhouse together with bags of chips which were leftover from teatime, but were still warm, so they went down well. Coming in from the midnight to 2am stag, the stewed tea would be a welcome refreshment - just to get both my hands around that warm mug was an absolute luxury!

On many a night we would come in from guard duty and collapse onto the bunk to try and get some sleep, when some `up and coming' young Officer would call out the guard. There would then be a mad scramble to get into our kit, which should not have been removed at all, and then outside to get into some kind of orderly file outside the Guard Room to be inspected and counted by the Guard Commander, as the Officer for that night was called. It was the same Officer who had inspected us earlier and who no doubt had a full six hours sleep. It must have been some sort of Army tradition, to wake up poor soldiers at that unearthly hour, just to inspect - or was it to keep us on our toes?

The following morning we would still have to be up at 8am for muster and carry out a full day's work.

Since leaving the Army I have been told that it was all to test the individual on how much he could take, and whether he would be suited for special training, the Para's or the SAS. Not many National Service lads qualified, I'm afraid. Although most of them readily accepted National Service, they did not ultimately see the Army as being a career.

I did have the chance of signing on and was promised a stay at the Depot if I signed `on the dotted line' for 3 years to play football and cricket for the Depot. I was very tempted. Incidentally, on the final night at Brecon, under the influence of alcohol, some of the lads did sign up the next day, and on that same night Lenny had tried to encourage Thommo and myself to also sign up for 3 years. These lads would most probably have stayed at the Depot as well on the MT section. Back then, 3 years seemed like a lifetime, and I often wondered how my life would have turned out if I HAD signed, because the Company that employed the National Service lads in Civvy Street, were not obliged to take them back if they signed regular Army forms for 3 or even 6 years - QUE SERA SERA!!!

CHAPTER FIFTY SEVEN

Dear John's and Oscar

Writing letters to my fiancée was my main occupation in the evenings; it was the only way I, and many other lads who also had partners, could keep in touch. Even though it was only 200 hundred miles away from Ellesmere Port, in those days it seemed like the other side of the World. Fortunately my fiancée wrote to me most days, but if a day was missed, I would immediately think the worse, because there were quite a few Squaddies in training who had received `Dear John' letters. Some of the lads would take it very hard and go AWOL in an attempt to patch things up, and would then be rounded up by the MP's and, unfortunately, receive further punishment. Some of the lads actually welcomed being in "Nick" and isolation just to contemplate their next move in life. Many of these men were married, and some, tragically, took their own lives. However, most of them would get over the shock after a few months.

It was a well known fact that some of the lads would try to hide their `Dear John' letters, but we always knew they had received one, because the individual would go very quiet for days on end, not speaking to anyone.

It was a difficult task trying to convince a young soldier who was in the Army through no fault of their own, that the girl who had sent the letter was not worth worrying about. Love will never be fully understood, and no one will ever be able to read another person's thoughts which, I suppose, is a blessing in disguise!

Having got over the traumatic experience of a broken marriage or the end of a courtship which had lasted for years, most of the lads would allow the offending letter be read out to the others in the billet, and a reply would be drafted by the "Barrack

Room Lawyer" (usually a `Geordie'). An extra page would be left aside for each member of the platoon to add his comments and the letter sent back to the ex-girlfriend. Some extremely naughty rude remarks would be made - some of them unprintable, but most, to a certain degree, were humorous. As you could imagine, once the girl in question had received the letter, she would certainly not show her face anywhere near the local cattle market.

I certainly admired the lads who did get over the experience. As for me, God only knows how I would have reacted should the same thing have happened to me. Luckily though, my fiancée must have thought as much for me, as I did for her, because our letters continued back and forth for the whole two years - and we are still together more than 30 years later.

"Oscar" was the Royal Welch Fusilier's RSM and had been in that role for almost 22 years, and RWF ran through his body like the letters in a stick of rock - he was due to retire from the Army at any time.

Oscar was known all over the World for his strict discipline and booming voice, which it was rumoured could be heard up to 10 miles away, and he was renown throughout the British Army, RSM HANKS. He was another one who was built like a brick shed, the back of his head shaved down to the wood. His head, his neck and his shoulder blades were perfectly in line - straight as a die. He was tall and had quite a belly on him - probably as a result of eating all that Army food over the years. However, when dressed in his uniform, the belly gave the appearance of solid muscle.

When striding out over the Parade Ground it was an amazing sight just to see Oscar with his pace stick swivelling in perfect unison, his back like a ramrod, counting to make sure he had enough room to manoeuvre the squad before they hit the boundary of the Parade Ground. I had often thought (just a thought!), of what fun it would have been to have shouted some of my own numbers in, just to confuse him at the point where he reached the turn, and to see his face turn to bright red in anger!

Regular soldiers had regaled us of the many incidents in his quest for discipline. On one such occasion he has ordered the `Juke Box' in the NAAFI to be put under close arrest and turned the guard out to carry it down to the Guard Room to be put in a cell for the night. He said it was "corrupting the men's minds." Songs like Pat Boone singing "I'll be home my darling, please wait for me." Songs directed at the servicemen.

This was why most of the Squaddies admired Elvis; at least he did do his stint in the Army. He was actually in at the same time as myself and my draft, and although he probably didn't have to go through the strict training and such like, at least he was there. Come to think of it, I cannot recollect many of the British singers or actors of the day entering the Army for National Service. (*Oh, yes, they were great in Army films weren't they?*) Many seemed to develop flat feet or something.

Eventually Oscar retired, and a big parade was organised; many of the lads thought they saw a tear glisten as he gave his farewell salute. Even the Regimental Mascot, the Goat, had a sorrowful look on his face. "Three cheers for RSM Hanks" the CSM shouted.

There followed a tumultuous cheer, and whether they were happy to see him going or not, I do not know, but I believe it was probably about 90% sorry. I cannot recollect whether the CSM who led the cheering did get Oscar's job or not.

I discovered that despite all the tales and rumours concerning Oscar, he was a very fair man and he proved it on one snowy and bitterly cold morning in January 1960, when we had to run into a snowdrift on top of the Cotswolds, travelling back to camp in Lenny's van.

CHAPTER FIFTY EIGHT

Blizzards and Barrack Rooms

The Battalion had arrived back from Cyprus the week before, and the Brigadier had ordered leave for most of the men. Lenny had a Bedford Dormobile van now, so we all had a 48 hour pass and, come Friday at 4.30pm, away we went, heading for the Wirral some 200 miles north.

After the weekend at home I was picked up at about 11pm on the Sunday, and it would then be a journey of about 5 to 6 hours to Bulford, depending on the weather.

We had been travelling for about 4 hours and most of the lads were nodding off in the back of the van, even though it was freezing and snowing moderately as we passed through Worcester. Once out of Tewkesbury, where we stopped for a coffee at an all night café in the main street, we started to climb as we headed for Cheltenham and the Cotswolds. Climbing out of Cheltenham and on the Cirencester Road (the A435), I could not help but notice the names of the villages in the area on the signposts; Royal-sounding names like: Charlton Kings, Charlton Abbots, Duntisbourne Abbots and so forth.

The snow was coming down much heavier now, driving into the windscreen horizontally and Lenny was having great difficulty seeing and controlling the van. Eventually, on a much steeper gradient, the van basically gave up. We all got out to lighten the load. The snow was now drifting and blowing across the top of the hedgerows, and there was no shelter at all as we all pushed for all we were worth - we had to keep that van moving.

Finally at the top of the hill, and what seemed like the top of the world, we were on a downward slope, so we all piled into the van again to add weight and to give it some bite on the icy road as we freewheeled through village after village.

Colesbourne and North Cerney were names of villages that could vaguely be seen on the snow covered signposts as we coasted along. As we arrived in Cirencester the roads were not as bad, and although the snow was only about 2 inches deep now, it would no doubt be 12 inches by the morning, as the snow was coming down very heavy.

Once out of Cirencester and more or less off the Cotswolds and on level ground, the van was able to cope quite well, although we were only dawdling along for safety reasons.

We reached Swindon and it was now almost 6am, and the snow had eased off. Lenny was coping very well increasing his speed as the roads got wider through the larger towns.

Dropping down into Marlborough, a very pretty village in the Summer no doubt, but on this particular night the snow was drifting up the walls of the houses to several feet high. There was a small amount of shelter as we travelled through the Severnake Forest, then passing through the small hamlets of Collingbourne Kingston and Collingbourne Ducis, not too far from Tidworth.

We eventually arrived back at the camp in Bulford at 7.30am and Oscar was standing outside the Battalion Orderly Room with the Guard Commander from the night's Guard. There was still a sprinkling of snow, but it was nowhere as deep as on the Cotswolds. "You lot - over here at the double!," screamed Oscar. We went over to him baffled, because we thought we were early and in plenty of time for muster at 8am.

"I told you to be back for Reveille!" he barked, "You'll get 7 days gaol for this," he continued.

"Guard, put these men under arrest!" he instructed.

Lenny then stepped forward.

"Sir, you definitely said be back for Muster - not Reveille," he said.

Oscar then looked puzzled.

"Did I?" he asked.

"Yes Sir, you did," we all replied in unison.

"Alright, get up to your billets and get ready for Muster - I'll let you off this time." said Oscar.

After the events we had endured that night, I thought to myself, there must be someone up there on our side after all.

Although we had not slept at all that night, we still managed to be on Muster for a thorough inspection at 8am sharp.

Being the Company Clerk meant that I had to move my kit down to the Company Office and sleep in the same room as the three Company Armourers, who gave me a dog's life! If I went home on a 48 hour pass, they would lock the door when I arrived back at 4am, when I would be hoping to get some sleep. I couldn't blame them I suppose.

I would have to sleep in one of the Landrovers parked on the Drill Square on many a Monday morning. The Armourers lived like pigs since there would be no inspection and, as Corporals, they were trusted.

One night I arrived back and the place stunk to high heavens. They had killed a lamb and had cooked it in the billet and the grease was running all over the floor. Two of them were lying asleep in their own vomit, having been out on the beer, and the third one lay on the floor, face down in the grease. As far as I was concerned, they acted like animals - although I feel that is an insult to animals. My first reaction was to pick up what remained of the lamb and throw it all over the three snoring, drunken excuses for human beings. I was almost sick myself and had to run out, relieved to get into the Landrover, where I didn't sleep at all.

One of the Armourer's was a drunken bachelor, and the other two had Wives who had left them, unsurprisingly! If only the CSM were aware of their antics, but no one was going to tell him - he lived in a world above all this. His world was Company Office 8am and mixing with the Officers, and he knew nothing of the slithering, slimy world that was more or less right under his nose, and the men who were in it, supposedly representing one of the best Regiments in the British Army. They were regular soldiers because they would be unable to hold a job down in Civvy Street, and they knew it. Their only strength was there in the Army, issuing a few rifles out to the National Service lads who had come in green, and were now being given the old soldier by these pillocks.

I hasten to say that these men were in no way representative of the Battalion NCOs who were very smart and disciplinarian. Maybe they were caught out in the end.

CHAPTER FIFTY NINE

Cricket and Dynamite

There would be many incidents in which I didn't comply with military orders and was duly punished. One such incident occurred during the cricket season. I had played a few games for the Battalion on Saturday afternoons at the Bulford ground, and unbeknownst to me, the next game was a very important game for the Battalion, as they were playing the RASC who were reputed to have players of County Standard in their team. The 1st Lieutenant who captained the team was determined to win this one.

During the week I was banging away on the old typewriter, one finger boogie, preparing company orders etc. I had insisted that I was not a Clerk, but they had given me the job with no previous experience whatsoever. "Grammar School lad - Company Clerk," they had said, at my training interview.

I felt that I would have been far more suited to the REME, but whatever your favourite choice was, the Army seemed to go the opposite way....anyway, back to the subject of cricket and the Saturday game.

Even while I was playing, my mind would be elsewhere - home mainly. I was mixing with Officers and could not converse with them, although they did try to make me feel at home.

Out of the blue on the Friday, CSM Anderson informed me that I could have a weekend pass, and as I had not been home for weeks, I readily accepted, not giving the cricket match a thought (had the CSM been nobbled by the RASC?). At about 3pm and after the CO had signed my pass and it was neatly tucked in my pocket, the office door was kicked open and there, standing in the doorway, looking a little red around the gills and tossing a new cricket ball from hand to hand, was the Captain of the cricket team - the 1st Lieutenant. "What's this Goolding? Going on a weekend pass?" he asked. I immediately stood up from the typewriter and gave a gesture of a salute, because I just knew that I was in for some sort of bollocking.

"Yes Sir," I replied. I was about to explain that I had not been home for quite a while, when the new cricket ball he was lobbing up and down, was thrown at the typewriter. The ball hit the desk just in front me, and then bounced and whistled pass my ear, before hitting the window behind. The CSM had jumped up and was about to placate the Officer.

"If you don't play on Saturday, you will NEVER play again!" he said.

I didn't play, and about a month later I was posted to the 1st Guard's Brigade at Winterbourne Gunner, which ultimately became the 51st Infantry Brigade.

The force at which that cricket ball was thrown, it would have gone for four byes anyway on a length, but going well down the leg side!

I was with the Battalion from December 1959 to September 1960, serving with Major Priestley - an extremely fit looking, dapper man with a neat moustache. He was our Company Commander at the time. CSM Newby had now retired and CSM Anderson had replaced him - another man of smart appearance with black hair and a thick, black moustache. Moustaches would appear to have been the `in-thing' back then for WO's and Officers. The CSM's were very often much better turned out than the Officers. They had shinier leather straps around their person and it was obvious that their batman would have spent hours cleaning all the regalia associated with a CSM.

Prior to our first big scheme on Salisbury Plain, the Major had taken it upon himself to appoint me the Company Runner, and had also sent me on a wireless operator's course. The old 88, battery and receiver fitted neatly into the ammunition pouches carried at the front of the body.

CSM Anderson had come into the office one day with a big smirk on his face. "Goolding, as you are somewhat of an all-rounder, the Major would like you to go on this course," he informed me.

I was quite proud that I was finally being given some responsibility.

The scheme was to last three weeks and all the Battalions in Southern Command would be involved. This was a new idea devised by the Army and the Government of the day, to get troops to any part of the world within 24 hours fighting fit.

The great day arrived!

We were ferried out into the middle of The Plain and our first task, as always, was to start digging out for the latrines and the trenches for defence, as soon as we landed from the back of the 3 tonners.

The Sergeants and Corporals were screaming their orders and there would be organised chaos with Fusiliers running everywhere. The older, more experienced soldiers appeared to take it all in their stride, obviously bored to tears with the whole charade. Picks were thrown from the back of the lorries. "What the hell are they for," I wondered, "Surely shovels are good enough for digging this terrain?" I realised how wrong I was as I bounced back off my shovel when I attempted to dig out my first sod of Salisbury Plain!

"Its chalk you dozy bastard!" screeched the Corporal.

After about three hours digging, our trench was eventually ready for inspection.

"Good," said the Corporal, "Now we want the command post digging 8 feet square for the Major and the CSM."

Wearily we started to dig, but it was not quick enough for the Sergeant.

"It is going to take us a month at this rate, and the Major will be here within the hour!" he shouted. I liked the "us" part!

"Put 18 inches overhead cover on your trenches, this will save you from a nuclear bomb attack," he said.

Our trench was about 10 feet away from the Command Post.

"Now get in and see if it's alright for size," he said, once we had completed it.

As we all squeezed in, it seemed OK, but within seconds of us settling down with our helmets on, there was an almighty bang. Unbeknown to us the Sergeant had ordered the Support Group to blast the Command Post out with dynamite and the resultant debris covered our trench. Our eardrums were ringing for hours afterwards.

The Sergeant then ordered other soldiers to start digging us out and when they had pierced a hole through with the pick, allowing some daylight through to our trench, the Sergeant then scraped more of the chalk away. "You have just survived a nuclear attack!" he announced through the small hole with his hands cupped around his mouth.

"Great," I thought to myself, "so long as the Major is alright!"

After scrambling out of the trench we had to then commence clearing up the debris which had been caused as a result of the explosion before the Major arrived. "Has anyone got a piece of chalk on them?" asked the Corporal jokingly.

A few of the lads then proceeded to go through their pockets before shaking their heads, not realising that we were stood on about 50 square miles of the stuff!

CHAPTER SIXTY

Camouflage and Air Strikes

As the manoeuvres progressed, going without sleep was becoming a major hazard and the novelty of playing soldiers was wearing off for many of us.

Some of the young Officers, fresh out of Sandhurst, were eager to test their newly acquired theoretical knowledge and put it to the practical test using our Platoon. They began to organise raiding parties into other Battalions' lines at night, arming us with thunder flashes to lob into trenches and Landrovers, where unfortunate Squaddies like ourselves, had no doubt gone without sleep for a few nights.

These Officers had, of course, had a full day's sleep and were suitably refreshed. No matter what sort of antics they ordered of us during the night, we still had to be up and ready to go to Reveille at 6.30am.

The weather had now turned to heavy rain, and as we trudged around Salisbury Plain looking for the imaginary enemy, somewhere out there in the miles and miles of open space, dotted by woods here and there, I wondered why regular Soldiers would sign up for this for 22 years.

National Service lads were mixed in with the regulars and soon picked up all the dodges and dives.

The rain was now literally bouncing off the poncho's as we marched into it, and as soon as it hit the poncho's it ran down onto our BD, and so soaked the legs, but fortunately never made it as far as our boots, because of the gaiters.

My 88 was now getting quite wet with the constant lifting of my arms to protect the rifle from the rain. Suddenly I heard a shout from the front of the file. "Company Runner double to CSM!" I heard.

It rang out three times before I realised that it was me. Unfortunately we were in a dell and the 88 sets could not pick up signals from HQ. With full kit, ammunition pouches, and 88 set, I had to run about 200 yards to the top of the hill to receive a message from HQ. Once the message had been received, I raced back, unravelling myself at the feet of Major Priestley who was not amused.

"Well - what are the orders Fusilier?" he asked.

"To open order formation and attack the coppice," I panted, but the map reference was scattered with raindrops, so it had to be deciphered.

Fortunately the Corporal worked it out and pointed to a rather large wood on our right.

"I hope you're right," I thought to myself.

The Corporal in question had only been made up to full Corporal a couple of weeks before the scheme.

The whole Platoon were now marching towards the wood on open ground in broad daylight, and we had supposedly been covered by mortar fire from behind. The OC then had a brilliant idea to call an air strike. "That'll weed the blighters out!" he snapped.

I had to radio HQ again to order the air strike.

"Roger and out," said HQ, once I had got through.

We were waiting and waiting for the air strike to arrive, rifle barrels getting full of rain.

"Camouflage," shouted the Sergeant, to let everyone know that he was still there.

We all dropped to our knees and started tugging at pieces of grass and stuffing it in pockets, gaiters, berets and other parts of the battle uniform until we were covered in wet, soggy grass. Some of the lads really had made a remarkable job of it, and resembled a hayrick; they could hardly stand up at the finish.

The whole Platoon then stood up as one (still no air strike!), to test the camouflage and to ensure it stayed on. We then dropped to the ground to blend in with the surroundings, some fell asleep as soon as they hit the deck (myself included), for a couple of minutes, only to be woken up by a loud shriek from the Lance Corporal. "Fix bayonets!" ordered the Sergeant.

The orders were now coming in thick and fast, probably to give us something to do to keep us awake ready for the offensive while we waited for the air strike; bayonets were eventually fitted with bits of grass and the soil hanging here and there, and a number of the platoon were taking on the appearance of scarecrows.

After about an hour, the Major was starting to get a little red around the gills, looking desperately at his watch and then towards the heavens and muttering - although I could not work out whether he was cursing or praying; a bit of both I should imagine.

"Here they are!" shouted one of the platoon suddenly, and pointed skywards.

Afterwards he was moved to the back of the attack, because the planes turned out to be a flock of rooks heading for the woods, and their nests. The enemy was certainly in there because we could see them lying down under their covers, smoking and joking just waiting for our Major to shout: "Attack." I thought I heard something in the distance, but I wisely kept my mouth shut as my ears were still ringing from two days previous, when the command post was blasted out with dynamite.

"We'll have to go in without the air strike," the Major eventually ordered, "the whole platoon is vulnerable out here."

"Yes, and most of the platoon would have been picked off by now anyway," I thought to myself.

By now the umpires had arrived on the scene advising that they had been judging another attack about 2 miles away. All the Officers were in the Landrovers and there was a good supply of sleeping bags in the back. "ATTACK!" shouted the Major suddenly, throwing all caution to the wind. "We can take them without an air strike," he continued.

We proceeded to move down towards the woods firing blanks which, luckily, were going off even with the torrential rain running into the barrels.

"You're dead, you're dead!" shouted the umpires to the enemy, as we entered the woods.

After a full 5 minutes of this game in the woods, there was a deafening noise which wasn't heard until the three Vampires had swooped low over the woods, turned and were on their way in to make another attack.

"DOWN!" screamed the Major.

"NO NO NO!" he shouted, as he turned towards the attacking jets, "For God's sake - NO!"

The RAF boys gave it hell and it doesn't take a Mastermind to realise what had happened. Yes, we were all dead really - the goodies and baddies alike.

"Are you sure you had a right map reference?" asked both the Sergeant and the Major, with a scowl on their faces.

An umpire shouted, "Fusilier you're dead.

Another one screamed, "Goolding, take that blasted beret off - you're dead!"

At that point in time, all I could think as I hit the ground again was that I desperately needed to sleep, and off I went, not even bothering to light a fag after the ordeal. I woke up saturated through to the skin.

After our 'triumphant' attack on the coppice, orders went out to march to another destination where it was rumoured we would rest and set up camp for the night. Marching along in single file, so that we were less vulnerable to the enemy attack, my thoughts wandered back to Civvy Street, and my fiancée and family. I thought to myself, if only they knew. There were 24 more Squaddies in the same situation with, no doubt, the same thoughts. I knew we were not an active service, so I thought, why do we have to go through this charade of hours of marching, and days of sleep deprivation. Surely we wouldn't be at our best if the enemy were for real.

We had now marched for about 10 minutes and I must have counted every blade of grass as my head hung low to stop the rain going into my eyes. We rested for 5 minutes and I thought what the hell those poor men in the trenches of the First and Second World Wars must have gone through with water up to their necks.

A crow flew over squawking, free, heading for his nest and home with nothing to worry about, just trying to avoid the odd pot shot from the farmers over at Tilshead. I was still soaked to the skin, even with my Poncho tied tightly around my neck; water was dripping off at my knees now and soaking into the KD's. I pinched myself a few times thinking that, perhaps, it was all just a bad dream - only to be brought back to reality by the Sergeant's voice. "Rest 5 minutes," he shouted.

Everyone dropped again in unison, lighting a fag as we hit the deck. Like many others in the platoon, I could not help falling asleep after I had finished my `soggy woodie' and, once again, drifting back to thoughts of Civvy Street - happily married and in my own home. But, again, I was woken by the Lance Corporal. "Come on! Get on those feet - we're moving out, move, double it!" he ordered.

Much to our surprise, we only marched for another 15 minutes and we were then ordered to make camp. Bivouacs were hastily erected and, in no time at all, I was inside and falling asleep.

"Goolding, Brown - you're on first stag; Oh, no, Guards as well!" How would we stay awake? Surely the Officers could do that for one night and then their man would be fully alert and ready for action come the morning. I only muttered under my breath, mind you.

Many of the lads were put on charges for sleeping too long - it was impossible to stay awake after being on the Plain for three weeks without any sleep. "500 days to go," said one of the lads. That was a morale booster - I must say! Some had even broken the time down to hours. Months were enough for me, because I was sure the time would go very slowly for those counting the hours off. It was now June 1960 and September 1961 seemed an eternity.

Army life kept us fit when we were not on schemes, and installed in us a certain amount of discipline, but it didn't work out that way for all National Servicemen. Some of the lads rebelled against the authority imposed on them from day one, and never changed for the whole two years - it must have seemed like a million years for them. Granted, some were victims of circumstance back home. It seems that Governments will always use the poor, working class to do their dirty work and say that it was for the `Good of the Country'. Some of us accepted this - others didn't.

.

CHAPTER SIXTY ONE

Dartmoor and Dinosaurs

I was destined to go on numerous schemes doing my part of Queen and Country. The scheme that stands out most in my mind was the short stay in the middle of Dartmoor amongst the ponies and other wild creatures.

We were dropped off by three tonners at Okehampton and then marched up to a Nissen hut in an elevated position on the outskirts of the town. It was a barbed wire area used as a prison by the Army for Grade 2 prisoners. I can only assume that they were either violent men or queers. Our hut had a cast iron fire in the middle of the floor with a sheet metal flue winding its way through the roof. The fire was eventually lit and fortunately it did generate a lot of heat, which was much needed as it was now the end of February and the snow was still lying thinly on the ground.

As I lay on my bunk, my mind went back to only 12 months before, while still in Civvy Street when I had passed through this small town on my way to Newquay for a week's holiday with my fiancée, Irene. We had travelled down by coach, again from Chester which, in itself, was an endurance test. However, when we arrived in Newquay the sun shone for the whole week just like it did the first year we visited. Buddy Holly was still being played on the juke box in the little café down by the cinema near the harbour. Now here, I was plodding around Dartmoor being told what to do and having to do it or else.

The following day we were woken by the well known voice of the Corporal. "Come on you lazy bastards - get out of those pits; we're moving out up into the Moors in 10 minutes!" shouted the Corporal.

The dawn was cold and the sky a clear, pale blue with a scattering of frost on the ground. We had been split up into section of 8 and were on the move to our first location. Yes-Tor, one of the highest points around this part of Dartmoor, to pick up a reading for a reference, so that if we did get lost or the weather suddenly turned, we had a position to move to and readjust.

The whole point of this exercise was the use of the map references and how to find one's way around with the compass and map. I had never before seen such desolation. Miles and miles of absolutely nothing - except for heather and swamps which we had to plough through. We had passed High Willhays and were still heading south and, after a couple of hours we decided to stop and try to work out where we were, but it was to no avail.

Night fell very quickly and we set up camp on the side of a hill inside some prehistoric hut circles. It must have been a lot warmer in this area during the days of the dinosaurs, because the hut circles were made from stones found in the vicinity and built up without any cementation.

Dozing on and off all night, then walking around and hearing roars in the distance (what they were, I will never know), it seemed as though we were actually there, in prehistoric times. Needless to say, my imagination ran riot with me, because it was very rare that I slept at all on any of the schemes.

As I looked up at the clear Devon sky, the stars were clear, each twinkle like a miniature explosion as it reached me after travelling billions of miles and taking light years in time. I lay there and calculated that when that twinkle left that star, there were dinosaurs on this planet - even on this very moor.

With that there was another roar and my sleepy eyes picked up a large shape moving away from us, followed by two smaller shapes. I estimated that the larger one was about 20 feet high. At this point I panicked and woke one of the lads to tell him to have a look. However, he would not wake up, or, maybe, he just wasn't interested in dinosaurs! I was left to my own imagination again. Perhaps I had been whisked through time (a Dartmoor Leap, maybe?), or was it an Army ploy to keep us on our toes? I narrowed my eyes because it was absolutely pitch black with just a very faint light coming from the horizon. An owl scooped low over my head and gave a hoot before disappearing into the cool night sky. I stood, motionless, only moving my eyes from side to side to try and detect what was going on in the distance.

The owl had frightened the life out of me, because I was half expecting a dinosaur to come ambling towards me. Had I nodded off for a couple of minutes and the whole episode been a dream, or had I actually seen that dinosaur and her offspring? Perhaps, like the Loch Ness Monster in Scotland, they are roaming the Moor at night!

Anyway, I did not mention any of this to the Corporal, because I knew what he would have said. However, I definitely heard those roars and saw them moving.

The following morning we had our bangers and it was time to move on. While we were having our breakfast news came through that one of the lad's in another section had been killed as a result of falling down a ravine. News in the Army is usually exaggerated as it travels through the grapevine, and we later found out it was a lad from the Wirral who had been in training with us at Brecon by the name of Kenny Bratley. He had broken his leg. The Army sent him to BMH at Chester and he remained there until his 2 years service was up, which, apparently was very close to where he lived in Moreton on the Wirral. When we found out that he had only (ONLY) broken his leg, the cry went up - "The Lucky Bastard - Chester!" No sympathy is there?

CHAPTER SIXTY TWO

Guards are a Go-Go!

Following my brush with the Lieutenant over the cricket match, I had now been posted to Winterbourne Gunner - a quaint little village on the outskirts of Salisbury with a stream running right through the village alongside the road. There was only one pub in the village which was hardly ever used by us. The camp, `Figsbury Camp," was impossible to find, unless there were map references to help you! It was situated under the shadow of `The Figsbury Rings' - an ancient Druids settlement; one of the many scattered around Salisbury Plain - hence the name for our camp. I never did get round to having a look at them; they were probably similar to Stonehenge (which was just up the road from our camp), but on a smaller scale.

To get to the camp we had to walk up a winding lane, under an old railway bridge, left, right and then, after half a mile, arriving at the Guard Room - a place I was destined to spend plenty of my time during the 12 months in the Old Sarum vicinity.

I was now attached to the 1st Guards Brigade (more latterly to become the 51 Infantry Brigade), with the Black Swan as our logo sewn onto our sleeves. "The Guards." Initially I was extremely proud to be part of the Guards set-up - seeing Grenadiers, Coldstream, Irish and Welsh in their full ceremonial regalia every so often. However, after my initial settling in period I realised when they say, "Guards," they mean just that, and I was to do more guards than I could keep up with. Sometimes it would be a Friday guard, sleep all day on Saturday, and then back on guard at 8am on Sunday.

At Bulford I didn't do any guards with the Battalion, because I was billeted in the office building. After a weekend guard there would be no rest on the Monday, and it was up at 6.30am as usual, and down to the Company Office. Guards took up about 25% of my time at Winterbourne Gunner.

Inside the Guard Room there were three double tiered bunk beds on which, after doing a 2 hour stag, one had to try and get some sleep. This was an almost impossible task, having to sleep in full kit, even leaving our boots on. My feet would swell and start to ache and, eventually, I would be looking forward to going out on stag again.

The radio would be on all night playing all the records requested by men in the forces - Reete Petite, Jackie Wilson and good old Pat Boone's `I'll be home my darling.'

We would march around the camp in pairs, 20 feet apart with a telephone on one shoulder and a pick helve on the other to protect ourselves from enemy attack. In the Winter it would take a couple of hours for my feet to thaw out after plodding around in the snow and rain. The tea, although very stewed towards the end of the night, was very welcome, and consequently my mouth would be like a vulture's armpit!

After guards, we would venture out the following evening, just to drink the cobwebs out of our system. Fortunately, Lenny still had his van, so we were able to get around the area and became familiar with most of the pubs in Salisbury.

CHAPTER SIXTY THREE

I Faced the Firing Squad
for You, Shirley

On one particular Sunday night, I was aware that Shirley Bassey was playing at the London Palladium which commenced at 9pm, so we managed to fiddle the right stag on guard -second 8 to 10. We patrolled around the camp for about an hour or so. I was with a lad named Fred Carter who was from Portsmouth and he was also an avid Shirley Bassey fan.

Our patrol just happened to take us past the NAFFI at 9.30pm, so it was right turn and in. We settled down to watch her, knowing that she would be top of the bill and therefore be the last performer. We got a couple of pints each, took off our BD jackets, lit our cigarettes and relaxed. The room was packed with Squaddies, and I was halfway down my pint when all the lights suddenly went on and there stood the Guard Commander Sergeant Cuxton, together with two MP's glaring at us. I glanced around at Fred and was already looking straight at me with a look of fear on his face, waiting for me to come up with a solution to get us out of this sticky situation. We were obviously in for some very heavy Army discipline. "Fusilier Goolding and Private Carter stand up!" screamed the Sergeant.

We were then doubled down to the Guard Room, after hearing only one of Shirley's songs - `I will love you as I love you.' If only she could have sung this to Sergeant Cuxton who, incidentally, had been informed by an unknown person in our presence in the NAFFI. He said he was only performing his duty and I believed him! We were then locked up in the cells for the night, where I hardly slept at all.

The following morning I had to report for duty to the Company Office as usual and I was informed that I would be on Company Orders at 10am. On arrival at the office there seemed to be a lot of muttering going on between Sergeant McDermott and Sergeant Gibbs (in charge of the office administration). They were discussing how many years `nick' I would get.

The CSM had now arrived at a much quicker pace than usual, and he was gloating that he had `got me at last.'

CSM Willis was a Yorkshire man from Skipton and had been in the Army forever - it was his life out and out. "I will see that you get 12 months on top of your time for this!" he screeched, as he carried on into the OC's office, `Big Jim' Major Cowley, one who had worked his way up through the ranks and like the CSM, a Coldstream Guardsman.

Sid Brown, who was also a National Service lad, attempted to smooth things over, but to no avail.

When I heard the CSM say "12 months extra," I had to dive in the toilet where I was as sick as a dog. The CSM then reappeared from the Major's office.

"If we were on active service and this had happened, it would have been classed as desertion, and we would have to be shot," said the CSM. Another visit to the toilet for me.

Fred, the other lad, wasn't here yet as he was with the DERR and carrying out other duties.

10 o'clock arrived and we were both lined up. The CSM was strutting up and down the corridor barking orders and glaring at us as if we had committed murder. "What do we plead?" asked Fred.

"Guilty," I replied, without any hesitation.

"Prisoners and Escort `SHUN', Double March!" screamed the CSM, and into the OC's office we slithered on the heavily polished floor, bulled up by myself only two hours earlier.

According to the CSM, we didn't get it right the first time and he was loving this. "About turn," he said, and doubled us out again.

I did get a glimpse of Major Cowley's face; it was red and was rather twisted, maybe as a result of listening to the CSM barking orders out first thing in the morning, or more likely because we had broken Army orders. "You horrible men!" the CSM snorted.

Eventually we arrived in front of `Big Jim', our Commanding Officer, a very smart, honest man and, I hoped, a very lenient man too. Boy! Did he go to town on us!! He was worse than the CSM!

The Sergeant Major read out the charges and Big Jim frowned and really laid into us about deserting posts and how the IRA could have got into the armoury while we were in the NAFFI. "Seven days nick," he said, at the end of the bollocking.

I looked at Fred and we were both so relieved that we almost keeled over. Of course, the Major had not heard all the comments that had been thrown around about an extra 12 months etc, and the anxiety that we had been through. "Prisoners and escort, about turn, off with your berets," the CSM bawled. "Double them down to the Guard Room!" he instructed, and he seemed to look somewhat disappointed.

Down at the Guard Room we were put into separate cells and as soon as I hit the bunk, I fell asleep, having had little sleep at all the previous night.

The next thing I knew, I woke up in a cold sweat because of a bad dream. In the dream the CSM was screaming orders to the firing squad, the blindfold was on and the last cigarette was drooping from the corner of my mouth. I could actually smell the smoke. "Take aim, fire!" Six shots rang out, but I was awake before they reached me.

""Breakfast," the Guard Commander ordered and I stood to immediate attention at the side of the bed, mess tins either side ready for the double march up to the cookhouse. I really didn't have an appetite that morning, but we had to go anyway as part of the prisoners' ritual of double marching around the camp. Other squaddies got used to seeing prisoners doubling around the camp, so we were completely ignored. There would be about 6 in the nick at any one time, mainly for going AWOL.

Seven days in the Guard Room turned out to be a complete rest from all duties. The lads on guard at night would pass cigarettes through the small eyehole in the cell door, and the food was not too bad so, all in all, it was almost like spending a week at Billy Butlins Holiday Camp.

Back on guard again a few weeks later, we noticed the Guard Commander was making more visits around the camp while we were `On Stag'. No doubt under the strict orders from the Commanding Officer.

CHAPTER SIXTY FOUR

Stars, And Out of the Time Warp

Of course it was not all doom and gloom. We would often venture out into the big wide world, mainly into Salisbury and the NAFFI Club which could get quite rough on some Thursday nights at around 10pm, which was when the different Battalions started to rub their antlers. It was wise to order two rounds at about 9.45pm because as soon as the trouble started, the shutters went down on the bar, and no more ale would be served that night.

MP's would patrol around at a cautionary distance, but would be into the NAFFI very quickly as soon as the entertainment started. After all, that is what they loved and that is why they were MP's.

The CSM was not very impressed with me at all after my little spell in the Guard Room. Back in the office sorting out all the mail, and getting orders ready for the next day, I came across the Army Bible - a booked called: `Queens Regulations'. I noted that I could continue my education at a College outside the Army jurisdiction.

In the Summer I was already away from the office every afternoon training for the athletics and all day Wednesday cricketing, so I thought I would have a go at this as well. I made enquiries at Salisbury Technical College and was informed that there was an engineering course available all day Thursday. `Big Jim' loved all the sporting activities and all the glory that would come if we won the 3rd DIV athletics at Tidworth (which we did!).

All in all, it was a good Summer for the HQ - winning the Cricket Final as well, so `Big Jim's' chest almost burst out of his immaculately pressed Battle Dress in 1961. Fair enough, the CSM's main job was to produce soldiers for action and he more or less kept to that, although his Yorkshire background did become evident when the football season commenced, because he would be seen on the touchline at many of our games shouting and moaning. I am sure that many First Division Clubs would have been happy at just hearing 100 of his voices in the crowd, as it would have seemed like a 1000.

"There is no way you will attend that College!" barked the CSM, once he had discovered that I had applied, smacking the palm of his hand with his pace stick and grimacing.

After marching me in on OC's orders again, the CSM gave all the reasons why I should not go, saying how much I was needed in the office. However, this was to no avail, because Major Cowley would not go against `Queens Regulations'.

The first Thursday at college I passed the CSM on my way out of the camp at the Guard Room wearing my civvies, and I detected a slight grimace and a twitch of the eye. "Good Morning, Sergeant," I said.

As my studies took off I began to notice that I was being selected for Wednesday night guards for more than usual, and consequently I was coming straight off guard and going to College, after having hardly any sleep. As a result I found it extremely difficult staying awake during lectures on moments of force, and all the calculations that went with them. In fact, it was very difficult for me to stay awake even WITH a full night's sleep for that lesson! Was this a cunning plot of the CSM's?

Eventually, after a few weeks when I arrived at College, the lecturer would tell me to go to the back of the class and there I would fall into a deep sleep for an hour. "Well, I hope you all understand that. I will ask questions next time," I heard the lecturer say, as I was coming round from my sleep.

Guards, I suppose, were a necessary component of Army life, and I have to admit that I covered some miles around that camp at Figsbury Rings. Patrolling the camp at 2 or 3am I often had a feeling of loneliness, even though I was accompanied by a fellow guardsman.

On some Winter nights the sky would be very clear and the air very cool and frosty. With a full moon and every star in the Northern Hemisphere visible, I would pause for a while and look into the swirling mass of stars and think of home, and my fiancée, and imagine the great times we had spent together. I would soon be snapped out of my thoughts by another member of the team usually asking me if I wanted a cigarette!

We would then get into the front of a 3 tonner and have a Woodbine, being extra careful to shield the glow with the hand. Looking out through the windscreen of the 3 tonner, I could see a lot of Salisbury Plain - still, mysterious and very barren.

I never wanted to go into the Army for two years, not knowing what I was walking into, and having to cope with the trauma of being away from home, but, let's face it, there were soldiers in the 1st and 2nd World Wars a lot younger than me who were in active combat for six years! Eventually I settled down without even realising it, and worked at being a soldier, because if you didn't, the Army would destroy you!

Whether the Army made me a better man or not, I do not know, and only other people can be the judge of that. I believe that character is laid out in the first five years of life, and nothing whatsoever can change that. I was never a rebel and would obey all of my superiors, and I believe this was just in my character, and was as a result of my Father's strict, disciplinarian upbringing - I would NEVER question his authority.

Obviously, on occasions, I did risk running the gauntlet against authority; I knew that if I were caught, I would be punished.

During my two years of service I met many soldiers with problems and they just plodded on, like myself, having to take orders whether they were right or wrong - nobody argued. Some say it was a waste of time and I, myself, have tried to convince myself that it was. However, I have come to the conclusion that I would never have met all the characters and Officers and men who were with me for the two years, and the memories would not have been written down here, if I hadn't carried out my National Service.

The lonely times were on Schemes in the middle of Salisbury Plain.

I can fully understand why the Druids chose Salisbury Plain to build Stonehenge, since there is no experience quite like being out there on guard in the middle of the night, watching the stars twinkling in an endlessly clear sky with the Russian Sputnik orbiting, adding one more twinkle to the millions already there.

If you were on the last stag from 4 to 6am, the eeriness of the sun rising over the horizon would send shivers down your spine, as colours merged and then changed and merged again.

We did visit Stonehenge on the night of the Summer solstice in 1961, and we waited patiently for the Druids to arrive. At about 3am they appeared, ethereal-like, in long white flowing robes. From a distance they looked like ghosts of Salisbury Plain. Then, as the sun came over the `Heel Stone', a lamb was sacrificed and there would be much chanting and moaning until, finally, they turned and, still chanting, made their ghostly departure. I wonder what they did for the rest of the year?

After weeks and weeks of demob parties, the day finally arrived for us to leave the Army and settle back into Civvy Street. It took a long time for me to adjust because in the two years that I had been away, many things had changed. Money was becoming a God to most people, and team work and community spirit was slowly dying out, as people started to look after number 1.

We received our last pay packets and demob papers, and it was over to the 3 tonners to take us to Salisbury Station. "All the best Don," Lenny shouted to CSM Willis, who was standing in the doorway of the Company Office shaking hands with everyone, and no doubt thinking to himself, thank God that crowds left. Although he had given many of the lads, including myself, a dog's life, I bore no grudge whatsoever, as if we had been called into action, we would have been well disciplined and quick to obey orders - essential elements in saving lives on active service.

As the 3 tonners trundled out of the camp and across `The Plain', hopefully for the last time, I glanced back and it was like coming out of a time warp. It was only two years earlier that I had glanced forward into the Plain and had got that feeling of loneliness and desolation. Now it was as if the event had never taken place.

At the station we strolled up to the platform in our Civvy clothes, the ones we had arrived in - Italian-style suits and winkle pickers which were well out of date now. It was the same lads who had gone through training at Brecon who were in the same compartment - Thommo, Lenny, Dennis and me; Fred Carter had gone South to Portsmouth. It was ironic really, because Dennis Fairbrother and I were recalling that this was where we came in.

The train was on its way to London where it would change for Liverpool. Of course, there was plenty of singing - `Quartermasters store' and `It wasn't the Yanks that won the War Parlez-Vous.` After a few beers Thommo wandered down to the guards van for a sleep. I will never know whether Thommo ever got out of the guards van, he was the only one from our area whom I didn't see again. For all we knew, we could all be back within a couple of weeks, because the Russians had started building the Berlin Wall, and Company Sergeant Major Willis would have the last laugh, because I can remember him jokingly saying that we'd all have to do another 12 months soon. Fortunately, it was not to be "23640068 Fusilier Goolding, Sir."

I was now back in Civvy Street, married to Irene and living at 4 Graham Avenue, Great Sutton, going to build a career for myself and earn a steady income to pay for all of life's necessities. I was 23 years old and back at Castrol Oil Company, Stanlow.

EPILOGUE

My father was now a friend and it was as if all the anxiety and disciple of my childhood had never happened. It was not a case of forgiving, because I was now beginning to understand as I talked to him more that he knew no better. It was if his job was complete and I had been put through the mill by being brought up in his disciplinary way. I could never bring myself to ask him why he had been the way he was over the years of our childhood because I realised that he wouldn't understand and would have instantly given me one of those bemused Goolding glares. I often thought top ask my mother, then I thought, "NO".

It had to be worrying about his job and the measly pension and of course the way he was made. When my father laughed all his chubby face would beam and he would throw his head backwards looking heavenwards and continue laughing for a good five minutes, tears running down his face stopping instantly as if an unknown force was telling him "now that's enough, we don't want people thinking your too happy, do we". My sister and I would look at him in amazement because we didn't know what had triggered off the bout of laughter. I wish we had known sometimes because we would have loved to have joined in, and no doubt my mother would as well. My mother would join in with us sometimes, obviously she knew when enough was enough. A case of support of the unknown.

Nobody, even his close policemen friends he had known all plodding life ever knew how to take him. All this is history now because I do tend to go on about him. I was never allowed to get too close to him to be shown a bit of affection as a child, in fact he was a one off.